Chapter	Exam Topic	CompTIA Health-care IT Technician Exam Objectives Covered
6	Identify commonly used medical terms and devices. Explain aspects of a typical clinical environment. Identify and label different components of medical interfaces. Determine common interface problems and escalate when necessary. Explain the basics of document imaging. Given a scenario, determine common clinical software problems. Describe change control best practices and its system-wide effects.	Objectives 4.1, 4.2, 4.3, 4.4, 4.5, 4.6, 4.7
7	Explain physical security controls. Summarize the different encryption types and when each is used. Apply best practices when creating and communicating passwords. Classify permission levels based on roles. Identify different remote access methods and security controls. Recognize wireless security protocols and best practices. Implement best practices in secure disposal of electronic or physical PHI. Implement back-sup procedures based on disaster recovery policies. Identify common security risks and their prevention methods.	Objectives 5.1, 5.2, 5.3, 5.4, 5.5, 5.6, 5.7, 5.8, 5.9

CompTIA® Healthcare IT Technician HIT-001 Authorized Cert Guide

Joy Dark
Jean Andrews, Ph.D.

800 East 96th Street
Indianapolis, Indiana 46240 USA

CompTIA® Healthcare IT Technician HIT-001 Authorized Cert Guide

ISBN-13: 978-0-7897-4929-1
ISBN-10: 0-7897-4929-7

The Library of Congress Cataloging-in-Publication data is on file.

Printed in the United States of America

Second Printing: July 2012

Trademarks

Warning and Disclaimer

Bulk Sales

Pearson IT Certification offers excellent discounts on this book when ordered in quantity for bulk purchases or special sales. For more information, please contact

U.S. Corporate and Government Sales
1-800-382-3419
corpsales@pearsontechgroup.com

For sales outside of the U.S., please contact

International Sales
international@pearson.com

Associate Publisher	David Dusthimer
Acquisitions Editor	Betsy Brown
Senior Development Editor	Christopher Cleveland
Managing Editor	Sandra Schroeder
Project Editor	Mandie Frank
Copy Editor	Apostrophe Editing Services
Indexer	Brad Herriman
Proofreader	Paula Lowell
Technical Editors	Chris Crayton, Isaias Leiva, Steve Picray, Ken Toth
Publishing Coordinator	Vanessa Evans
Multimedia Developer	Tim Warner
Book Designer	Gary Adair
Cover Designer	Sandra Schroeder
Composition	Bronkella Publishing

Contents at a Glance

Table of Contents

About the Authors

Joy Dark has worked in the healthcare IT field in several capacities. She first worked as a help desk technician providing first-level support at a company that supports more than 130 hospitals in 29 states. Later she focused on providing second-level support for clinical information systems, specializing in perioperative information systems and the emergency department information systems. Next she switched gears to become a support operations specialist, helping to design support protocols and structures as well as managing the transition of support when hospitals converted information systems. Now she has authored the *CompTIA Healthcare IT Technician HIT-001 Cert Guide* and contributes in writing other technical books. Before healthcare IT, Joy was an elementary school teacher in both the United States and in South America. She lives in Dalton, Georgia, with her sister and Doberman dog. She has two sisters who are physicians (anesthesiology and emergency medicine) who have shared plenty of stories, facts, and opinions about the healthcare environment that have helped to shape the content in this book.

Jean Andrews, Ph.D., has more than 30 years of experience in the computer industry, including more than 13 years in the college classroom. She has worked in a wide variety of businesses and corporations designing, writing, and supporting applications software; managing a PC repair help desk; and troubleshooting wide area networks. She has written a variety of books on software, hardware, and the Internet. She lives in northeast Georgia.

About the Reviewers

Chris Crayton is an author, technical editor, technical consultant, and trainer. Formerly, he worked as a computer and networking instructor at Keiser University; as network administrator for Protocol, a global electronic customer relationship management (eCRM) company; and at Eastman Kodak Headquarters as a computer and network specialist. Chris has authored several print and online books on PC Repair, CompTIA A+, CompTIA Security+, and Microsoft Windows. Mr. Crayton has also served as technical editor and contributor on numerous technical titles for many of the leading publishing companies. He holds MCSE, A+, and Network+ certifications.

Isaias Leiva is a professor at city college of San Francisco where he teaches computer networking and information technology topics. He is also a technical training manager at the stride center, a very successful non-profit organization where he develops curriculum and manages the training program that prepares students for industry certifications. Proffessor Leiva has also written and implemented a set of life skills and professional skills that prepare students for the work place. He has also contributed very valuable training videos through his YouTube channel which has gained worldwide audience. He is A+, Network+, IC3, MOS, MCP, MCDST certified and holds an AS in CNIT from CCSF.

Steven M. Picray is a medical surgical registered nurse in a major metropolitan hospital. He has also been a Baptist pastor and a computer programmer. He has bachelor's and master's degrees in Theology, and is a few months away from obtaining his BSN in preparation for advanced practice nursing.

Kenneth J. Toth is a Business and Information Technology instructor who has worked at Coloma Community Schools (1989–1998), Careerline Tech Center (1999–present), and Lake Michigan College (2110–present). He holds Certiport IC3 GS3, ETA CSS, Oracle Data Modeling/SQL/Java, CompTIA A+, Network+, Security+, and Healthcare IT certifications. Ken serves on the CompTIA Education Advisory Council and he is an active member of the Marketing, Attendance, and Scholarship committees at Careerline Tech Center.

Dedication

This book is dedicated to the covenant of God with man on earth.

Acknowledgments

Being my first book, I have a lot of people to thank for helping me. Without their support and mentorship, this book might never have happened.

First, I would like to thank Pearson for giving the book and me this opportunity. David Dusthimer took a leap of faith in me and believed in the potential of this book. Betsy Brown encouraged me as a new author with a little hand-holding when deadlines seemed overwhelming. Chris Cleveland guided this project and provided helpful feedback. The reviewers have been fantastic and have helped to polish this book: Chris Crayton, Steve Pickray, Ken Toth, and Isaias Leiva. The researchers who contributed to this book: Bambi Cannon, Casey Jo Baldridge, Shelia Howard, Pam Ownby, and Jill West (photo research), raised this book to the next level of quality with the information they each provided. I also acknowledge various people who have also contributed to the success of this book: Sandra Schroeder, Vanessa Evans, Tim Warner, and Gary Adair.

Finally, I acknowledge my mother, Jean Andrews. She has been my mentor and support through the entire writing process. She has been there in moments of stress, helping me figure out how to fix things, and in moments of celebration, helping me to rejoice in the victories to encourage me to keep going.

—Joy Dark

Would "I'm a proud mama!" be appropriate to say here? When Joy and I took on this daughter/mother mentoring arrangement, we both had hopes this would work, but actually my expectations have been greatly exceeded. It's been fun! Joy, I'm proud of you! Way to go!

—Jean Andrews

We Want to Hear from You!

As the reader of this book, you are our most important critic and commentator. We value your opinion and want to know what we're doing right, what we could do better, what areas you'd like to see us publish in, and any other words of wisdom you're willing to pass our way.

As an associate publisher for Pearson IT Certification, I welcome your comments. You can e-mail or write me directly to let me know what you did or didn't like about this book—as well as what we can do to make our books better.

Please note that I cannot help you with technical problems related to the topic of this book. We do have a User Services group, however, where I will forward specific technical questions related to the book.

When you write, please be sure to include this book's title and author as well as your name, e-mail address, and phone number. I will carefully review your comments and share them with the author and editors who worked on the book.

Email: feedback@pearsonitcertification.com

Mail: **David Dusthimer**
Associate Publisher
800 East 96th Street
Indianapolis, IN 46240 USA

CompTIA.

CompTIA Healthcare IT Technician

The CompTIA Healthcare Technician specialty certification is a vendor and technology neutral exam designed to ensure IT professionals have the operational, regulatory and security knowledge necessary to provide hardware and software support in medical environments where Electronic Health Record systems are being deployed or maintained.

It Pays to Get Certified

In a digital world, digital literacy is an essential survival skill—Certification proves you have the knowledge and skill to solve business problems in virtually any business environment. Certifications are highly valued credentials that qualify you for jobs, increased compensation and promotion.

Ten of the twenty fastest growing occupations in the US are healthcare-related, potentially yielding 3.2 million new jobs over the next decade.

- **U.S. HITECH ACT**—Funded imperative for US healthcare industry

- **Transition paper records**—Iin U.S medical facilities by year-end 2015

- **Individual physicians receive $40K+**—Installing EHRs and demonstrating "meaningful use."

- **More than $88.6 billion**—Spent by providers in 2010 on developing and implementing EHRs, health information exchanges (HIEs) and other HIT initiatives, HIT and consulting vendors expected to see a 10% to 20% hike in revenues in 2012

Healthcare IT: A Growing Opportunity

U.S. officials estimate healthcare IT jobs will grow

by at least 50,000

between February 2010 and February 2015

That's more than

12,000 new jobs per year

34 new jobs every day

1,0000 jobs a month

The average base salary for a Healthcare IT tech is

$78,000

How Certification Helps Your Career

IT Is Everywhere	IT Knowledge and Skills Gets Jobs	Retain Your Job and Salary	Want to Change Jobs	Stick Out from the Resume Pile
IT is ubiquitous, needed by most organizations. Globally, there are over 600,000 IT job openings.	Certifications are essential credentials that qualify you for jobs, increased compensation, and promotion.	Make your expertise stand above the rest. Competence is usually retained during times of change.	Certifications qualify you for new opportunities, whether locked into a current job, see limited advancement, or need to change careers.	Hiring managers can demand the strongest skill set.

CompTIA Career Pathway

CompTIA offers a number of credentials that form a foundation for your career in technology and allow you to pursue specific areas of concentration. Depending on the path you choose to take, CompTIA certifications help you build upon your skills and knowledge, supporting learning throughout your entire career.

POTENTIAL CAREER PATH

Steps to Getting Certified and Staying Certified

Review Exam Objectives	Review the certification objectives to make sure you know what is covered in the exam: http://certification.comptia.org/Training/testingcenters/examobjectives.aspx
Practice for the Exam	After you have studied for the certification, take a free assessment and sample test to get an idea of what type of questions might be on the exam: http://certification.comptia.org/Training/testingcenters/samplequestions.aspx
Purchase an Exam Voucher	Purchase your exam voucher on the CompTIA Marketplace, which is located at: http://www.comptiastore.com/
Take the Test!	Select a certification exam provider and schedule a time to take your exam. You can find exam providers at the following link: http://certification.comptia.org/Training/testingcenters.aspx

Join the Professional Community

Join IT Pro Community http://itpro.comptia.org	The free IT Pro online community provides valuable content to students and professionals Career IT Job Resources ■ Where to start in IT ■ Career Assessments ■ Salary Trends ■ US Job Board Forums on Networking, Security, Computing and Cutting Edge Technologies Access to blogs written by Industry Experts Current information on Cutting Edge Technologies Access to various industry resource links and articles related to IT and IT careers

Content Seal of Quality

This courseware bears the seal of **CompTIA Approved Quality Content.** This seal signifies this content covers 100% of the exam objectives and implements important instructional design principles. CompTIA recommends multiple learning tools to help increase coverage of the learning objectives.

Why CompTIA?

- **Global Recognition**—CompTIA is recognized globally as the leading IT non-profit trade association and has enormous credibility. Plus, CompTIA's certifications are vendor-neutral and offer proof of foundational knowledge that translates across technologies.

- **Valued by Hiring Managers**—Hiring managers value CompTIA certification, because it is vendor- and technology-independent validation of your technical skills.

- **Recommended or Required by Government and Businesses**—Many government organizations and corporations either recommend or require technical staff to be CompTIA certified. (For example, Dell, Sharp, Ricoh, the U.S. Department of Defense, and many more.)

- **Three CompTIA Certifications ranked in the top 10**—In a study by DICE of 17,000 technology professionals, certifications helped command higher salaries at all experience levels.

How to obtain more information

- **Visit CompTIA online**—www.comptia.org to learn more about getting CompTIA certified.

- **Contact CompTIA**—Call 866-835-8020 ext. 5 or email questions@comptia. org.

- **Join the IT Pro Community**—http://itpro.comptia.org to join the IT community to get relevant career information.

- Connect with us—

CompTIA Healthcare IT Technician HIT-001 Official Exam Objectives

Objective	Chapter	Pages
■ Desktop support	4	113-127
■ Database administrator	4	113-127
■ Business Associate Access and Contractor Access	4	113-127
■ Access limitations based on role and exceptions	4	113-127
■ Emergency access (break the glass)	4	113-127
■ Access based on sensitive patient data	4	113-127
■ Sensitivity labels and clearance	4	113-127
2.3 Apply proper communication methods in the workplace.	4	105-112
■ Email	4	105-112
■ IM vs. secure chat	4	105-112
■ EMR system	4	105-112
■ Fax	4	105-112
■ Secure FTP	4	105-112
■ Phone	4	105-112
■ VoIP	4	105-112
2.4 Identify organizational structures and different methods of operation.	4	127-132
■ Organizational Structures:	4	127-132
■ Hospital	4	127-132
■ Private practice	4	127-132
■ Nursing homes	4	127-132
■ Assisted living facilities	4	127-132
■ Home healthcare	4	127-132
■ Hospice	4	127-132
■ Surgical centers	4	127-132
■ Methods:	4	127-132
■ Differences in scope of work	4	127-132
■ Availability of resources	4	127-132
■ Formality of procedures	4	127-132

CompTIA Healthcare IT Technician HIT-001 Official Exam Objectives   Continued

Objective	Chapter	Pages
■ Fax printer	5	198-213
■ Camera	5	198-213
■ Signature pads	5	198-213
■ Physical interfaces:	5	198-213
■ USB	5	198-213
■ IEEE 1394	5	198-213
■ SCSI	5	198-213
■ Serial	5	198-213
■ Bluetooth	5	198-213
■ Mobile storage devices:	5	198-213
■ Flash drives	5	198-213
■ External hard drives	5	198-213
■ DVDs	5	198-213
■ CDs	5	198-213
■ Tapes	5	198-213
■ SD cards	5	198-213
■ Mobile devices:	5	198-213
■ Tablet PCs	5	198-213
■ Smart phones	5	198-213
■ Portable media players	5	198-213
3.5 Compare and contrast basic client networks and tools.	5	172-192
■ DHCP vs. static IP	5	172-192
■ Adhoc vs. infrastructure	5	172-192
■ Command line prompts	5	172-192
■ ping	5	172-192
■ ipconfig	5	172-192
■ tracert	5	172-192
3.6 Setup basic network devices and apply basic configuration settings.	5	172-192
■ Wireless access point	5	172-192
■ Security settings	5	172-192

Objective	Chapter	Pages
■ SSID	5	172-192
■ Guest network	5	172-192
■ Access point placement	5	172-192
■ Router	5	172-192
■ DHCP	5	172-192
■ Port forwarding	5	172-192
■ Internet modem	5	172-192
3.7 Given a scenario, troubleshoot and solve common network problems.	5	172-192
■ Cabling	5	172-192
■ Power	5	172-192
■ IP settings	5	172-192
■ ISP	5	172-192
■ Interference	5	172-192
■ Signal issues	5	172-192
3.8 Explain the features of different backup configurations and the associated maintenance practices.	5	192-197
■ Daily	5	192-197
■ Differential	5	192-197
■ Incremental	5	192-197
■ Archive flags	5	192-197
3.9 Classify different server types, environments, features, and limitations.	5	192-197
■ Database server	5	192-197
■ Application server	5	192-197
■ Interfaces	5	192-197
■ Physical connections	5	192-197
■ Server load and utilization	5	192-197
■ Application services	5	192-197
■ OS and application interoperability	5	192-197
■ Storage space limitations based on application usage and electronic record storage	5	192-197

CompTIA Healthcare IT Technician HIT-001 Official Exam Objectives   Continued

Objective	Chapter	Pages
3.10 Compare and contrast EHR/EMR technologies and how each is implemented.	5	192-197
■ ASP/Cloud vs. client-server (locally-hosted)	5	192-197
■ Browser vs. installed application vs. terminal/remote access	5	192-197
■ Hardware requirements	5	192-197
4.0 Medical Business Operations	6	
4.1 Identify commonly used medical terms and devices.	6	227-264
■ Interfaces:	6	245-264
■ HL7	6	259-264
■ e-prescribing	6	245-259
■ CCD	6	259-264
■ CCR	6	259-264
■ ICD10	6	245-259
■ CPT	6	245-259
■ SNOMED	6	245-259
■ NDCID	6	245-259
■ PACS	6	245-259
■ E/M codes	6	245-259
■ Devices:	6	227-244
■ Portable x-ray machine	6	227-244
■ MRI	6	227-244
■ Vitals cuff	6	227-244
■ EKG	6	227-244
■ EEG	6	227-244
■ Ultrasound	6	227-244
■ PET	6	227-244
■ CT	6	227-244
■ Vascular/Nuclear Stress Test	6	227-244
■ Glucose monitor	6	227-244
■ Clinical software and modules:	6	245-259
■ Patient tracking	6	245-259

CompTIA Healthcare IT Technician HIT-001 Official Exam Objectives   Continued

Objective	Chapter	Pages
■ Site surveys	7	302-303
■ Access point placement	7	302-303
5.7 Implement best practices in secure disposal of electronic or physical PHI.	7	307-308
■ Secure shredding	7	307-308
■ Degaussing	7	307-308
■ Sanitizing	7	307-308
5.8 Implement backup procedures based on disaster recovery policies.	7	306-307
■ Deployment, configuration and testing of backups	7	306-307
■ Backup storage:	7	306-307
■ Offsite	7	306-307
■ Courier	7	306-307
■ Onsite	7	306-307
■ Methods of secure transfer	7	306-307
■ Backup inventory	7	306-307
5.9 Identify common security risks and their prevention methods.	7	281-283
■ Social engineering—User training	7	281-283
■ Phishing—User training	7	281-283
■ Spamming—Filters	7	281-283
■ Malware—Access control	7	281-283
■ Spyware—Anti-spyware	7	281-283

Introduction

Welcome to the *CompTIA Healthcare IT Technician HIT-001 Cert Guide*. The CompTIA Healthcare IT Technician certification was created due to a growing need for it in the healthcare IT field. The CompTIA Healthcare IT Technician certification is designed to be a vendor-neutral exam that measures your knowledge of industry-standard technologies and methodologies. It serves as a gateway to transition from IT into healthcare IT. This book was developed to be a resource while studying for the exam and also to be a reference while working on the job.

The Healthcare IT Technician exam objectives were designed with the suggestion that the test taker would already have the CompTIA A+ certification. Although having the CompTIA A+ certification before attempting the CompTIA Healthcare IT Technician exam can greatly benefit you, the book does review and explain the CompTIA A+ objectives as needed to pass the exam.

While writing this book, the author imagined how to share what she knows with a new employee at the healthcare company where she used to work. Most new employees have a strong IT background but don't actually have much experience on the medical side of healthcare IT. This book completes a picture from IT to healthcare IT.

Good luck as you explore the new world of healthcare IT and prepare to take the CompTIA Healthcare IT Technician exam. As you read this book you can learn how to combine two worlds into a familiar environment, armed with knowledge and skills to pass the exam.

Goals and Methods

The number one goal of this book is to help you pass the 2011 version of the CompTIA Healthcare IT Technician certification exam (number HIT-001).

The CompTIA Healthcare IT Technician certification exam involves familiarity with healthcare and the information systems used in the healthcare environment. To aid you in mastering and understanding the Healthcare IT Technician certification objectives, this book uses the following methods:

- **Opening topics list**: This defines the topics covered in the chapter; it also lists the corresponding CompTIA Healthcare IT Technician objective numbers.

- **Topical coverage**: The heart of the chapter that explains each objective from a practical perspective relative to the exam and potential future jobs. This includes in-depth descriptions, tables, and figures geared to build your knowledge so that you can pass the exam. The chapters are broken down by objective domains.

- **Exam Tips**: The Exam Tips indicate important subjects, tables, and lists of information that you should know for the exam. They are interspersed throughout the chapter.

- **Notes**: The Notes offer bits of information that help you to understand a topic covered or direct you to where you can find more information on a topic.

- **Key Terms**: Key Terms are definitions of important vocabulary you need to know to pass the exam and succeed in healthcare IT. Key terms are interspersed throughout the chapter and listed without definitions at the end of each chapter.

- **HIT in the Real World**: Each chapter has a story that provides a real-world experience. These stories demonstrate at least one topic covered in the chapter and how it is important to learn the objectives for success in healthcare IT.

- **Chapter Summary**: At the end of each chapter, you can find a summary of the key topics covered in the chapter.

- **Acronym Drill**: In healthcare IT there are so many acronyms it is easy to get confused by them. The acronym drill reinforces learning the acronyms so that they become second nature.

- **Review Questions**: At the end of each chapter is a quiz. The quizzes, and answers with explanations, are meant to gauge your knowledge of the subjects. If an answer to a question doesn't come readily to you, be sure to review that portion of the chapter.

- **Practical Application**: There are critical thinking questions at the end of each chapter. These questions or challenges are intended to put to use what you have learned in the chapter to reinforce your learning the content of the chapter.

Who Should Read This Book?

This book is for anyone who wants to start or advance a career in healthcare IT. Readers of this book can range from persons taking a healthcare IT course to individuals already in the field who want to keep their skills sharp. Many readers will be individuals who have earned the CompTIA A+ certification and want to broaden into healthcare for more job opportunities. This book is designed to offer an easy transition from IT to healthcare IT.

This book also offers opportunity for individuals in healthcare to transition into healthcare IT. This book offers an IT background of all objectives. Whether your background is in healthcare or IT, this book prepares you for the CompTIA Healthcare IT Technician exam.

Although not a prerequisite, CompTIA Healthcare IT Technician candidates should have at least one year of technical experience. The CompTIA A+ certification is also recommended as a prerequisite. It is expected that you understand basic computer topics such as how to install operating systems and applications and so on. The focus of this book is on the technologies used in the healthcare environment and the rules and regulations about how to use these technologies.

Important! If you do not feel that you have the required experience or are new to the IT field, consider an IT course that covers the CompTIA Healthcare IT Technician objectives. You can choose from plenty of technical training schools, community colleges, and online courses. Use this book with the course and any other course materials you obtain.

CompTIA Healthcare IT Technician Exam Topics

Table I-1 lists the exam topics for the CompTIA Healthcare IT Technician exam. This table lists the chapter in which each exam topic is covered. Chapters 1 and 2 are introductory chapters and as such do not map to any specific exam objectives.

Table I-1   CompTIA Healthcare IT Technician Exam Topics

Chapter	Exam Topic	CompTIA Healthcare IT Technician Exam Objectives Covered
1	Overview of the HITECH Act, healthcare, and healthcare IT.	Applies to the entire exam.
2	Overview of data flow used in healthcare information systems.	Applies to the entire exam.

Table I-1 Continued

Chapter	Exam Topic	CompTIA Health-care IT Technician Exam Objectives Covered
3	Identify standard agencies, laws, and regulations. Explain and classify HIPAA controls and compliance issues. Summarize regulatory rules of record retention, disposal, and archiving. Explain and interpret legal best practices, requirements, and documentation.	Objectives 1.1, 1.2, 1.3, 1.4
4	Use best practices for handling PHI in the workplace. Identify EHR/EMR access roles and responsibilities. Apply proper communication methods in the workplace. Identify organizational structures and different methods of operation. Given a scenario, execute daily activities while following a code of conduct.	Objective 2.1, 2.2, 2.3, 2.4, 2.5
5	Identify commonly used IT terms and technologies. Demonstrate the ability to set up a basic PC workstation within an EHR/EMR environment. Given a scenario, troubleshoot and solve common PC problems. Install and configure hardware drivers and devices. Compare and contrast basic client networks and tools. Set up basic network devices and apply basic configuration settings. Given a scenario, troubleshoot and solve common network problems. Explain the features of different backup configurations and the associated maintenance practices. Classify different server types, environments, features, and limitations. Compare and contrast EHR/EMR technologies and how each is implemented.	Objectives 3.1, 3.2, 3.3, 3.4, 3.5, 3.6, 3.7, 3.8, 3.9, 3.10

Chapter	Exam Topic	CompTIA Health-care IT Technician Exam Objectives Covered
6	Identify commonly used medical terms and devices.	Objectives 4.1, 4.2, 4.3, 4.4, 4.5, 4.6, 4.7
	Explain aspects of a typical clinical environment.	
	Identify and label different components of medical interfaces.	
	Determine common interface problems and escalate when necessary.	
	Explain the basics of document imaging.	
	Given a scenario, determine common clinical software problems.	
	Describe change control best practices and its system-wide effects.	
7	Explain physical security controls.	Objectives 5.1, 5.2, 5.3, 5.4, 5.5, 5.6, 5.7, 5.8, 5.9
	Summarize the different encryption types and when each is used.	
	Apply best practices when creating and communicating passwords.	
	Classify permission levels based on roles.	
	Identify different remote access methods and security controls.	
	Recognize wireless security protocols and best practices.	
	Implement best practices in secure disposal of electronic or physical PHI.	
	Implement back-sup procedures based on disaster recovery policies.	
	Identify common security risks and their prevention methods.	

Pearson IT Certification Practice Test Engine and Questions on the CD

The CD in the back of the book includes the Pearson IT Certification Practice Test engine software that displays and grades a set of exam-realistic multiple-choice questions. Using the Pearson IT Certification Practice Test engine, you can either study by going through the questions in Study Mode or taking a simulated exam that mimics real exam conditions.

The installation process requires two major steps: installing the software and then activating the exam. The CD in the back of this book has a recent copy of the Pearson IT Certification Practice Test engine. The practice exam—the database of exam questions—is not on the CD.

> **NOTE**   The cardboard CD case in the back of this book includes the CD and a piece of paper. The paper lists the activation code for the practice exam associated with this book. Do not lose the activation code. On the opposite side of the paper from the activation code is a unique, one-time-use coupon code for the purchase of the Premium Edition eBook and Practice Test.

Install the Software from the CD

The Pearson IT Certification Practice Test is a Windows-only desktop application. You can run it on a Mac using a Windows Virtual Machine, but it was built specifically for the PC platform. The minimum system requirements follow:

- Windows XP (SP3), Windows Vista (SP2), or Windows 7
- Microsoft .NET Framework 4.0 Client
- Microsoft SQL Server Compact 4.0
- Pentium class 1GHz processor (or equivalent)
- 512 MB RAM
- 650 MB disc space plus 50 MB for each downloaded similar to other software installation processes. If you have already installed the Pearson IT Certification Practice Test software from another Pearson product, you do not need to reinstall the software. Simply launch the software on your desktop and proceed to activate the practice exam from this book by using the activation code included in the CD sleeve.

The following steps outline the installation process:

Step 1: Insert the CD into your PC.

Step 2: The software that automatically runs is the Pearson software to access and use all CD-based features, including the exam engine and the appendix. From the main menu, click the **Install the Exam Engine** option.

Step 3: Respond to windows prompts as with any typical software installation process.

The installation process gives you the option to activate your exam with the activation code supplied on the paper in the CD sleeve. This process requires that you establish a Pearson website login. You need this login to activate the exam, so register when prompted. If you already have a Pearson website login, you do not need to register again; just use your existing login.

Activate and Download the Practice Exam

After the exam engine is installed, you should then activate the exam associated with this book (if you did not do so during the installation process) as follows:

Step 1: Start the Pearson IT Certification Practice Test software from the Windows **Start** menu or from your desktop shortcut icon.

Step 2: To activate and download the exam associated with this book, from the My Products or Tools tab, select the **Activate** button.

Step 3: At the next screen, enter the Activation Key from the paper inside the CD sleeve in the back of the book. When it's entered, click the **Activate** button.

Step 4: The activation process downloads the practice exam. Click **Next**, and then click **Finish**.

After the activation process completes, the My Products tab should list your new exam. If you do not see the exam, make sure you have selected the **My Products** tab on the menu. At this point, the software and practice exam are ready to use. Simply select the exam and click the **Open Exam** button.

To update a particular exam you have already activated and downloaded, simply select the **Tools** tab, and select the **Update Products** button. Updating your exams ensures you have the latest changes and updates to the exam data.

If you want to check for updates to the Pearson Cert Practice Test exam engine software, simply select the **Tools** tab, and select the **Update Application** button. This ensures you are running the latest version of the software engine.

Activating Other Exams

The exam software installation process, and the registration process, must happen only once. Then, for each new exam, only a few steps are required. For instance, if you buy another new Pearson IT Certification Cert Guide or Cisco Press Official Cert Guide, extract the activation code from the CD sleeve in the back of that book—you don't need the CD at this point. From there, all you need to do is start the exam engine (if it's not still up and running), and perform steps 2 through 4 from the previous list.

Premium Edition

In addition to the two free practice exams provided on the CD, you can purchase one additional exam with expanded functionality directly from Pearson IT Certification. The Premium Edition eBook and Practice Test for this title contains an additional full practice exam as well as an eBook (in both PDF and ePub format). In addition, the Premium Edition title also has remediation for each question to the specific part of the eBook that relates to that question.

If you purchased the print version of this title, you can purchase the Premium Edition at a deep discount. There is a coupon code in the CD sleeve that contains a one-time-use code as well as instructions for where you can purchase the Premium Edition.

To view the premium edition product page, go to http://www.pearsonitcertification.com/store/product.aspx?isbn=0133104761.

CHAPTER 1
Introducing Healthcare IT

In this chapter you learn about:

- The importance of the HITECH Act
- The basic types of healthcare facilities as well as patient registration
- The basic goals of healthcare IT

Most healthcare facilities and healthcare providers depend on computer systems to provide the best possible healthcare for patients. Knowledgeable information technology (IT) technicians who install, support, and maintain these computer systems are an integral part of the healthcare organization responsible for patient care.

Suppose you are an IT technician who wants to branch into the healthcare IT field. If you don't know much about healthcare, your first day in a hospital might be an overwhelming experience. You might feel like you're in the way and don't know where you're supposed to be or what you're supposed to do. This book can help you know your place as healthcare IT personnel and the vital row you play as support for **healthcare providers**. Healthcare providers depend on **healthcare IT (HIT)** for timely and accurate information being available in the computer systems to make decisions on how to treat patients' afflictions. To get you up to speed on the job roles of IT personnel in the healthcare environment, you first need to know about the functions and processes that happen in a hospital. As you become familiar with how a hospital works, you can start to see how the healthcare world benefits from what the IT world has to offer.

healthcare provider—A qualified person or facility that provides healthcare to patients; for example, a doctor, nurse, or hospital.

healthcare IT (HIT)—The personnel, equipment, and procedures that provide and support the computer systems used in the healthcare environment.

The Importance of the HITECH Act

Healthcare IT is drastically changing because of the **Health Information Technology for Economic and Clinical Health (HITECH) Act**, which Chapter 3, "Regulatory Requirements," explains in greater detail. The HITECH Act regulates how HIT interacts with third parties and requires healthcare facilities to move toward electronic solutions to store patient data and to no longer use paper forms and charts for retaining patient records. The **electronic medical record (EMR)** and **electronic health record (EHR)** store and gather the same patient data as does a medical record using forms and paper charts, except the EHR/EMR stores the data in electronic format. A patient's EMR is a collection of all patient information about a patient from all visits to a particular hospital. A patient's EHR is a collection of all patient information about a patient from all visits to any hospital. EHR and EMR systems are quickly replacing the outdated paper form and chart filing systems. EHRs and EMRs are more accurate because of fewer chances for human error because the record is touched fewer times by a person, which risks a mistake being made by someone who, for example, might be distracted and put a document in the wrong person's medical record.

Health Information Technology for Economic and Clinical Health (HITECH) Act—An act of the U.S. congress enacted as part of the American Recovery and Reinvestment Act (ARRA) of 2009. Its purpose is to promote the meaningful use of technology in healthcare so that technology ultimately results in improved healthcare for the patient.

electronic medical record (EMR)—Information about a patient's care and health that was previously captured on paper forms and charts, collected from all visits at one hospital and stored electronically. The term *EMR* is sometimes used interchangeably with Electronic Health Record (EHR), although the two terms are not exactly the same.

electronic health record (EHR)—Information about a patient's care and health collected and stored electronically. This record is not limited to the visits at only one hospital but is a collection of all visits at all hospitals. The term *EHR* is sometimes used interchangeably with electronic medical record (EMR), although the two terms are not exactly the same.

Because of the HITECH Act, older paper charts must be scanned and stored electronically, and then the paper charts must be properly disposed of so that the information cannot be recovered. For example, one method to properly dispose of a document with patient information is to shred the document. New EHR/EMR information systems must be built, installed, and supported to retain patient data. This push toward EHRs/EMRs creates job opportunities for IT technicians to branch into the healthcare industry. Healthcare IT is one of the fastest-growing fields for job employment in the United States.

With the increasing demand from job openings in healthcare IT, HITECH has funded a group of colleges across the nation to train students for these jobs at minimal cost to the student. These programs focus on filling positions needed for hospital information systems to convert to EHR/EMR information systems from the paper chart archives. The programs train students for the following positions:

- Practice workflow and information management redesign specialists
- Clinician/practitioner consultants
- Implementation support specialists
- Implementation managers
- Technical/software support
- Trainers

Be sure to check out the website for the HITECH education programs; see Figure 1-1.

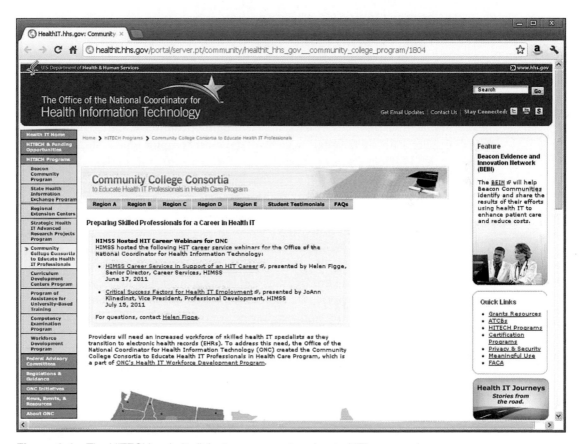

Figure 1-1   The HITECH website links to programs to educate HIT personnel.

Photo credit: http://www.healthit.hhs.gov/communitycollege

Getting to Know Healthcare

To understand healthcare IT, you must first understand healthcare. Patients might not go untreated because a computer crashes, but the level of healthcare provided will likely diminish. Before there were computers in a hospital, a healthcare provider had to call or walk to the lab to find out the results of **blood work** or to the Medical Records department to find out the patient's history. With HIT, this information is readily available with the click of a mouse. This speed of access to information assists the doctors and nurses to make more timely decisions about a patient's care, which leads to saving more lives. A patient receives diagnosis and treatment faster, and healthcare providers have more time to see more patients. HIT technicians can facilitate healthcare providers by making available to them more accurate and timely information so that they can make proper decisions on the health of patients.

> **blood work**—Examination of a blood sample to test for certain diseases, medications, or other data.

The following sections introduce healthcare by looking at the different types of healthcare facilities and the departments you might encounter in these facilities, focusing specifically on hospitals, which are the most complex type of healthcare facility. Then you focus on a high-level view of what happens from the time a patient steps through the door of a hospital until the patient care cycle completes.

Types of Healthcare Facilities

When a person gets sick, she has several options for where she can go for help. Her choice depends on the type of affliction or the proximity to the closest care. Two types of facilities are **acute care** facilities and **long-term care** facilities. Acute care facilities are for patients who have a short-term need for help or diagnosis or the patient needs immediate attention for a severe condition. Long-term care facilities are for patients who have already been diagnosed with a condition and need ongoing care. A long-term care patient's condition is stabilized as long as he has the ongoing medical or nursing care. Healthcare can also be provided by agencies that travel to where the patients are.

> **acute care**—Care that is given short term and for severe afflictions. For example, a patient experiencing a heart attack goes to an acute care facility.
>
> **long-term care**—Ongoing treatment or care. For example, a patient with Alzheimer's goes to a long-term care facility.

Nine types of acute care facilities or agencies are listed in the following Key Term box.

> **ambulatory care facility**—A facility used for outpatient services. Basically, if patient care takes less than 24 hours, the patient goes to an ambulatory care facility rather than a hospital.
>
> **primary care facility**—A facility that contains the private practice of a doctor where a patient receives preventive, diagnostic, treatment, and management services. When a person has an annual check-up, he schedules an appointment with his primary care provider (PCP), such as a family doctor, nurse practitioner, or physician assistant.

ambulatory surgery center—A facility used for surgical procedures in outpatient services.

birth center—A facility that offers services for prenatal and labor and delivery low-risk patients. This can be a department of a hospital or a separate facility.

rehabilitation hospital or center—A facility that offers care for patients with ongoing recovery from a disability. This can include medical, psychiatric, or physical therapy.

general acute care hospital—A facility that offers diagnosis, treatment, or care for patients in a variety of specialties. Patient care is uniquely approached and not all patients are there for the same type of care.

home health agency—An organization that offers preventative, rehabilitation, and therapeutic care to patients in their homes.

hospice agency—An organization that offers medical, nursing, social work, and counseling to terminally ill patients in their homes or as an inpatient hospice service at a facility.

psychiatric hospital—A facility that specializes in the care of patients with mental illness. Services include diagnosis, treatment, care, and rehabilitation. This can be on an inpatient or outpatient basis.

Three types of long-term care facilities or agencies are listed in the following Key Term box.

adult day care facility—A facility that offers medical and nursing supervision of adults. Patients cannot be at one of these facilities for longer than 12 hours in one day.

assisted living residence—A facility that offers an apartment-style living situation for patients or residents who need assistance in daily activities. Most assisted living residences have different levels of assistance. A resident might live independently where help is available only if needed, or a resident lives in an apartment, but almost everything is done for the resident.

nursing home—A facility that provides a residence for disabled and elderly patients who need medical supervision or ongoing nursing care. Patients in a nursing home do not need the level of care required to be admitted into an acute care hospital.

Focus on Hospitals

This book focuses on hospitals mostly because they are the most complex of healthcare facilities and require the most complex computer systems. For example, a general acute care hospital offers multiple levels of care for patients in a variety of areas of practice, such as surgery, emergency care, psychiatric care, **oncology**, labor and delivery, and so on. The wide variety of healthcare specialties in the hospital works together for patient care. For example, an oncology patient needs regular blood work provided by the laboratory and medicine provided by the pharmacy. The same patient might need **medical images** made in the radiology department to see how successful the treatments are working. The patient might need to have surgery to remove a tumor. A single patient can make use of multiple **clinical departments** in one hospital stay.

---

oncology—Field of medicine dealing with cancer or tumors.

medical image—Visuals made of body parts, tissues, or organs for clinical study, treatment, or diagnosis.

clinical department—A department in a healthcare facility that offers specific medical services for patient care, treatment, or diagnosis. Sometimes called ancillary departments.

From the IT perspective, if you can learn how the computer systems in each of these departments work individually and together, you can learn the other computer systems in other departments and facilities as well. A hospital is likely to have all these different departments, and other facilities might not have them all. If you understand the more complicated computer systems in a hospital, the simpler systems will be easier to understand later when you work and learn on the job at any kind of healthcare facility. For example a doctor's office uses fewer and simpler computer systems because it is a smaller facility with fewer services offered. Therefore, this book focuses on hospitals.

Departments in the Hospital

Every hospital has a few departments that are standard for all hospitals. Each of these departments plays a crucial role in patient care, and IT supports every one of them. These departments are as follows:

- Administrative offices, which maintain patient records, schedules, billing, payment, and reimbursements.
- Outpatient clinics, which offer specialized care.
- Inpatient units, which manage patients during their stay at the hospital.
- Surgery or operating rooms, which provide surgical services.
- Radiology, which provides imaging services such as X-ray, **MRI**, **CT**, and more.

- Emergency department, which provides emergency care for trauma patients.
- Pathology and laboratory (lab), which perform lab work to research the condition of a patient.
- Pharmacy, which provides medicine for patients. *Rx* is a common abbreviation for the pharmacy or a prescription of medicine.

---

magnetic resonance imaging (MRI)—Imaging that uses strong magnetic fields and radio signals to create an image of a patient's body. A patient lies down in an MRI machine and must remain still for extended periods of time in a noisy, cramped space.

computed tomography (CT)—Imaging that uses X-rays along with computing algorithms. A patient lies down in a CT machine while the CT machine rotates around the patient producing cross-sectional images (tomography) of the patient's body.

Patient Flow Through a Hospital Stay

To understand how computer systems track patient data used by a hospital, you must first understand patient flow through a hospital stay from beginning to end. The three ways a patient can be admitted to a hospital are to enter as an inpatient, outpatient, or through the emergency department. First, let's walk through an inpatient process.

Inpatient Admittance

Inpatient status is for patients who are admitted to the hospital by a doctor's order for more than 24 hours for care. A patient can arrive at a hospital as an inpatient through a number of methods. The two most common ways are by a referral from another healthcare provider, such as a PCP, or through the emergency department. Follow the diagram in Figure 1-2 to understand the process for an inpatient. When someone arrives as an inpatient, her information goes to **registration**, so the hospital is aware of who is in the hospital for care. The Registration office maintains the **patient census**. The patient's medical record is retrieved from the **medical records office** for reference during her stay.

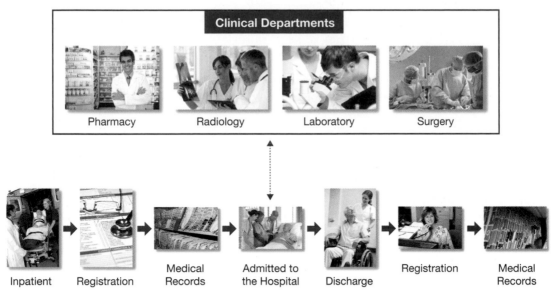

Figure 1-2 Inpatients are at the hospital for more than 24 hours.

Photo credits: Petr Kurgan, goodluz, WavebreakMediaMicro, Jordan Edgcomb, Chad McDermott, and-reiorlov, carlosseller, and Monkey Business

> **inpatient**—A patient admitted to a healthcare facility who stays longer than 24 hours by a doctor's order.
>
> **registration**—The administrative office that maintains a patient census of the facility through patient admissions, transfers, and discharges.
>
> **patient census**—A recording of the number of patients with the location, registration status, and other data about the patient in a healthcare facility. Patient census usually applies to inpatients or occupied beds.
>
> **medical records office**—The administrative office that stores and archives patients' medical records.

During the time a patient is admitted, they might receive services from the clinical departments. A hospital might have many clinical departments; although, the four primary departments follow:

- Pharmacy
- Radiology
- Lab
- Surgery

Other clinical departments might include respiratory, dietary, or physical therapy.

When a patient is well enough to leave the hospital, he is discharged. His discharge information is sent to registration, so the hospital has an accurate patient census showing the patient is no longer admitted in the facility. His medical record is completed and submitted to the medical records office for storage.

Outpatient Admittance

Outpatient status is for patients who are at the hospital for less than 24 hours for care or are under observation that can last two or three days. The most common way to arrive at a hospital as an outpatient is because someone is scheduled for a procedure or service that doesn't take more than a day, start to finish. For example, the procedure might be minor surgery or imaging. Follow the diagram in Figure 1-3 to understand the flow of an outpatient. When the patient arrives as an outpatient, his information is sent to registration. His medical record is retrieved from the medical records office for reference during his stay. An outpatient might receive services from the clinical departments while at the healthcare facility.

> **outpatient**—A patient who is scheduled for medical treatment, care, or a service. The patient's stay in the healthcare facility lasts less than 24 hours unless being observed. Ambulatory facilities are specifically for outpatient services.

When a patient is well enough to be discharged, his information is sent to registration again for a correct patient census. His medical record is completed and submitted to the medical records office for storage.

The alternative path shown in Figure 1-3 happens if the level of care an outpatient needs unexpectedly requires more than the 24-hour period. In this situation, the outpatient is admitted to the hospital as an inpatient. The Registration office updates the registration status of the patient from outpatient to inpatient. The inpatient might continue to receive services from the clinical departments. When the patient is well enough to be discharged, his information is sent to registration again, so the hospital's patient census is accurate. His medical record is completed and submitted to the medical records office for storage.

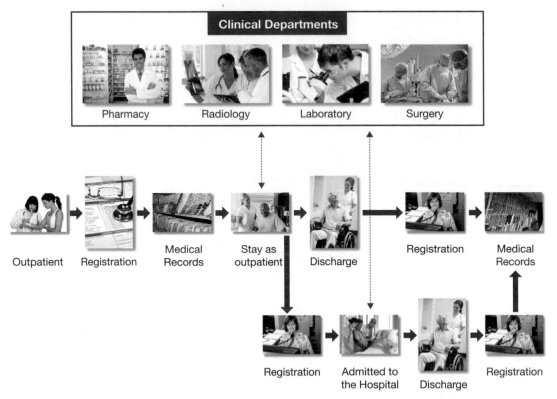

Figure 1-3   Outpatients are at a hospital for less than 24 hours unless they need to be admitted as inpatients or require only observation.

Photo credits: Petr Kurgan, goodluz, WavebreakMediaMicro, Jordan Edgcomb, Chad McDermott, andreiorlov, carlosseller, Monkey Business, and auremar

Emergency Department Patient

The **Emergency Department (ED)** is sometimes referred to as the front door of the hospital. Most patients at the hospital enter this way. When people have a sudden and acute affliction, they go to the ED. All patients are treated in the ED. The ED staff uses a specialized computer system designed specifically for the ED as a registration system. The **tracking board** displays the status, assignments, and conditions of patients in the ED for the staff to use for quick reference. The tracking board can either be on a large flat screen display for all staff to use or on regular computer monitors viewed individually; see Figure 1-4. Information that might identify a patient displays in code to prevent a violation of patient privacy.

emergency department (ED)—The department in a healthcare facility that treats patients with acute and sudden afflictions. The ED is often referred to as the emergency room (ER) by nonmedical people, but in the healthcare world, it is called the ED.

tracking board—A display showing the patients in the ED, where they are, and who is caring for them. Because the tracking board contains confidential information, it is for the use of the ED staff only and is primarily kept out of view of the waiting area and patients.

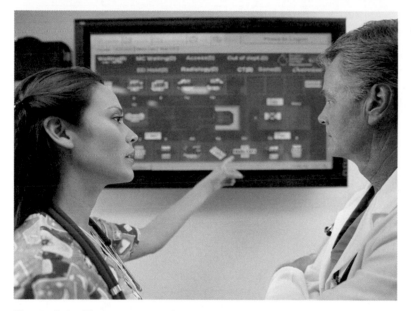

Figure 1-4   The emergency department (ED) uses a tracking board to make sure no patients are overlooked.

ED patients are **triaged** for the **acuity** level for their **chief complaint** to determine which patients need care first. Every ED determines the protocols for triaging patients as they arrive and sets their own version of the acuity index. Many EDs are moving toward using a five-level acuity index, as outlined in Table 1-1. Use Figure 1-5 to follow the patient flow of an ED patient.

triage—The assessment of the level of care a patient needs when she arrives at the hospital used to determine the priority of the patient for being seen by a physician.

acuity—The level of severity of an affliction.

chief complaint—The primary reason a person goes to the ED.

Table 1-1   One Possible Description of an Acuity Level Index

Acuity Level	Description of Patient's Condition
1	Severely unstable, seen by a physician immediately, usually requires an intervention
2	Potentially unstable, seen by a physician within 10 minutes, usually requires testing and medication
3	Stable, yet urgent, seen by a physician within 30 minutes, usually requires testing and medication
4	Stable and nonurgent, seen by physician when available, requires minimal testing and medication
5	Stable and nonurgent, seen by physician when available, requires no testing or procedure

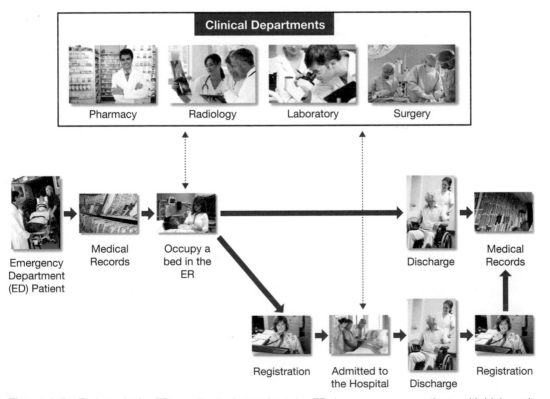

Figure 1-5   Patients in the ED usually discharge from the ED; however, some patients with high acuity are admitted to the hospital as inpatients.

Photo credits: Petr Kurgan, goodluz, WavebreakMediaMicro, Jordan Edgcom, Monkey Business, andreiorlov, carlosseller, and Andrew Gentry

Emergency physicians use a patient's medical record if available from the medical records office. An ED patient might receive services from the clinical departments. Most patients are discharged from the ED without being admitted to the hospital for inpatient care. The patient's completed medical record is sent to the medical records office for storage.

If a patient needs to be admitted to the hospital, her information goes to registration. While she is admitted, she might receive services from the clinical departments. When the patient is well enough to be discharged, her information is sent to registration again. Her medical record is completed and submitted to the medical records office for storage.

The Goals of Healthcare IT

Healthcare IT is more than providing a functioning computer for a doctor or nurse to use in a patient room or other area of the hospital. Your role as a healthcare IT professional goes far beyond that. You must understand the needs of HIT users and know how to support those needs. It is rare to find someone who can speak both techie and medical languages. You are responsible for bridging the communication gap between the IT and healthcare worlds when HIT is concerned. You champion the cause of HIT to the healthcare providers and administration. You become the advocate for the HIT user who needs a functional computer in a patient room, has the software she needs, and can access the information she needs to do her job successfully.

HIT staff also performs some of the traditional IT roles as well. You are there to provide technology and solve problems with that technology. When a problem arises, you need to interpret what your HIT user is saying to understand the IT problem so that you can resolve it. You are there to maintain the quick and accurate flow of electronic patient data. You are in the hospital to ensure the meaningful use of computer systems so that patient care benefits from these systems. This goal requires that you know what make these computer systems useful to healthcare providers. You absolutely must understand their needs and how computers can meet those needs. Meaningful use of HIT results in better patient care. Not a single aspect of HIT is without effect to the function and success of a hospital.

Why Have IT in Healthcare?

Healthcare providers are doing everything within their power to keep patients alive and healthy. They pool all resources available to accomplish this goal. As IT support in the hospital, this becomes your goal as well. Everything you do must be done with the goal of patient care in mind. As an IT professional, you don't treat patients directly; however, your job is to help make the healthcare providers' jobs easier and more efficient. When you quickly and readily provide patient data stored in databases including patient history, current conditions, and possible treatments, you are helping the healthcare providers to be better equipped with more information to make wiser decisions for their patients. Your number one goal is to provide accurate and timely information about patients to healthcare providers.

For example, you might get a request to reset a password. Don't take even this simple and seemingly benign task as insignificant. If a nurse cannot log into her computer to enter orders for a patient to receive a **stat** MRI, the lag time of having to communicate those orders manually could mean life and death for a patient. If the billing department can't correctly charge for the services provided, the hospital might not have the revenue needed to provide proper patient care for future patients. Everything is significant. The most important concept you can get out of this book is to remember that what you do every day in healthcare IT affects patient care. Don't let the mundane daily activities distract you from this goal.

> **stat**—Derived from the Latin word *statim*, which means *immediately*. It is often used in the medical environment to expedite something.

IT professionals are not expected to know how to set a broken bone. Medical professionals are not expected to manage a database holding patient data. Because HIT professionals work in both the IT and medical worlds, they are uniquely positioned to interpret what a user is saying to what he is asking for in IT terms. As an HIT professional, you often serve as the middle man between the medical users and the IT support; for example, with a vendor. It is your job to learn how to communicate with the "customers"—the HIT users. It is also your job to learn what users are experiencing and how to create a solution for them that they need, whether it is reprogramming, fixing a glitch, or implementing a new solution.

Prepare for a Career in Healthcare IT

With career opportunities in HIT rising, a need for a certification in this field rose as well. CompTIA has fulfilled this need with the Healthcare IT Technician certification, as shown in Figure 1-6 on the comptia.org website. In the past, HIT positions were filled by IT technicians who were simply open to learning the healthcare field on the job. With this certification, the first day you walk onto the job you will understand HIT terminology, regulations, troubleshooting skills, security, and organizational behavior in healthcare. This book aligns with the objectives for this exam listed in the table in the "Introduction" of the book.

Figure 1-6   CompTIA offers a certification for Healthcare IT Technician.

Photo credit: http://certification.comptia.org/getCertified/certifications/hittech.aspx

Now that you understand more about healthcare facilities, the flow of patients in a hospital, and the goals of healthcare IT, the next chapter looks at the flow of patient data as this data follows a patient through the cycle of a hospital stay.

HIT in the Real World

While working on a help desk for a healthcare company in Tennessee, I got a call from an IT Director at one of our hospitals in Texas. The **VPN** connection to NightHawk, a remote radiology company, was down and they needed it restored…stat. Usually this kind of request could take up to 24 hours to complete due to the workload of the network engineers. The urgency in the voice of the IT Director clearly communicated criticality as he explained there was a patient in the ED dying, and the doctors were waiting for the results from the imaging to know how to treat the patient.

I tried calling the network engineers, even though they were notorious for avoiding calls from the help desk because we usually were pushing for them to complete a request they didn't have time to do. No answer. I informed my team lead of the call and trekked across the building to hunt down a network engineer. I told him someone was about to die unless he immediately restored this VPN connection! He jumped right to the task, and the VPN connection was immediately up.

I think everyone realized in that moment that our jobs were not just about phone calls, routers, software, and interfaces. Our jobs actually affect patient care. People's lives are at stake, and doctors depend on us to get our work done in a timely manner.

virtual private network (VPN)—The secure and private networking of computers through the Internet.

Chapter Summary

The Importance of the HITECH Act

- The HITECH Act regulates how HIT interacts with third parties.
- The HITECH Act requires healthcare facilities to use EMR/EHR systems.
- With HIT, patient information has fewer chances of human error by electronically transferring and storing information.

Getting to Know Healthcare

- Acute care facilities are for patients with short-term, immediate needs for healthcare. Nine types of acute care facilities and agencies are an ambulatory care facility, a primary care facility, an ambulatory surgery center, a birth center, a rehabilitation hospital or center, a general acute care hospital, a home health agency, a hospice agency, and a psychiatric hospital.
- Long-term care facilities are for patients who need ongoing care after receiving a diagnosis. Three types of long-term care facilities and agencies are an adult day care facility, assisted-living residence, and nursing home.
- The IT systems in hospitals are the most complex of healthcare facilities. Other facilities are limited to fewer IT systems.
- The departments in a hospital each have specific roles to play in healthcare. Eight standard departments in a hospital are administrative offices, outpatient clinics, inpatient rooms, surgery or operating rooms, radiology, emergency department (ED), pathology and lab, and pharmacy.
- Three entrances for patients to the hospital system are outpatient, inpatient, and the ED.
- Outpatient care lasts less than 24 hours, and patients are usually not admitted into the hospital for inpatient care.
- Inpatient care is when patients are admitted to the hospital and stay longer than 24 hours.
- ED patients can usually be discharged without being admitted to the hospital for inpatient care; however, most patients who are admitted enter through the ED.
- Medical records are maintained for every patient at the hospital for future use if needed.

Goals of Healthcare IT

- The primary goal of HIT is to assist healthcare providers to have more accurate and timely information about their patients.

- Patients might not go untreated without IT; however, the quality and speed of treatment can diminish without the timely assistance of IT.

- HIT technicians are responsible for bridging the gap of communication between the medical staff and the IT support staff.

- HIT personnel are responsible for communicating with healthcare providers to understand their technology needs and try to meet these needs to provide better patient care.

- HIT staff is an advocate for HIT users to find ways IT can improve the quality of work of the medical staff.

Key Terms

For definitions of key terms, see the "Key Terms Glossary" near the end of the book.

- acuity
- acute care
- adult day care facility
- ambulatory care facility
- ambulatory surgery center
- assisted living residence
- birth center
- blood work
- chief complaint
- clinical department
- computed tomography (CT)
- electronic health record (EHR)
- electronic medical record (EMR)
- emergency department (ED)
- general acute care hospital
- healthcare IT
- healthcare IT Health Information Technology for Economic and Clinical Health (HITECH) Act

- healthcare provider
- home health agency
- hospice agency
- inpatient
- long-term care
- magnetic resonance imaging (MRI)
- medical image
- medical records office
- nursing home
- oncology
- outpatient
- patient census
- primary care facility
- psychiatric hospital
- registration
- rehabilitation hospital or center
- stat
- tracking board
- triage
- virtual private network (VPN)

Acronym Drill

Acronyms sometimes get confusing, especially when a single sentence can have four or five. As an HIT professional, you must know the acronyms and what they stand for. Fill in the blank with the correct acronym for the sentence.

1. Healthcare providers depend on _____ for timely and accurate information being available in the computer systems to make decisions on how to treat patients' afflictions.

   Answer: _____

2. The _____ Act regulates how _____ interacts with third parties and requires healthcare facilities to move toward electronic solutions to store patient data and to no longer use paper forms and charts for retaining patient records.

   Answer: _____

3. A patient's _____ is a collection of all patient information about a patient from all visits to a particular hospital. A patient's _____ is a collection of all patient information about a patient from all visits to any hospital.

   Answer: _____

4. An X-ray, _____, and _____ are examples of medical imaging created in the Radiology department.

   Answer: _____

5. A _____ is a secure and private network of computers through the Internet.

   Answer: _____

Review Questions

1. Is a birth center an acute care facility or a long-term care facility?

   Answer: _____

2. Describe the difference between acute and long-term care.

   Answer: _____

   _____

3. Why are hospitals a good starting point for learning about HIT?

   Answer: _____

   _____

4. Which department in a hospital is responsible for billing?

   Answer: _____

5. Where does a patient go in a hospital to get an X-ray?

   Answer: _____

6. List the three ways to enter a hospital. Which is the most common?

   Answer: _____

   _____

7. If a patient comes to a hospital for a surgical procedure that will take 8 hours, from beginning to end, which classification of patient is this?

   Answer: _____

8. If a patient in the ED has an acuity level of five, what is the general condition of that patient?

    Answer: _____

9. What is the primary goal of HIT staff?

    Answer: _____

10. Whose responsibility is it to communicate with the medical staff concerning IT functions?

    Answer: _____

Practical Application

1. Research on the Internet to find the government website that explains the HITECH Act. Which U.S. Department sponsored the HITECH Act and in what year was it signed into law?

    Answer: _____

2. Research on the website you found in the preceding question to find the purposes of Electronic Health Records and Meaningful Use. Using information on the site, write a statement describing the purpose of Electronic Health Records, and write another statement describing Meaningful Use.

    Answer: _____

    _____

    _____

3. Search on the Internet for possible job specializations in healthcare IT. What websites did you visit to find job ideas? Which jobs did you find? What is the job description? What interests you about a particular field of HIT?

    Answer: _____

    _____

    _____

    _____

    _____

CHAPTER 2
Introducing Data Flow in HIT

In this chapter you learn about:

- The technical support that hospitals might use
- The interfaces among HIT information systems
- How data flows among healthcare information systems

As always, remember that getting patient data to healthcare providers in a timely manner makes for better patient care. For example, data about patients needs to move from the bedside to the lab, and then to the pharmacy and back to the bedside. The data can be moved using paper and phone calls, and that is how healthcare data moved for years; however, to save healthcare providers' time and energy, computerized information systems have been installed. In the past, someone had to call the lab to get results from blood work, call the pharmacy to request medication, and walk to the pharmacy to pick up the medication. Now, lab results are viewed on the computer near the patient, an order for medication can be entered on that same computer, and medication can be picked up from an automated dispensing medicine cabinet located near the patient. To learn how all this works, you learn about the information systems used to compute and communicate this data, the interfaces that connect them, and what is in the data that is sent.

Learning Support Flow

A hospital requires technical support for the computer systems it uses. This support can be provided in many ways. For example, some smaller hospitals might have one or two IT technicians to support the computers with the help of support provided by vendors. Larger hospitals might have a team of IT technicians who specialize in each of the different systems. For example, one person might support the servers used at the hospital, and another person might support the network.

Many hospitals are managed by corporations. These management corporations have teams of analysts in the IT department who provide remote technical support to the local IT technicians at each hospital. The local IT personnel handle the support issues to the best of their ability and according to the time they have and the security access they are allowed. When they need help beyond their abilities or access, they call the corporate office IT department and ask for help.

The IT department at the corporate office is made up of several smaller teams. These teams offer focused and specialized support to cover all needs of healthcare IT. To properly route the calls from the local IT, the corporate office has a help desk or call center, as shown in Figure 2-1. The help desk receives requests and creates a trouble ticket to track requests. Usually the help desk can resolve the incident. If, however, the help desk cannot resolve the incident, it escalates the trouble ticket to a higher-level team that can resolve the issue. The local IT and the help desk are both responsible for all trouble tickets. This means they will both follow up with the team resolving the issue until a satisfactory resolution is reached.

Even though multiple hospitals across the country might be managed by the same corporation, these hospitals do not usually share patient information. Sharing patient information among hospitals might happen if several hospitals are in the same geographic area managed by the same corporation. For example, hospitals in the same city managed by the same corporation might share patient information. This sharing of patient information improves the continuity of care for patients because the healthcare providers have access to patient medical records from a neighboring hospital. **Health information exchange (HIE)** is the practice of sharing patient information among multiple providers. This practice is quickly growing in the HIT field.

health information exchange (HIE)—Sharing of patient information among multiple providers. These providers do not need to work in the same hospital to have access to patient information. Currently, this is typically done for hospitals in close geographic locations, but the goal is to make HIE nationwide.

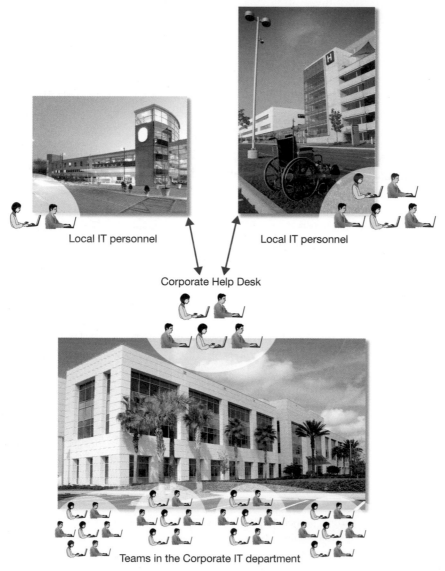

Figure 2-1   The corporate help desk connects the local IT personnel with the support teams in the corporate IT department.

Photo credits: SeanPavonePhoto, blondsteve, btmedia

Now that you know about the support system, the next section discusses the computer systems you support.

Getting to Know Information Systems

A computerized **information system (IS)** is a group of components that collect, process, store, and communicate information. The IS contains a database to store the information it collects and uses instructions stored in the database to process data. An example of an IS in a hospital is the electronic medical record (EMR) IS. The purpose of the EMR IS is to collect patient medical records, store these records, process queries to access the records, and communicate the records to another system upon request.

> **information system (IS)**—A computerized system used to facilitate the functions of an organization. An IS is a group of components that collect, process, store, and communicate information.

Other information systems in the hospital work the same way. They collect, store, process, and communicate data to and from other information systems in the hospital. Hospitals have standard departments, and these departments each have an IS. There is an IS for the lab, radiology, surgery, and pharmacy. These four information systems are classified as **clinical information systems (CIS)** because each is an IS that directly relates to the medical care of a patient. The primary IS that centralizes patient data while a patient is admitted is called the hospital IS (HIS). Hospitals might use other, smaller information systems that support other ancillary clinical departments such as dietary or respiratory. The smaller systems are usually supported by the vendor and not the HIT department. Other information systems in the hospital work to manage the administrative side of hospital functions. This includes an IS for time management for hourly paid staff, billing, medical coding, or scheduling.

> **clinical IS (CIS)**—An information system directly related to the care of patients. Examples are the information systems for radiology, lab, surgery, pharmacy, and order entry.

As a member of the IT staff at a hospital, you are responsible for understanding the flow of data at your hospital. This is true if you are the IT director, project manager, implementation analyst, or technician. You must know where the data needs to be to make it useful to patient care. It's easier to understand the HIT data flow if you know where the patient is in the hospital. For example, if a patient needs an MRI in the Radiology department, that patient's information needs to go into the radiology information system (RIS). Makes sense, right?

Each IS is a bit unique and is not exactly the same at every hospital. Many vendors have developed their own **solutions** for an information system or systems. Each solution is unique and functions differently even though multiple solutions might work for the same purpose and all share common goals in patient care. For example, one vendor's user interface looks nothing like the user interface of another vendor, yet both serve as the RIS. Some solutions have many different systems networked together, and others have all functions of the entire hospital housed in the same system. Hospitals customize vendor products, so even within a product from the same vendor, two hospitals won't be configured the same. Hospitals pick and choose if they want the HIS to handle all IS operations or if they want to use subsystems for more options offered by specialized systems.

When you are on the HIT staff, you should create a data flow diagram for your particular hospital. You can use this graphic many times as you troubleshoot where a breakdown occurs, as you explain to users why they don't see what they expect, or as you program data to go where it needs to go.

> **solutions**—Products or programs offered by vendors to provide an answer to a need.

Getting to Know HIS

The **hospital information system (HIS)** is the primary IS in a hospital. The HIS has six primary functions, which do the following:

- Manage patient registration.
- Maintain centralized patient information.
- Provide software for order entry.
- Manage charges and billing.
- Manage scheduling for patient arrivals and procedures.
- Maintain the master patient index (MPI).

> **hospital information system (HIS)**—The primary information system used to manage data flow and maintain databases in a hospital. An HIS usually manages patient administration and order entry. HIS is sometimes called a healthcare information system (HIS).

The responsibilities of the HIS might expand to include other functions, or the HIS might delegate responsibilities of any of the six primary functions to ancillary systems. Each HIS component maintains its own databases, as shown in Figure 2-2. Any of these components—for example, billing—can be outsourced to a separate IS.

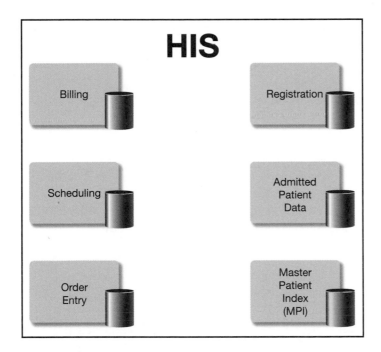

Figure 2-2   The HIS contains components that have databases of information to perform functions of the hospital information management.

Large hospitals have greater need for a more complex HIS. For example, they might have labs inside the hospital that smaller hospitals might outsource. Small hospitals that need only basic information systems can purchase an HIS solution that handles all IS functions, including the clinical systems and administrative systems. The decision on which solution to use is determined by the cost and functionality of the solution.

The following sections focus on explaining each function of an HIS.

Functions of an HIS

Patient registration is how the HIS knows how many patients are in the hospital, where they are, and who they are. The Registration office is responsible for the patient census. Registration has three components:

- **Admission**: Recall from Chapter 1, "Introducing Healthcare IT," that admission is when a patient has doctor's orders to be admitted and needs care that exceeds 24 hours, unless under observation.

- **Discharge**: When a patient leaves a hospital.
- **Transfer**: The HIS tracks all transfers. A patient can transfer within a hospital to a different unit or even transfer/discharge to another hospital if the patient requires care that the current hospital cannot provide.

Patient information is the data about a patient that healthcare providers need to know to make decisions for patient care. Portions of this information include patient demographics, such as age, sex, allergies, current medications, address, next of kin, insurance provider, and history. Patient information also includes patient vital signs, such as heart rate, blood pressure, temperature, height, and weight. The HIS is where nurses record these patient vital signs, and doctors enter their notes about the patient.

Order entry is exactly as it sounds. Healthcare providers enter their orders for treatment, tests, imaging, or medicine in the HIS system for services and procedures. Order entry is used primarily by nurses. Figure 2-3 shows a sample order entry screen. New information systems called **computerized physician order entry (CPOE)** are implemented so that doctors can conveniently enter their own orders.

> **order entry**—A component of an HIS where healthcare providers enter orders for patient care. Orders can be for procedures, imaging, or maybe tests. Order entry is sometimes written as OE but still read as "order entry."
>
> **computerized physician order entry (CPOE)**—An order entry system designed specifically for doctors' use.

Each hospital is unique, and a hospital might have nonelectronic methods for entering some orders. Hospitals are widely still in transition of adopting computerized information systems, so paper information systems might still be used while a computerized system is implemented. For example, there might not be an order entry for the pharmacy, and therefore pharmacy orders must be faxed, called, written, or sent by some other method. Even while using a computerized system, occasionally paper is still relied on as a backup plan in case the computerized system requires down time, such as during a power outage or system maintenance.

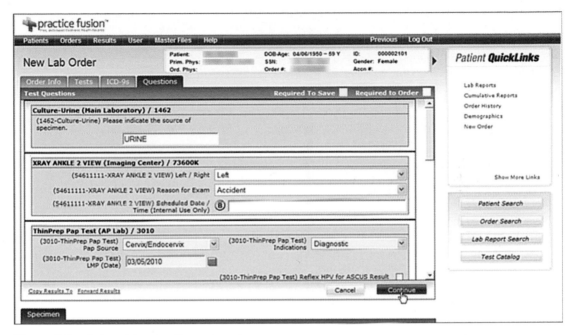

Figure 2-3 Order a lab using the order entry screen.

Photo credit: http://www.practicefusion.com

The HIS manages charges and billing. For example, an HIS might be used to charge a patient for a procedure, supplies, or medication. In addition, patients are charged depending on the level of care needed. If the care of a patient requires significant intervention, the level of care charge will be higher than if the patient needs only an evaluation and advice. In the emergency department (ED), charges are based on the acuity of the patient's condition. The IS that fulfills the service or manages the supplies calculates charges, sends a charge message to the HIS, and the charges are added to a patient's account. Billing is maintained in the financial segment of the HIS. The finances of a hospital are sometimes managed by an ancillary financial IS in larger hospitals.

The HIS maintains the scheduling of procedures. Each department has its own schedule to consider, so having a centralized system for maintaining the schedule helps to streamline patient care. When procedure schedules are streamlined, patients get the care they need as quickly as possible. Figure 2-4 shows an example of an appointment schedule screen.

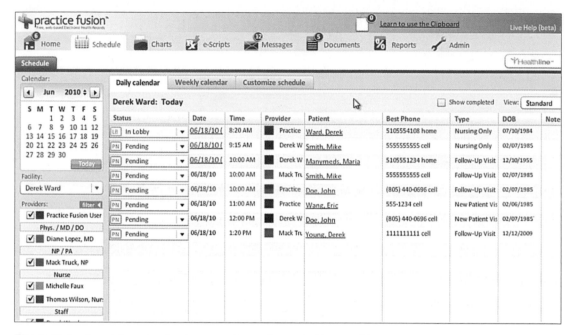

Figure 2-4   Appointment calendars are often color-coded by provider.

Photo credit: http://www.practicefusion.com

The HIS maintains the database of **medical record numbers (MRNs)** and **account numbers** called the **master patient index (MPI)**. MRNs are used to reference the collective medical history of a patient. Each patient must have a unique MRN at a hospital. It works similarly to a Social Security number (SSN). A patient is assigned an MRN during his first visit at the hospital and retains that MRN in every subsequent visit to that hospital. MRNs do not cross to other hospitals unless multiple facilities are in the same network and share HIS data. A patient might have multiple account numbers at a hospital. The account number is assigned per visit by a patient. No two patients have the same account number, and the account number is different for one patient for each visit.

> **medical record number (MRN)**—The number assigned to a patient to reference the care of that patient for all visits at one particular hospital. An MRN is unique to a patient within a hospital's network.
>
> **account number**—The number assigned to a patient to reference the care of that patient for the current visit. The account number is sometimes referred to as an encounter number, accession number, or registration number in different information systems.
>
> **master patient index (MPI)**—The database of all MRNs and account numbers. This centralized database is responsible for preventing duplication of MRNs and account numbers.

The MPI contains fields of data easily searched for a match to a patient record. When searching for a patient, enough information should be entered to limit the number of results to easily find the correct patient. Some of the recommended data fields follow:

- MRN
- Patient's first name, middle initial (optional), or last name
- Date of birth (DOB)
- Gender
- Ethnicity
- Address: street, city, state, and ZIP code
- Alias
- SSN
- Account number
- Admission date
- Discharge date
- Service type (inpatient or outpatient)

Now that you know what the HIS offers, let's look at the interfaces.

Getting to Know the Interface

All hospital information systems have interfaces of one sort or another. The purpose of an **interface** is to communicate data from one IS to another IS. What travels between the information systems are messages. **Messages** contain the data about a patient and his visit to the hospital. To understand the message and the path it takes, you need to know what the message is, the format the message uses, and how it travels from IS to IS.

> **interface**—The connection between two information systems for the purpose of exchanging data.
>
> **message**—The information sent from one system to another.

The Message

Messages containing data about patients are sent across the hospital network from one IS to another IS. This data contains information about the patient demographic, encounter, or charges. The data is formatted in a standard used across healthcare organizations. This standard is called **Health Level 7 (HL7)** as developed by the HL7 organization. HL7 is an interface protocol at the application level designed for healthcare applications and systems. A standard format for sending messages means that the destination IS understands the data presented. This also means that the same message can be used to communicate to several different systems who all "speak the same language." You can learn more about the all-volunteer, nonprofit organization called HL7 and its accreditations on its website, hl7.org.

> **Health Level 7 (HL7)**—The standard protocol of formatting a message for healthcare interfacing. HL7 is ANSI certified. HL7 operates at the seventh or application layer of the OSI communication model.

> **NOTE**   The American National Standards Institute (ANSI) is responsible for standards in products, services, processes, and systems. You can find out more about ANSI on its website at www.ansi.org.

> **NOTE**   The Open Systems Interconnection (OSI) model explains the communication process of a network in layers.

HL7 has several different types of messages. Table 2-1 describes the most commonly used HL7 messages. Don't worry yet about knowing what each of these mean or the details of the message because Chapter 6, "Medical Business Operations," covers HL7 in more detail. The three you need to pay attention to at this time are the ADT, ORM, and ORU message types. These message types create the most pathways in the interfaces. The ADT message is sent when a patient's registration status in the hospital changes. The ADT acts like an alert to the information systems that a patient is heading its way and to expect possible further transmissions of messages. "A"dmit for when a patient enters the hospital, "d"ischarge when the patient leaves the hospital, and "t"ransfer when the patient moves to a different unit or to a different hospital. All information systems need to receive this message if they have any interaction with the patient's data. The ORM message, or order message, is sent when a healthcare provider requests a service, procedure, or treatment for a patient. Any IS involved to fulfill this order needs to receive this message. The ORU message is returned in response to the ORM message and contains the results from the request. For example, the ORU transmits the results from a test or image.

Table 2-1 Some HL7 Message Types

Abbreviation	Message Type	Description
ACK	General acknowledgment	Return message confirming message was received
ADT	Admit discharge transfer	Changes the registration status of a patient
ORM	Order	Requests a service or treatment
ORU	Observation result (Unsolicited)	Results from orders request
BAR	Add/change billing account	Makes additions or changes to a patient's billing account
DFT	Detailed financial transaction	Transmits charges and credits
MFN	Master files notification	Makes a change to master drug formulary record

Figure 2-5 shows an example HL7 message so that you can see what is sent. This message has been parsed, or split into lines, so it can be read more easily. The vertical bars indicate each of the fields available for content in the message. The carets indicate a separation within a field.

```
MSH|^~\&|PATACCT|999|MCKESSON|999|20120320115714||ADT^A03|3163|P|2.3|3
163||||US|
EVN|A03|20120320115400|||GDC|
PID|1||2||MOUSE^MICKEY||17620824|M||W|2525 OAK STREET^^DES
MOINES^IA^50302|153||||D|C|2000008|||||CO|||||
PD1|||||||Y||||N|N^N|
PV1|1|O|RAD|3|||107^DUCK^DAFFY^L|||RAD||||1||N|107^DUCK^DAFFY^L|E||H||
|||||||||||||||01^DC TO HOME OR SELF CARE (RO
DISCHA)|||||||||20120320115400|20120320115400||||||
DG1|1|I9||HEADACHES||||||||||||||
GT1|1|2|JAMES^TEST||324 6TH AVE^^CEDAR
RAPIDS^IA^52402||||M|||||1||||||||||||||||||||||||||||||||||||||||
IN1|1|2|411|AETNA|REG TO ENTER^^REG TO
ENTER^OK^00000|||||||||||C|JAMES|G8^OTHER
RELATIONSHIP|||Y|CO|1|||||Y|||||||||||||||1|M|SAME^^^^|Y||3|||
```

Figure 2-5 An example ADT message using HL7 formatting.

> **NOTE** When working in a test environment, use names of patients that are obviously fake, such as Daffy Duck, Mickey Mouse, or James Test. This protects the patient information of real patients and is additional assurance that you are working in the test environment, and not the live environment.

The Message Path

Messages travels across the network from a source IS to the destination IS. The interface can be set up using one of the following two common methods: point-to-point or through the interface engine. A **point-to-point connection** is when the message leaves one IS and goes directly to another IS. In this type of connection, the originating system is responsible for sending the message to the right destination and for ensuring the data is in a format the receiving system can interpret.

> **point-to-point connection**—A one-to-one interface between two information systems. Point-to-point connections require the IS at each end of the connection to guarantee the delivery and interpretation of the data.

When a message needs to go to more than one destination IS or needs to be filtered or changed in any manner, an **interface engine** is used. An interface engine is a complex system and yet a simple concept. An interface engine is a communications hub. If the interface engine were not implemented, each IS would need an interface set up with all other information systems it needs to communicate with. This can look messy, as shown in Figure 2-6. The interface engine can organize the transfer of data in a one-to-one relationship or a one-to-many relationship. The interface engine can receive data from one IS and broadcast that data to as many other information systems that need the data. A point-to-point interface can be used only if both systems on each end of the interface use the same platform or operating system (OS). For a Linux system to communicate with a Windows system, the interface must translate the data so that it can be received by the different IS.

> **interface engine**—An application that serves as a communications hub and offers services to the messages as they travel through a network. These services include but are not limited to forwarding, filtering, translation, and queue management.

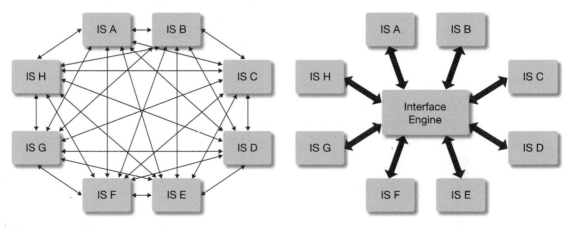

Figure 2-6   Without an interface engine, each IS must have a separate interface with any other IS with which it needs to communicate.

The interface engine does much more than just direct traffic. Data is forwarded, filtered, translated, and sent to the destination information systems. The interface engine manages the message queues, archives messages, and guarantees delivery of messages. Now take a closer look at some possible functions of an interface engine in Table 2-2.

Table 2-2   Functions of an Interface Engine

Function	Description
Forward	A single inbound message can be sent to multiple destinations.
Filter	Sorts through all the incoming messages from one source and deciphers which needs to go to each of the various destinations. For example, only lab orders go to the lab.
Translate	Translates a message from one platform, or OS, to another. For example, if the lab IS is based on Linux and the HIS is based on Windows, the interface engine translates the data so that both systems understand the data they receive.
Queue management	If a connection goes down, the interface engine maintains the queue of messages until the connection is reopened by the destination IS and then sends the waiting messages.
Archive messages	Stores messages that have been received and sent so a technician can troubleshoot problems regarding the messages. This archive keeps only a few days of messages due to the amount of data that passes through an interface engine: The memory would fill to capacity.

Interface engine applications offer a **dashboard** that gives a status of each inbound and outbound interfaces on the message engine. Some interface engine vendors provide a visual by using a dashboard display, so there is a green light when messages are flowing properly, a yellow light when the message queue backup reaches a threshold, or a red light when messages are no longer flowing. The dashboard ensures the IT department is the first to know of a problem with the interface engine. This proactive approach is preferred rather than hearing about a problem through a complaint of information not showing up that a doctor has been waiting on.

> **dashboard**—An application's graphic user interface (GUI) that provides status information at a quick glance and commands to manage the application.

Now that you understand a little about what is in a message and how messages get across the network, look at where these messages come from and where they go.

Following the Data Flow

Following the data flow is crucial to understanding how an HIS works. You need to understand what is in the data, how it is communicated, where it comes from, and where it goes. This knowledge enables you to troubleshoot errors and glitches in the system, implement new systems, and update changes to the current system. HL7 is highly customizable and makes it possible for a technician to change the fields of the messages. If you change the HL7 fields in one interface, you need to understand the downstream effect of that change on the other interfaces. The rest of the chapter uses diagrams that represent a possible configuration of a hospital's data flow. As you work through the diagrams, keep in mind that each hospital is unique in its data flow based on the information systems installed, the vendors, and the phase of implementation. Also keep in mind that some hospitals are not going to be as complex.

Remember from Chapter 1 that the three types of patient entrances into a hospital are through inpatient services, outpatient services, and the ED. As a patient enters the hospital, his registration status is changed to "admitted" by an ADT message. Because a patient can only enter the hospital through three entrances, only the information systems used in these departments can create an ADT message. These three departments are the Registration office, the ED, and outpatient surgery. The Registration office uses the HIS directly to admit patients. The ED uses the EDIS. Outpatient surgery uses the **perioperative IS**. After an ADT message, other HL7 messages can originate from other information systems.

perioperative IS—The information system that manages patients in surgery. The perioperative IS starts with scheduling for surgery through discharge or transfer out of surgery. The perioperative IS works largely independent from other information systems because there is rarely a need for interaction with the other clinical departments.

The next section looks at the data flow of an ADT message from the three IS sources. Then you learn about the data flow of other HL7 messages.

Three IS Sources of an ADT Message

Inpatient and outpatient patients are entered into the HIS directly unless the patient is a surgical outpatient. ED patients are entered through the **emergency department information systems (EDIS)**. The following sections look at the data flow from each of these systems. Surgical outpatients use the perioperative IS.

emergency department IS (EDIS)—The information system that manages patient flow, orders, patient history, and record healthcare providers' notes on the patient's visit, and more. The stage of a patient's visit to the ED, who is caring for the patient, and other information are displayed on the tracking board from the EDIS for convenient reference to a healthcare provider's current caseload.

NOTE   As you follow the flow of data, note the HIS and the EMR/EHR are collecting data from all the other systems.

HIS-originated ADT Data Flow

Figure 2-7 shows the data flow when the HIS originates an ADT message. This first diagram is for the first two entrances into a hospital, through inpatient and outpatient services, when a patient's registration is entered directly into the HIS.

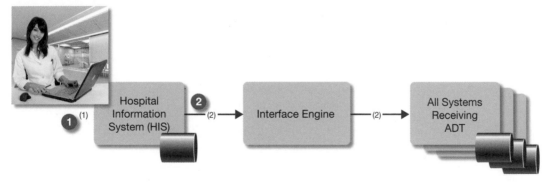

Figure 2-7   The general ADT data flow is dispersed to all systems through the interface engine.

Photo credit: Monkey Business

As shown in Figure 2-7, the steps in the ADT data flow are as follows:

1. The patient is registered in the HIS by hospital staff. This happens bedside or in the Registration area of a hospital.

2. The HIS sends the ADT notification through the interface engine to all systems receiving ADT messages.

The ADT data flow must interact with the HIS because the HIS maintains the MPI.

EDIS ADT Data Flow

The emergency department IS (EDIS) is an independent IS that manages the patient flow in the ED. Arriving patients must have their information entered into the MPI for record keeping. Remember that the HIS maintains the MPI, so the EDIS must query or ask the HIS if this patient already exists in the database before creating a new entry in the MPI. This ADT message data flow must happen before any ORM (order) and ORU (result) messages may be sent or received. For example, a message follows the ADT message path when an ED patient needs an order from the pharmacy or an image made in the radiology department. Order flow for the ED will be explained later in this chapter. Figure 2-8 shows the data flow as it originates in the ED and is sent to all the other information systems.

Patient already exists in MPI

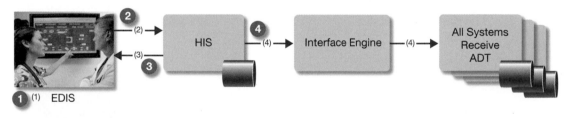

Patient does not exist in MPI

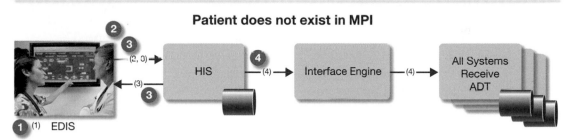

Figure 2-8   Messages from the EDIS go through the HIS and the interface engine to reach the other information systems.

The first diagram in the figure shows the data flow when a patient already exists in the MPI. Here are the steps to follow the data flow in the diagram.

1. The patient is registered in the EDIS by ED staff.

2. The EDIS sends a data query to the HIS with identifiers to find out if the patient already exists in the MPI to prevent patient duplication in records.

3. If the patient exits, the HIS sends an ADT message to the EDIS with the patient information.

4. The HIS sends the ADT notification through the interface engine to all systems receiving ADT messages.

The second diagram shows what happens when a patient does not yet exist in the MPI. Here are the steps to follow the data flow in the diagram.

1. The patient is registered in the EDIS by ED staff.

2. The EDIS sends a data query to the HIS with identifiers to find out if the patient already exists in the MPI so that patient duplication in records is prevented.

3. If the patient does not exist, the HIS sends a message back to the EDIS with no patient information. The patient information is entered into the EDIS and sent back to the HIS to create a new entry in the MPI.

4. The HIS sends the ADT notification through the interface engine to all systems receiving ADT messages.

Perioperative IS Data Flow

The third entrance into the hospital is through outpatient surgery. Surgery consists of three phases:

1. Preoperative (before surgery)
2. Intraoperative (during surgery)
3. Postoperative (after surgery)

These three phases are known collectively as *perioperative*. The perioperative IS manages the entire patient flow of a patient having a surgical procedure. The perioperative IS treats both inpatient and outpatient patients the same way. The perioperative IS must query the HIS for the MRN and send charges to the HIS for billing. Finally, the perioperative IS sends the records of the procedure to the EMR/EHR IS. Follow the data flow for the perioperative IS, as shown in Figure 2-9.

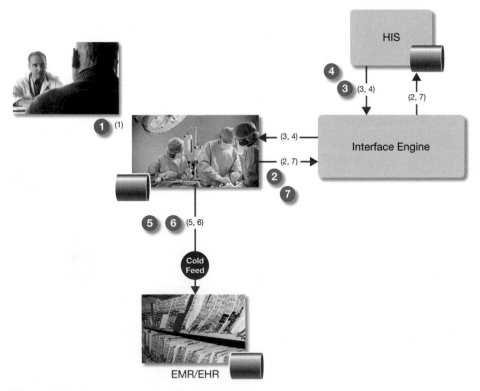

Figure 2-9   The perioperative IS manages the patient from scheduling the procedure through the end of postoperative care.

Photo credits: Jordan Edgcomb, andreiorlov, and carmeta

Following is the data flow prior to surgery:

1. The patient is scheduled in the perioperative IS by the surgery department staff.

2. The perioperative IS sends a temporary account number through the interface engine to the HIS. The perioperative IS uses this temporary account number to track the patient until the HIS can assign a permanent account number to the patient needing surgery.

3. The HIS sends a permanent account number to the perioperative IS through the interface engine after verifying if the patient already exists in the MPI.

The following happens at the time of surgery:

4. The patient is registered in the HIS on the day of the procedure, and an MRN is attached to the appointment. The HIS sends the ADT message to the perioperative IS to acknowledge that the patient is present and ready to begin the surgery process.

5. When the intraoperative phase is complete, the **surgical summary report** is sent to the EMR/EHR in a **cold feed**.

6. When all operative phases are complete, the **operative record** is sent to the EMR/EHR from the perioperative IS through a **dictation** cold feed.

7. The charges are calculated by the perioperative IS and sent to the HIS for billing.

---

surgical summary report—A brief accounting of the surgical case report for immediate referral during the postoperative phase.

cold feed—The real-time transfer of data from a source IS to a destination IS that does not receive acknowledgment of receipt of data. The data transfer is not guaranteed in a cold feed. Other data transfers require a receipt of data acknowledgment, called an ACK message, that guarantees the data was received.

operative record—A complete and detailed accounting of the surgical case happenings from preoperative through postoperative phases. This document is written to be used for legal reference if ever needed.

dictation—A typed transcript of a recorded healthcare provider's oral report of patient care as spoken into a voice recorder.

Now that you know the ADT message paths, the sections that follow outline the message paths of other types of HL7 messages used by the following clinical information systems: pharmacy IS, radiology IS, lab IS, and the EDIS.

Data Flow Other Than ADT

The data flow for the other types of HL7 messages happens after the ADT messages have been sent and received. The ADT messages have made all the information systems in the hospital aware that a patient is present and ready for care. (Refer to Figure 2-7 to see the general ADT data flow diagram.) After the ADT messages, other HL7 messages are sent and received that reference care, records, and the administration for providing care. The following sections begin with an understanding of the message paths of other HL7 messages in the pharmacy IS and then proceed with other clinical information systems.

Pharmacy IS Data Flow

The pharmacy receives orders from healthcare providers and fulfills them. The pharmacy also accounts for all medications consumed in the hospital by using a **medication administration record (MAR)**. The MAR is a legal record that ensures patients receive the prescribed medication. Many hospitals are streamlining this process, which also offers more security in the process, by implementing an **electronic MAR (eMAR)**. An eMAR is recorded using hand-held scanners. These scanners look like those used at checkout lines in a retail store, as shown in Figure 2-10. They track meds from the pharmacy to the nursing station to the bedside, scanning the medication in each location. The eMAR tracks individual doses of medicine for more accurate accounting of the medicine. Another tool used to contribute to the eMAR is the **automated dispensing cabinet (ADC)**. An ADC is an electronic cabinet with drawers containing medications stocked by pharmacy staff, as shown in Figure 2-11. These cabinets are found in various locations in the hospital, usually somewhere close to a nursing station for convenient access to administer medicine quickly to a patient. ADCs have enhanced an important aspect of patient care by providing better accessibility to medication used to treat patients. An ADC can be accessed only by an order or security code. All ADCs have an emergency override in case the system is down.

---

medication administration record (MAR)—The legal record of medication consumption in a hospital. The MAR tracks all medications in the hospital. Sometimes called drug charts.

electronic MAR (eMAR)—The medication administration record (MAR) recorded electronically using hand-held scanners at several locations from the pharmacy to the patient bedside.

automated dispensing cabinet (ADC)—An electronic cabinet with drawers containing medications that are placed throughout the hospital for convenient access by healthcare providers to quickly administer medicines.

Figure 2-10   A barcode scanner is used to track medication.

Figure 2-11   The automated dispensing cabinet (ADC) offers healthcare providers convenient and ready access to critical or commonly used medications.

The **pharmacy IS** is responsible for tracking all activity regarding medications within the entire hospital. The pharmacy IS is linked to the ADCs, updates the eMARs, and sends charges to the HIS. Doctors use a physician portal to check on their patients' records. A **physician portal** is a view into the HIS and EMR/EHR records. Doctors can view their patients' information, test results, orders, and enter notes. They can also sign documents electronically using a physician portal. Physician portals differ from CPOE because the CPOE application is designed specifically for physicians to enter orders for their patients. The physician portal is used to check on patients electronically and enter notes into patient charts. Many vendors offer both solutions and might offer them as a package that uses the same user credentials for both applications.

> **pharmacy IS**—The information system used by the pharmacy. The pharmacy IS supports but is not limited to order entry, management, dispensing of medications, monitoring, reporting, and charging.
>
> **physician portal**—A user interface that accesses the HIS or EHR/EMR. The physician portal is where doctors go to view patient records, add notes, and electronically sign off on charts.

Figure 2-12 shows the data flow for the pharmacy IS.

Follow these steps in the pharmacy IS to follow the pharmacy data flow, which are shown in Figure 2-12:

1. A healthcare provider enters an order for a medication from the pharmacy in the hospital using the order entry component in the HIS.
2. The HIS sends the order to the pharmacy through the interface engine.
3. The pharmacy IS sends an order message to the ADC through the interface engine.
4. The order can be viewed in the physician portal.
5. When the healthcare provider collects and administers the medicine, the dispense information is sent from the ADC to the pharmacy IS through the interface engine.
6. The pharmacy IS charges at the time the medicine is dispensed. The pharmacy IS sends charges to the billing component in the HIS through the interface engine.
7. The eMAR is updated in the pharmacy IS.

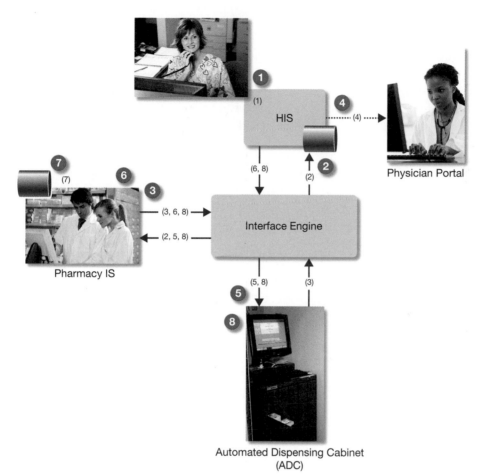

Figure 2-12   The pharmacy IS tracks medication consumption in the hospital. The dashed line in step 4 indicates that this is primarily a view-only access.

Photo credits: Lisa F. Youn, lightpoet, and diego cervo

8. ADC medication credits for orders that were not used are sent to the pharmacy IS and then to the billing component of the HIS through the interface engine. For example, if a nurse removes medicine from the ADC for a patient, the charge is sent for that medicine. If for some reason the patient did not consume that medicine, the patient's account is credited for the unused medicine.

Here is an excellent opportunity to show how each facility can differ. Suppose a pharmacy had not yet implemented its order interface with the HIS. The pharmacy would still receive orders the old-fashioned way. Orders would come in through a fax, a handwritten prescription, or a phone call. This extra step to communicate an order to the pharmacy costs the healthcare provider time and resources until the new pharmacy IS is fully installed. Let this remind you how one ORM interface saves healthcare providers a lot of time.

RIS Data Flow

The radiology department in a hospital fulfills orders for patient imaging. The **radiology IS (RIS)** is responsible for receiving imaging orders, charging, and sending results. If a hospital is not big enough to offer after-hour radiology services, a remote radiology service may be used to read an image and provide a report explaining the results about the image. The RIS is responsible for the link to these remote services as well.

> **radiology IS (RIS)**—The information system responsible for orders, charging, and results of medical imaging.

Figure 2-13 shows the data flow of the RIS.

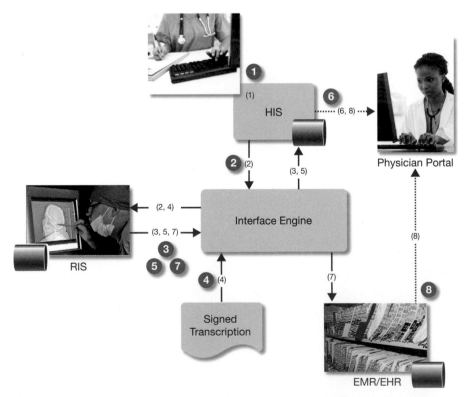

Figure 2-13   The RIS manages the orders, charges, and results of imaging services.

Photo credits: andreiorlov, lightpoet, Yuri Arcurs, and Konstantin Sutyagin

Use these steps to follow the RIS data flow shown in Figure 2-13:

1. A healthcare provider places an order for a radiology service in the HIS.

2. The HIS sends an order message to the RIS through the interface engine, and then the images are taken by a radiology technician.

3. The RIS sends the charge for the procedure to the HIS through the interface engine.

4. After the procedure is completed and interpreted, the final results from the transcription signed by the radiologist are sent to the RIS through the interface engine.

5. Final results are communicated from the RIS to the HIS through the interface engine.

6. Radiology results are viewable in the physician portal.

7. The RIS sends the image of the signed report to the EHR/EMR through the interface engine.

8. The final patient chart is viewable in the EHR/EMR using the physician portal.

LIS Data Flow

The **Lab IS (LIS)** is a bit of a beast to create a flow diagram. This challenge is because a lab includes many components used to fulfill multiple types of lab orders. The LIS is developed and sold by vendors with various levels of complexity. The diagram shown in Figure 2-14 is actually a simple configuration compared to many. Some lab information systems actually have their own miniature interface engine and require a separate server because of the complexity.

> **lab IS (LIS)**—The information system responsible for orders, charging, and results of laboratory tests.

Labs do more than just run test tubes through centrifuges. Labs perform the following tasks.

- Test blood for the **blood bank**, which has an IS.

- Coordinate with a **diagnostic lab**, which is often remote.

- Send work off to a **pathology lab**, which has its own IS.

- Print labels and forms for tracking specimens.

- Provide a hardcopy of the results along with the electronic results through the interface engine.

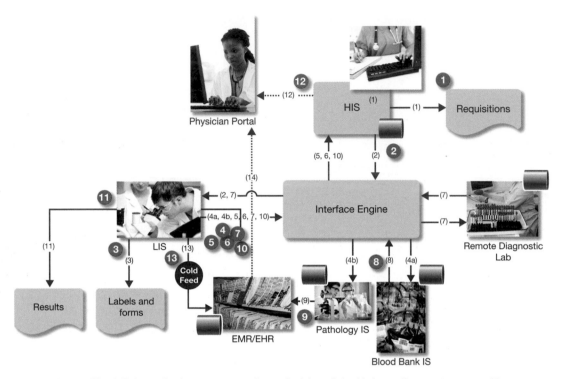

Figure 2-14   The LIS is easily the most complicated of the clinical information systems used in a hospital.

Photo credits: WavebreakMediaMicro, andreiorlov, lightpoet, Yuri Arcurs, Alexander Raths, Donald Swartz, and withGod

The data flow (refer to Figure 2-14) is representative of an LIS in one hospital.

---

blood bank—A reserve of donated blood used to replenish blood supply of patients who experience extreme blood loss. Testing is performed on the blood to reduce risk of problems during blood transfusions.

diagnostic lab—A service used for advanced testing for disorders or diseases through laboratory analysis. Most diagnostic labs are remote from the hospital.

pathology lab—A service that focuses on the diagnosis of diseases through laboratory analysis.

Use the following steps to follow the data flow shown in Figure 2-14:

1. A healthcare provider places a lab order in the HIS for a patient. The HIS prints nursing **requisitions** to let the nurses know which **specimens** need to be collected and when.

---

requisitions—The list of requests sent to the nursing staff for collection of specimens from patients. The timing of the collection is sometimes critical for accuracy of tests.

specimen—Sample of bodily fluids or tissue taken for analysis.

---

2. An order message is sent from the HIS to the LIS through the interface engine.

3. The lab receives the order message and prints a label and collection form for the specimen as needed.

4a. The LIS sends an order message to the blood bank IS through the interface engine.

4b. The LIS sends an order message to the pathology IS through the interface engine.

5. The lab collects and receives the specimen. An order update message is sent from the LIS to the HIS through the interface engine so that healthcare providers know the progress of the order.

6. The LIS sends test data (charge code, quantity, patient name, account, and so on) for the charge to be generated in the HIS through the interface engine.

7. The LIS sends data to the remote diagnostic lab through the interface engine and receives results back through the interface engine.

8. The blood bank result message is sent to the HIS through the interface engine.

9. The pathology final transcription result message is sent directly to the EMR/EHR.

10. The ordered test is resulted. A status update of the result is sent from the LIS to the HIS through the interface engine.

11. The result is printed/delivered/faxed from the LIS as needed.

12. Physician reviews the reports in the HIS using a physician portal.

13. The LIS feeds the reports directly to the EMR/EHR.

14. The final patient chart is viewable in the EMR/EHR using the physician portal.

EDIS Data Flow

The EDIS handles the patient flow for ED patients, but it needs help from the other clinical information systems for treatment of the ED patients. The interface engine connects the EDIS to the other clinical information systems, but only after the HIS has recorded that data. Figure 2-15 shows the data flow of the EDIS orders and charges.

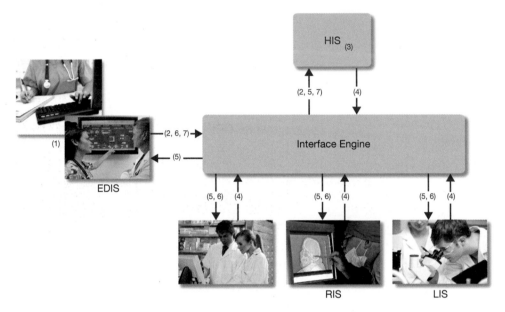

Figure 2-15   The HIS manages the order requests from the EDIS before the orders are sent to the other clinical information systems.

Photo credits: WavebreakMediaMicro, diego cervo, Yuri Arcurs, and Konstantin Sutyagin

Use these steps to follow the data flow shown in Figure 2-15:

1. The healthcare provider enters an order in the EDIS.
2. The EDIS sends an order to the HIS for assignment of an order number through the interface engine.
3. The HIS assigns an order number to the test.
4. The HIS sends the order message to the system fulfilling the order (pharmacy IS, RIS, or LIS) through the interface engine.
5. Results are returned through the interface engine to the HIS and the EDIS.
6. The charge is sent to the HIS from the system fulfilling the order.
7. The EDIS sends a charge for the patient care provided to the HIS through the interface engine.

HIT in the Real World

The corporate office where I worked managed hospitals. When the company acquired a new hospital, we would send out a team to switch the hospital to computer systems that we could support. The support structure at corporate was organized into three levels. First was the call center. The call center staff members resolved most trouble tickets during the initial phone call. If they could not resolve a more complicated issue, they escalated the ticket to level 2 support teams. I worked at the second level, where my team was dedicated to triaging tickets for the level 3 CIS support teams that resolved trouble tickets my team could not resolve.

For about 2 months we kept getting trouble tickets about broken communications from a hospital that had just installed new computer systems. When a help desk analyst reads "Data is not passing from the blood bank IS to the HIS," he usually thinks there's a problem with the interface because it's responsible for data communication: but not so in this case. Our interface team members knew these tickets were not their problem because the interface engine is assertive. It is always "banging on the door" to the other systems asking to reestablish any down or idle connections. So if an interface is down, it's not due to lack of trying on the interface engine's part. That didn't matter; the application teams saw "communication down," and interpreted that to mean the interface team had to take the trouble ticket.

There was quite a bit of push-back from all the teams claiming the problems weren't with the IS they support. So my team and I decided to take matters into our own hands. We created diagrams like the ones you see in the chapter for this hospital. When we heard that blood bank results weren't showing up in the HIS, we used these diagrams to know where all the possible breaking points were. We were able to ask more relevant questions to pinpoint where the breakdown was. With this ammunition, we were able to convince teams that the problem did lie with their IS, and they needed to accept the trouble ticket and resolve it. We got the trouble tickets resolved.

Because of the overwhelming amount of trouble tickets the interface team members were getting, they started sharing the knowledge of the dashboard. We held cross-training sessions where they showed us how they can see when an interface is down, and how they can see if it's on their side because if they have an outgoing message queue that builds up, it's the destination IS that is not receiving the messages. We created a service-level agreement (SLA) with the interface team members to be more proactive about sharing their knowledge with the application teams. So now whenever they start to see a message queue building up, they create their own trouble ticket and send it to the team that supports the destination IS. This way the application team is aware of the problem before the local IT calls to complain; for example, because a doctor cannot see results from her ordered test.

Taking proactive measures to better understand your systems before they break down greatly reduces your time to resolution for problems. You can even solve some problems before healthcare providers even notice they're not seeing what they should on their screens.

Chapter Summary

Learning Support Flow

- Hospitals employ local IT technicians to support the information systems in the hospital.

- If a hospital management corporation is involved, local IT personnel request help from the corporate IT department when they encounter a problem beyond their skill or security access levels.

- The local IT and the help desk at the corporate office are responsible for all trouble tickets.

- Health information exchange (HIE) is the sharing of patient information among multiple providers.

Getting to Know Information Systems

- A computerized information system (IS) is a group of components that collect, process, store, and communicate information.

- A clinical IS (CIS) is an information system used directly for the care of patients.

- Some HIS solutions have many different systems networked together, and others have all functions of the entire hospital housed in the same system.

Getting to Know HIS

- The hospital information system (HIS) is the primary IS in a hospital.

- The HIS has six primary functions:
  - Manages patient registration
  - Maintains patient information
  - Provides software for order entry
  - Manages charges and billing
  - Manages scheduling for patient arrivals and procedures
  - Maintains the master patient index (MPI)

Getting to Know the Interface

- An interface is used to communicate data in the form of messages from a source IS to a destination IS.

- Health Level 7 (HL7) is an organization and a standard protocol for formatting the communication of data between information systems.

- An ADT message is used to communicate the admission, discharge, or transfer of a patient.

- An ORM message is used to order a service or treatment for a patient.

- An ORU message is used to communicate the results from orders requested of the radiology, lab, or other department that might provide a written result.

- A point-to-point connection interface depends on the source and destination IS to control all aspects of the communication.

- An interface engine serves as a communications hub on a network. The interface engine forwards, filters, and translates data received in messages. The interface engine also manages the message queue and archives messages that pass through.

- The application dashboard on the interface engine offers a quick glance of the status of the interfaces.

Following the Data Flow

- The ADT message is the first to be communicated. It serves as an alert to the other systems that more communication might be coming about this patient.

- When a patient comes into the hospital through the ED or outpatient surgery, these information systems must check with the MPI on the HIS for a record of the patient to be used rather than creating a new entry.

- Perioperative indicates all three phases of surgery: preoperative, intraoperative, and postoperative.

- A cold feed means the interface is one directional. No acknowledgment message (ACK) is sent back to the source IS to confirm the destination IS received the data.

- The medication administration record (MAR) tracks medicine as it is ordered and consumed. The eMAR does the same thing, but electronically.

- An automated dispensing cabinet (ADC) is an electronic cabinet that contains medicines at a convenient and quickly accessible location for healthcare providers. Records made when the ADC is used contribute to the eMAR.

- A physician portal is used by physicians to view patient information, sign charts, and enter notes.
- Requisitions are reports used to inform healthcare providers which patients need specimens collected and when and where.

Key Terms

- account number
- automated dispensing cabinet (ADC)
- blood bank
- clinical information system (CIS)
- cold feed
- computerized physician order entry (CPOE)
- dashboard
- diagnostic lab
- dictation
- electronic medication administration record (eMAR)
- emergency department information system (EDIS)
- health information exchange (HIE)
- Health Level 7 (HL7)
- hospital information system (HIS)
- information system (IS)
- interface
- interface engine
- lab information system (LIS)
- master patient index (MPI)
- medical record number (MRN)
- medication administration record (MAR)
- message
- operative record
- order entry
- pathology lab

- perioperative information system
- pharmacy information system
- physician portal
- point-to-point connection
- radiology information system (RIS)
- requisitions
- solutions
- specimen
- surgical summary report

Acronym Drill

Acronyms sometimes get confusing, especially when a single sentence can have four or five. As an HIT professional, you must know the acronyms and what they stand for. Fill in the blank with the correct acronym for the sentence.

1. _____ is the practice of sharing patient information among multiple providers.

   Answer: _____

2. The _____ is the primary information system used to manage data flow and maintain databases in a hospital.

   Answer: _____

3. _____ is an information system implemented so that doctors can conveniently enter their own orders.

   Answer: _____

4. The _____ maintains the database of _____ and account numbers called the _____.

   Answer: _____

5. The _____ message is returned in response to the _____ message and contains the results from the request.

   Answer: _____

Review Questions

1. In what situation might the IT technicians at a hospital request support help from vendors of the information systems used in the hospital?

   Answer: _____

2. What happens if the corporate help desk cannot resolve a trouble ticket?

   Answer: _____

3. In question 2, who is responsible for following up on a trouble ticket to ensure a satisfactory result is reached?

   Answer: _____

4. What is the practice of sharing of patient information among multiple providers called?

   Answer: _____

5. Is the billing system considered part of CIS? Why or why not?

   Answer: _____

6. What are the six primary functions of the HIS?

   Answer: _____

   _____

   _____

   _____

   _____

7. What is the difference between an account number and an MRN?

   Answer: _____

   _____

   _____

   _____

8. Where is the MPI located?

    Answer: _____

9. What is the URL of the website for the HL7 organization?

    Answer: _____

10. What is the benefit of having an interface engine rather than a point-to-point interface?

    Answer: _____

    _____

11. Why must the EDIS and perioperative IS query the HIS when new patients are registered in its system?

    Answer: _____

    _____

12. What is the benefit of using an eMAR over a paper MAR?

    Answer: _____

    _____

13. Which application is used for order entry by physicians?

    Answer: _____

14. Why would an ADC send an HL7 credit message?

    Answer: _____

    _____

15. Why is the LIS usually more complex than other clinical information systems?

    Answer: _____

    _____

Practical Application

1. Match the IS to the solution provided by vendors. Use the website of the vendor if you need help. Hint: Some information systems have more than one solution.

   Type of IS:

   A. RIS

   B. LIS

   C. Remote radiology IS

   D. Interface engine

   E. ADC

   F. HIS

   G. EDIS

   H. Pharmacy IS

   I. Perioperative IS

   J. Physician portal

   K. EMR/EHR IS

   L. Pathology IS

   M. Blood bank IS

	Solution	Vendor Website
1	ONRAD	www.onradinc.com
2	Pyxis	www.carefusion.com
3	Pro-MED	www.promed-services.com
4	Nighthawk	www.nighthawkradiology.net
5	Wyndgate	www.wyndgate.com
6	Horizon Clinical Infrastructure	www.mckesson.com
7	Horizon Physician Portal	www.mckesson.com
8	Horizon Patient Folder	www.mckesson.com
9	Horizon Surgical Manager	www.mckesson.com
10	Surgical Information System	www.sisfirst.com
11	Horizon Lab	www.mckesson.com
12	Horizon Meds Manager	www.mckesson.com

13	Healthcare Management System	www.hmstn.com
14	PowerPath	www.elekta.com
15	Pathways Healthcare Scheduling	www.mckesson.com
16	Omnicell	www.omnicell.com
17	PathNet	www.cerner.com
18	Cloverleaf	www.lawson.com
19	Horizon Radiology Manager	www.mckesson.com
20	Mirth	www.mirthcorp.com
21	Corepoint	www.corepointhealth.com

Answers:

1. _____

2. _____

3. _____

4. _____

5. _____

6. _____

7. _____

8. _____

9. _____

10. _____

11. _____

12. _____

13. _____

14. _____

15. _____

16. _____

17. _____

18. _____

19. _____

20. _____

21. _____

2. Assume the pharmacy data flow shown in Figure 2-12 still uses paper for receiving orders. How might that affect the flow of data? A healthcare provider would not enter the order in the HIS. Redraw the diagram and indicate that paper is used for direct input into the pharmacy IS. Rewrite the steps to reflect these differences.

Answer: _____

_____

_____

_____

_____

_____

_____

_____

_____

_____

_____

_____

_____

_____

3. You arrive at your new job at a new facility. You ask around to have people explain to you how the data flow works at your facility. You learn your system has an automatic discharge for outpatients who become inpatients and are registered under a new account number for the inpatient stay. Because of this, the information systems need to purge all unneeded outpatients because they are no longer an outpatient, but an inpatient. Following are the steps as explained to you. How would you show this in a diagram?

Step 1. An outpatient is registered in the HIS.

Step 2. A process to discharge outpatients runs in the HIS at 11 p.m. for admit date and time greater than 24 hours.

Step 3. The ADT and the auto discharge are sent through the interface engine to all receiving systems. The auto discharge is suppressed for the patient according to a filter list in the interface engine.

CHAPTER 3
Regulatory Requirements

In this chapter you learn about:

- Agencies, laws, and regulations
- HIPAA controls and compliance issues
- Types of health records and rules of record retention and disposal
- Legal best practices, requirements, and documentation

Regulatory requirements don't sound like fun to read about. No matter how boring this topic is, it is relevant to HIT. The requirements keep you and others out of trouble. The agencies and laws are in place to protect patients' rights and privacy and help you find resources.

Laws and regulations change and can be updated, so the most important point of this chapter is to know where to go to find current information. Also agencies, laws, and regulations vary from state to state, so you need to be aware of local policies in your state.

Use government websites and Internet search engines to find information. The government or .gov sites are the authoritative sources. Other websites might offer insight about where to look for answers or how other facilities handle issues. If you cannot find what you need, look within your facility. Often all it takes to find information about a policy is to visit the department in your hospital that handles matters of policy on a daily basis.

This chapter begins by identifying and explaining the roles of some important agencies and laws.

Identifying Standard Agencies, Laws, and Regulations

HI001 Objectives:

1.1 Identify standard agencies, laws, and regulations.

HHS, ONC, CMS, HIPAA, Medicare, Medicaid, ARRA, HITECH, Meaningful use, Eligible provider, NIST

EXAM TIP Notice all the acronyms as you read this book. Pay attention to them because you absolutely will see them again on the exam and on the job.

Each of the agencies, laws, and regulations described in the following sections play a role in healthcare. The agencies of the U.S. government are responsible for implementing the laws and regulations created by Congress and enacted by the President. The common goal of the agencies, laws, and regulations is to improve the healthcare available to citizens. First, learn about the agencies.

Agencies Governing Healthcare

With changes in the government over the last few years, generous resources have been provided for the development and implementation of HIT. The government has focused funding toward advancing healthcare technology in the United States. The government created agencies to filter the monies to **covered entities**. Covered agencies work toward this same goal to advance healthcare technology. The government and covered agencies are tasked with ensuring the laws and regulations have compliance by healthcare providers and facilities.

covered entity—Health Insurance Portability and Accountability Act (HIPAA) is designed to protect health information used by health insurance plan providers, **healthcare clearinghouses**, and healthcare providers. These three entities are classified as covered entities. Basically, a covered entity is anyone or any organization required to submit to HIPAA rules.

Health Insurance Portability and Accountability Act (HIPAA)—A law created in 1996 to provide a standard set of rules that all covered entities must follow to protect patient health information and to help healthcare providers transition from paper to electronic health records.

> **EXAM TIP**   The Healthcare IT exam focuses on HIPAA quite a bit. Pay close attention to what it is and how it affects IT and healthcare providers.

> **healthcare clearinghouse**—A business that receives healthcare information and translates that information into a standardized format to be sent to a health plan provider. A healthcare clearinghouse is sometimes called a billing service. Basically, a healthcare clearinghouse is a middle person that processes healthcare information.

Following is a list of agencies that govern healthcare in the United States:

- Department of Health and Human Services (HHS)
- National Institute of Standards and Technology (NIST)

Department of Health and Human Services

The Department of Health and Human Services (HHS)—http://www.hhs.gov—is an agency of the U.S. government tasked with the following responsibilities:

- Protect the health of Americans.
- Provide a means for Americans who are least able to help themselves to access healthcare.
- Contain and treat any national health emergencies.
- Test and regulate food and drug supplies.

Figure 3-1 shows the HHS website.

> **EXAM TIP**   For the Healthcare IT exam, you need to be familiar with the HHS, as well as its operating divisions. Be sure you understand the purpose of the CMS.

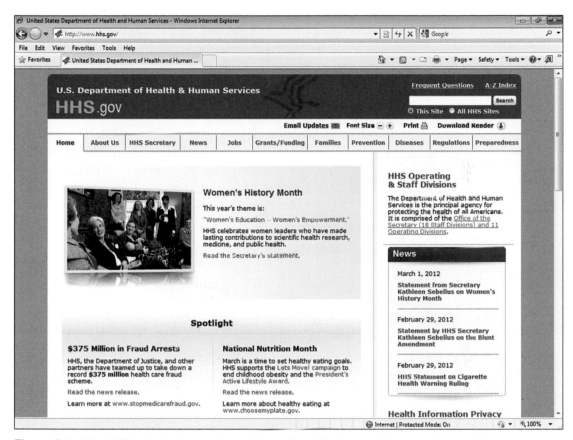

Figure 3-1   The HHS website is current and informative with the need-to-know facts and how to access resources the HHS provides.

Photo credit: http://www.hhs.gov

The HHS contains several operating divisions, as shown in Table 3-1.

Table 3-1   Operating Divisions of the HHS

Division	Abbreviation
Administration for Children and Families	ACF
Administration on Children, Youth, and Families	ACYF
Administration on Aging	AoA
Agency for Healthcare Research and Quality	AHRQ

Table 3-1 Continued

Division	Abbreviation
Centers for Disease Control and Prevention	CDC
Centers for Medicare & Medicaid Services	CMS
Food and Drug Administration	FDA
Health Resources and Services Administration	HRSA
Indian Health Service	IHS
National Institutes of Health	NIH
National Cancer Institute	NCI
Office of the Inspector General	OIG
Substance Abuse and Mental Health Services Administration	SAMHSA

The more notable divisions of the HHS include the Food and Drug Administration (FDA), Centers for Disease Control and Prevention (CDC), and the National Institutes of Health (NIH). Now take a closer look at the divisions of the HHS involved in healthcare:

- Centers for Medicare & Medicaid Services (CMS)
- Office of the National Coordinator for HIT (ONC)
- Office for Civil Rights (OCR)

Centers for Medicare & Medicaid Services (CMS)

The Centers for Medicare & Medicaid Services (CMS) branch—http://www. cms.gov—of the HHS is responsible for administrating Medicare and Medicaid. CMS also regulates the transaction standards of billing codes used to price healthcare expenses, such as electronic claims, remittance, eligibility, and claims status requests/responses. The current version of HIPAA transaction standards is **Version 5010**. All HIPAA-compliant facilities adopted this version January 1, 2012. CMS regulates medical diagnosis and inpatient procedure coding in healthcare. The current version is **ICD-9**. The new version, **ICD-10**, is required to be adopted by HIPAA-compliant facilities by October 1, 2013. Figure 3-2 shows the CMS website homepage.

Version 5010—HIPAA mandated a standard format for electronic claims transactions. This standard was updated to grow with the functional needs of the healthcare industry. The http://www.cms.gov website offers more details about Version 5010.

ICD-9—HIPAA mandated a standard format for electronic provider and diagnostic codes. The current standard has limitations that restrict the full use of EMR/EHR software.

ICD-10—HIPAA mandated a standard electronic format for provider and diagnostic codes. The new standard is intended to grow with the functional needs of the healthcare industry. The http://www.cms.gov website offers more details about ICD-10.

Figure 3-2 The CMS website is current and informative with the need-to-know facts and how to access resources the CMS provides.

Photo credit: http://www.cms.gov

The purpose of coding is to equate expenses in a hospital into numbers. For example, whenever a doctor examines a patient, a nurse uses a syringe to administer a drug, or a patient receives a diagnosis, a code must be generated to represent the expense associated with providing this patient care. When healthcare providers enter information into a patient's chart, that information eventually is sent to a medical coding specialist. This person is responsible for translating charted documentation about a patient's stay in a hospital into codes so that insurance companies can be properly billed for the hospital's expenses.

Covered entities must upgrade to Version 5010 billing codes to be prepared for the ICD-10 diagnostic and procedure codes. ICD-10 codes accommodate Version 5010. The reason for the transition to Version 5010 over a year and a half before the transition to ICD-10 is to make sure any kinks in the transition to Version 5010 have been addressed to reduce the possibilities of problems in the transition to ICD-10.

The need for the transition from ICD-9 to ICD-10 is because ICD-9 is too restrictive in the amount of information the code can communicate. With ICD-10, a code can report more specifically what was wrong with a patient and how the patient was treated. ICD-10 uses more character fields in the code and approximately 55,000 more available codes. For example, if a physician charts "initial encounter for a stress fracture of the right tibia," in ICD-9, a coder could use only the code 733.9 to mean the limited information "stress fracture of the tibia." This ignores a lot of specific information about this patient's condition. Because this was the first encounter and of the right tibia would be coded using separate codes. With ICD-10, the coder can report more details in a single code using a longer code with more options to choose from. To report "initial encounter for a stress fracture of the right tibia" in ICD-10, a coder would report M84.361A as the code.

Office of the National Coordinator for Health Information Technology (ONC)

Office of the National Coordinator for Health Information Technology (ONC)—http://www.healthit.hhs.gov: This office of the HHS was created to promote national HIT infrastructure and oversee its development. The ONC was created by executive order in 2004 and written into legislation by the HITECH Act in 2009, which requires healthcare providers to move toward using electronic solutions to store and process patient data. The ONC tests and certifies all EMR/EHR solutions to be HIPAA-compliant. Healthcare providers and hospitals may use only the certified EMR/EHR solutions if they want to qualify for monetary incentives. Figure 3-3 shows the ONC website.

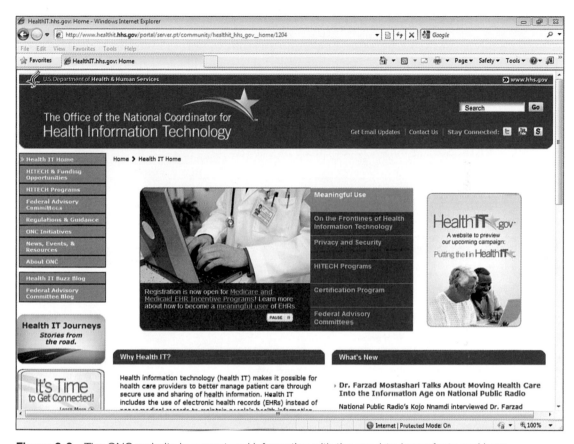

Figure 3-3 The ONC website is current and informative with the need-to-know facts and how to access resources the ONC provides.

Photo credit: http://www.healthit.hhs.gov

> **EXAM TIP** For the Healthcare IT exam, you need to know about the ONC, what it does, and why it was created.

The U.S. government provides funding through various venues to encourage covered entities to transition to advanced healthcare technology. Covered entities are encouraged to meet deadlines for stages in the transition, for example, to EMR/EHR information systems. If they meet these goals, they are given money. The deadlines for the incentives are set before the deadlines of when covered entities are required to transition to advanced healthcare technology. If a covered entity misses the latter required deadline, the U.S. government starts applying penalties for not complying with the required deadline. It serves the covered entities well to be ahead of the game by transitioning to advanced healthcare technologies sooner rather than later.

Office of Civil Rights (OCR)

Office of Civil Rights (OCR)—http://www.hhs.gov/ocr: This office of the HHS is responsible to protect Americans against discrimination and enforce the Privacy and Security Rules of HIPAA. The OCR fulfills this responsibility through education to prevent violations and through investigation of complaints about violations of these rules. The OCR usually enables a covered entity to enforce rules and reprimand violations without intervening. Complaints about violations are filed through the OCR. See Figure 3-4 to see the OCR website.

Figure 3-4   The OCR website is current, informative, and offers instructions on how to file a complaint about a privacy violation.

Photo credit: http://www.hhs.gov/ocr

National Institute of Standards and Technology (NIST)

National Institute of Standards and Technology (NIST)—http://www.nist.gov—This agency is part of the U.S. Department of Commerce. The goal of the NIST is to promote

U.S. innovation and industrial competition. The NIST aims to advance standards
and technology to improve American economic security and quality of life. In
healthcare, the NIST aims to do the following:

- Create opportunities for accelerated research and development of HIT.
- Improve the usefulness of HIT and remote healthcare.
- Develop the security of HIT.

Figure 3-5 shows the NIST website.

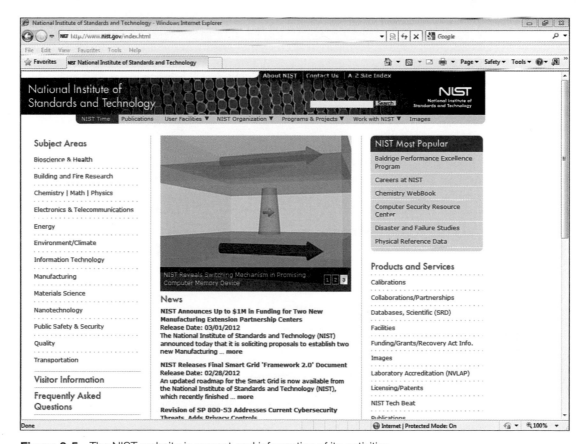

Figure 3-5   The NIST website is current and informative of its activities.

Photo credit: http://www.nist.gov

EXAM TIP   Expect to see the NIST on the Healthcare IT exam in the context of how
it aims to improve healthcare IT.

Now that you have learned about the agencies for healthcare, turn your attention to the programs and laws that these agencies offer and enforce.

Healthcare Programs

Government agencies use social programs to fulfill responsibilities tasked to the agency. Programs ensure accessibility of benefits to those who qualify. The two most significant healthcare programs are Medicare and Medicaid. Medicare and Medicaid are impressive by the numbers of beneficiaries and expense.

The Medicare—http://www.medicare.gov—social insurance program is for hospital and medical care for elderly and certain disabled citizens. Medicare is provided by the U.S. government. Medicare was created as an amendment to the Social Security Act in 1965. Medicare is regulated and administered at the federal level. Figure 3-6 shows the Medicare website homepage.

Figure 3-6 The Medicare website is current and informative with the need-to-know facts and how to access resources Medicare provides.

Photo credit: http://www.medicare.gov

EXAM TIP For the Healthcare IT exam, you need to understand what Medicare and Medicaid are and how funding comes to healthcare providers.

The Medicaid—http://www.medicaid.gov—social welfare program is for health and medical services for certain citizens and families with low incomes and few resources. Medicaid is provided by the U.S. government. Medicaid was created as an amendment to the Social Security Act in 1965. Primary oversight of Medicaid is regulated at the federal level. All states participate in Medicaid; however, state participation to use Medicaid funding is voluntary. Each state administers this program using Medicaid funding. States also have control over eligibility standards, scope of services, and rate of payment for services. Figure 3-7 shows the Medicaid website.

Figure 3-7 The Medicaid website is current and informative with the need-to-know facts and how to access resources Medicaid provides.

Photo credit: http://www.medicaid.gov

Healthcare Laws

Government agencies use laws to define the scope of responsibilities tasked to the agency. Laws clarify the manner and intent of the government. HIPAA, ARRA, and HITECH are all acts of Congress meant to improve healthcare in the United States.

Health Insurance Portability and Accountability Act (HIPAA)

The Health Insurance Portability and Accountability Act (HIPAA)—http://www.hhs.gov/ocr/privacy—was created in 1996 to provide a standard set of rules for all covered entities to follow to protect patient health information and to help healthcare providers transition from paper to electronic health records. The Office of Civil Rights (OCR) enforces the following HIPAA rules:

- **Privacy Rule**: Establishes national standards to protect individuals' health information whenever a covered entity accesses this information. This rule establishes safeguards to regulate who can access **e-PHI (electronic protected health information)** and the reasons why someone needs to access e-PHI.

> **electronic protected health information (e-PHI)**—HIPAA protects the electronic information that can be used to identify an individual. e-PHI is information created, used, or disclosed about a patient while providing healthcare.

- **Security Rule**: Establishes national standards to protect the e-PHI of an individual. This rule establishes safeguards for how e-PHI is accessed.

- **Breach Notification Rule**: Requires covered entities to notify affected individuals, the HHS secretary, and possibly the media when protected health information (PHI) has been breached.

- **Enforcement Rule**: Establishes penalties for violations to HIPAA rules and procedures following a violation, such as investigations and hearings.

Figure 3-8 shows the enforcement activities and results on the HIPAA website.

Figure 3-8   The HIPAA website is current and informative of the need-to-know facts.

Photo credit: http://www.hhs.gov/ocr/privacy/hipaa/enforcement

American Recovery and Reinvestment Act (ARRA)

The American Recovery and Reinvestment Act (ARRA)—http://www.recovery. gov—was created in 2009 at the urging of President Obama to help citizens through the economic recession. This act is called the Recovery Act. The Recovery Act provided hundreds of billions of dollars for tax cuts, funding for entitlement programs, and federal contracts, grants, and loans. Specific to healthcare, the Recovery Act provides funding to HHS branches, such as the CMS and ONC. The Recovery Act is intended to help preserve and improve affordable healthcare in the United States. The Recovery Act also creates plans and incentives to assist Americans through challenges faced as a nation. Figure 3-9 shows the Recovery Act website.

Figure 3-9   The Recovery Act website is current and informative with the need-to-know facts and how to access resources the Recovery Act provides.

Photo credit: http://www.recovery.org

> **EXAM TIP**   For the Healthcare IT exam, you need to know how the ARRA has affected healthcare and healthcare IT.

Health Information Technology for Economic and Clinical Health (HITECH) Act

The Health Information Technology for Economic and Clinical Health (HITECH) Act—http://www.healthit.hhs.gov—focuses on creating incentive and opportunity for the advancement of HIT through the ONC. The programs funded in the HITECH Act collectively aim to make EMRs/EHRs relevant and beneficial resources to all Americans. The HITECH Act provides grants for education programs and monetary incentives. The HITECH Act also encourages communication within the healthcare community, within a state, and between states as HIT is advanced and implemented.

> **EXAM TIP**   For the Healthcare IT exam, you need to know about the HITECH Act and how its funding and regulations affect healthcare and healthcare IT.

Now that you are familiar with programs and laws about healthcare, the following sections explain how these programs and laws are regulated.

Regulations of Healthcare Laws

Government agencies use regulations to ensure the intent of the government is carried out. It is in these regulations that healthcare providers and hospitals begin to understand the means and extent of the laws' intent.

Two new buzzwords in HIT are **meaningful use** and **eligible provider**. The Recovery Act requires covered entities to use HIT in a meaningful way, which is where the term "meaningful use" came from. The meaningful use of HIT justifies the push to advance in technology and offer incentives to accomplish this goal. Starting in 2011, grants from the HITECH Act provide incentives with deadlines for healthcare providers to comply with the regulations identified by meaningful use. By 2015, all healthcare entities must demonstrate meaningful use to avoid financial penalties. Eligible providers are covered entities that want to receive monetary incentives by meeting meaningful use criteria. This qualification makes them eligible to receive incentive money.

> **meaningful use**—The goals of meaningful use are to help healthcare providers know more about their patients, make better decisions, and save money by using HIT in a meaningful way.
>
> **eligible provider**—Hospitals or professionals participating in incentive programs must meet meaningful use criteria to be eligible to receive incentive money.

> **EXAM TIP**   To pass the Healthcare IT exam, you need to understand the terms "meaningful use" and "eligible provider" and use both terms appropriately when discussing how the ARRA has affected healthcare IT.

Now that you know some background on the agencies, laws, and regulations, the following section shifts the focus to how the agencies and acts from the government regulate privacy.

Learning HIPAA Controls and Compliance Issues

HI001 Objectives:

1.2 Explain and classify HIPAA controls and compliance issues.

PHI, Covered Entity, Security, HIPAA Security, Violations, Fines, Requirements, Release of information, and Access permissions

The HHS publishes rules and regulations through HIPAA to provide standards that control and require compliance for the security of e-PHI. HIPAA Privacy and Security Rules provide the regulations that covered entities must follow to protect e-PHI. The HIPAA Enforcement Rule explains the consequences of violating the Privacy and Security Rules. These three rules are not just technical safeguards but also physical and administrative safeguards, including auditing, enforcement, and punishment standards. To fully understand these rules, you must understand the issues concerning these rules and the reasons for creating the rules. The following issues are explained as they relate to HIPAA.

- **Security**: Keeping e-PHI secure is a concern for HIPAA because HIPAA is designed to protect e-PHI. The security measures include all the administrative, physical, and technical safeguards in any IS containing or processing e-PHI. This includes security protocols that HIT technicians must follow, such as administrating security access.

  HIPAA security protects e-PHI created, received, used, or maintained by a covered entity. The OCR is responsible for enforcing HIPAA security. The following portions of HIPAA security ensure the confidentiality, integrity, and availability of e-PHI.

- **Violations**: The breach of a HIPAA rule must be defined for covered entities to know boundaries of what is not acceptable behavior to maintain privacy of patients. A breach can be theft, unauthorized access or disclosure, loss, or improper disposal of e-PHI.

- **Fines**: Normally, the OCR does not intervene when there is a violation to HIPAA rules. Instead, the covered entity that violates the rule issues voluntary compliance and corrective action that reaches a satisfactory resolution with the

OCR. If the violating entity does not handle the offense properly, there are monetary penalties. HIPAA states the fine for each incident should not exceed $100 or $25,000 for identical violations within a calendar year. In 2009, the ARRA increased these amounts into a tiered structure, as outlined in Table 3-2.

Table 3-2   The ARRA Defines These Penalties If a Covered Entity Violates a HIPAA Rule

HIPAA Violation	Minimum Penalty	Maximum Penalty
Individual did not know (and by exercising reasonable diligence would not have known) that he/she violated HIPAA.	$100 per violation, with an annual maximum of $25,000 for repeat violations	$50,000 per violation, with an annual maximum of $1.5 million
HIPAA violation due to reasonable cause and not due to willful neglect.	$1,000 per violation, with an annual maximum of $100,000 for repeat violations	$50,000 per violation, with an annual maximum of $1.5 million
HIPAA violation due to willful neglect but violation is corrected within the required time period.	$10,000 per violation, with an annual maximum of $250,000 for repeat violations	$50,000 per violation, with an annual maximum of $1.5 million
HIPAA violation is due to willful neglect and is not corrected.	$50,000 per violation, with an annual maximum of $1.5 million for repeat violations	$50,000 per violation, with an annual maximum of $1.5 million

- **Requirements**: States have the capability to tighten the rules for security. When you start a new job, especially if you are in a new state, be sure to check with your local state regulations because the state may have different rules than what you knew from your last job. Covered entities must

    - Ensure confidentiality, integrity, and availability of e-PHI they create, receive, maintain, or transmit.

    - Identify risks to e-PHI and implement resolutions to anticipated threats.

    - Ensure compliance by their workforce.

HIPAA enables certain hospital personnel to access patient information to perform job duties. However, if a patient wants his patient information released to a person or organization that is not a covered entity, the covered entity must receive written permission to access and distribute the e-PHI.

This website shows an example of a release form used in New York: http://www.nycourts.gov/forms/Hipaa_fillable.pdf. For example, a patient might need this form to release medical information to an athletic program.

A covered entity might access e-PHI to distribute to the individual or its own personnel for treatment of the patient or to retrieve payment from the patient's insurance provider without acquiring a release form. Access permission is restricted based on the role of the personnel, called role-based access control. Personnel should have access to e-PHI only as required to fulfill their job descriptions, no more, no less. Ultimately the CFO has the final say in what access to the information systems used in the hospital is granted to hospital personnel. The CFO makes these determinations by approving access to each job role when each IS is initially configured. Therefore, the CFO does not need to be involved with assignments for each employee. When a professional starts a job at a healthcare facility, he is given access to e-PHI as defined by his job. For example, all lab technicians should have access as defined for a lab technician. All nurses should have access as defined for a nurse. A lab technician and a nurse might not have the same access. While performing duties of their job, these personnel do not require signed release forms from patients. The personnel is required to sign an acknowledgment of understanding HIPAA rules. These access policies are controlled by the covered entity and are expected to comply with HIPAA and state regulations.

The HHS offers case studies of HIPAA violations on its website. An example of one case study was a hospital employee who left a voicemail for a patient on the patient's home answering machine. The message included the medical condition and treatment plan of the patient. However the patient did not live alone and others in the household listened to the message. The patient had specifically asked to be contacted at her work phone number. The hospital employee did not follow confidential communication requirements as set by the hospital. To resolve this violation, the hospital implemented new policies for communication. For example, the policy set rules for the minimum information required to leave in a voicemail so as to not reveal PHI. The hospital also trained employees how to review registration information from patients to verify special instructions from the patient on how to contact them. Finally, the hospital integrated training for these new policies into the annual refresher series for employees.

With the background surrounding agencies, laws, and regulations covered, now turn your focus to a topic a little more practical: the rules of record retention and disposal.

Learning Rules of Record Retention and Disposal

HI001 Objectives:

1.3   Summarize regulatory rules of record retention, disposal, and archiving.

Documentation requirements, Time of storage, Types of records, Public records, Private records, Legal health record, Methods of record disposal

Documentation requirements are defined by HIPAA, but some requirements vary from state to state. The state defines how long records must be kept, called record retention. HIPAA defines how records are disposed of and how they are kept in storage (archived). The three types of records are public, private, and legal. All these follow the same rules for retention and disposal.

Types of Health Records

Health information comes in three different types. A patient's **public health record** is used for research and to create reports for public health data. For example, if a state requires a hospital to report how many patients are at risk for getting the flu, the public health records are accessible to calculate this information. Figure 3-10 shows the reporting function of an example EHR IS. Public health records are not intended to connect individuals to their health records.

public health record—Researchers need access to health records to analyze data. For this reason a public health record is made available for the collection of public health data in an anonymous manner.

A **private health record** is the health record created and maintained by an individual. The benefit of a private health record is the individual is completely aware of all healthcare received and is available to the individual no matter where she may be a patient. A private health record is great for chronically ill patients or for an individual who is a guardian of another individual.

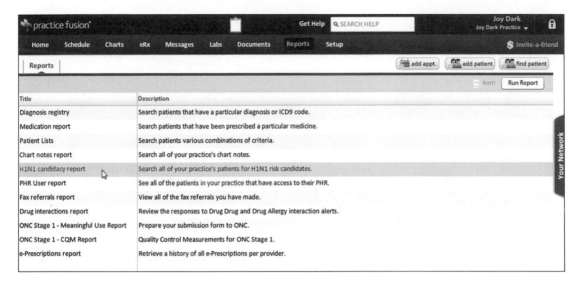

Figure 3-10   The reporting feature of an EHR IS provides a list of patients at risk for the H1N1 virus.

Photo credit: http://www.practicefusion.com

> **private health record**—A health record created and maintained by an individual.
> Sometimes called a personal health record (PHR).

An individual may keep a private health record in any format she prefers. She may simply place her health records in a file folder on her computer or move it to a jump drive for added security and mobility. She might decide to keep her health records with a web-based service designed for private health records. The benefit of using a web-based service is that many healthcare providers can access and easily format the data from these services for the HIS used at the facility with the permission from the individual.

A **legal health record** is the health record created by healthcare providers. The regulations for legal health records are set by the state and healthcare organization with a few basic standards set by the federal government. The legal health record can be requested by the patient or legal services. For example, if a patient brings up a lawsuit due to received healthcare, the court might need the legal health record to know what was charted in the patient's health record.

> **legal health record**—Health organizations must retain a health record of patients for use by the patient or legal services.

Record Retention

HIPAA sets a minimum timeframe for record retention of six years and for two years after a patient's death, and Medicare requires Medicare beneficiaries' records be retained for five years. HIPAA enables the states to create laws to dictate their own policy for record retention so long as the state law meets minimum HIPAA requirements. If a state requires more time for record retention, covered entities in that state must comply with the state law.

States have the freedom to determine how long documents need to be stored before disposal. States retain records anywhere from 6 to 20 years. Some states choose to vary the length of record retention based on resources, type of patient, events during the course of care, or any other stipulation.

When you start a new job, check with your state's legislature website or ask someone in the medical records department at your facility. For example, if your new job is to implement a new EMR/EHR IS in a hospital, you would need to know how long to program the EMR/EHR IS to retain the health records.

Record Disposal

HIPAA states that record disposal is the responsibility of covered entities. Physical documentation can be shredded, burned, or pulverized. PHI on electronic media is sometimes disposed of by cleaning, purging, or destroying the device. The covered entity is at fault if any physical or electronic PHI is recovered at any point after the disposal of records.

The basic rule when disposing of an electronic device that contained e-PHI is to make sure the data on the device is unreadable, is indecipherable, and cannot be reconstructed. Following are three ways records on electronic media can be disposed of :

- Cleaning the device is when irrelevant data (1s and 0s) is written on the memory several times. This method is considered unacceptable in the healthcare environment by many technicians. The only reason cleaning a device is okay is when the device has never had PHI on it; for example, the gift shop computer or the server used to control HVAC in the facility.

- Purging or degaussing is when exposure to a strong magnetic field is used to purge data from the device.

- Destroying a device is when physical destruction is used to render a device useless. For example, you can drive a nail through a hard drive to make sure no one can recover the data that was once on that hard drive.

Learning Legal Best Practices and Documentation

> **HI001 Objectives:**
>
> **1.4 Explain and interpret legal best practices, requirements, and documentation.**
>
> Waivers of liability, Business Associate Agreements (BAA), and Third-party vendor review agreements (SLA, MOU)

Whether or not it is convenient, HIT technicians must deal with legal issues. You need to make sure you are covered for all possible legal issues, so if any issues come up you will be prepared. Best practices and documentation need to be established for HIT technicians because of the necessity to be prepared for a legal issue. For example, HIT technicians are responsible for having the ability to audit all PHI accessed. With the ability to audit activity in information systems, if someone in the hospital violates HIPAA by viewing a patient's record they should not, the IS can track who accessed the e-PHI that was violated. As another example, when you depend on a vendor to support the equipment in the lab, a contract with the vendor is needed to know the time frame the vendor has to reply to repair needs. If the vendor is slow to respond to your repair requests, you have the contract to remind the vendor of its agreements with consequences to not meeting the commitments outlined.

Hospitals and healthcare providers must use legal best practices to protect themselves from unwarranted lawsuits. **Waivers of liability** are forms used by healthcare entities to be protected from being inappropriately responsible or sued for harm or debt. An example of a waiver of liability relates to Medicare. Medicare has a law that states healthcare providers are only responsible for providing services that are reasonable and necessary for a patient's health. However if a patient wants further healthcare, the patient can sign a waiver of liability to receive services not covered by Medicare if he agrees to pay out-of-pocket for the expense of the extra services.

> **waiver of liability**—A contract used to protect healthcare entities from being inappropriately responsible or sued for harm or debt.

HIPAA requires that when a covered entity requires the services of a person, company, or organization outside the organization, the covered entity must enter into contracts with these third parties. The purpose of this **business associate agreement (BAA)** is to establish rules for safeguarding e-PHI. Third parties need access to e-PHI to fulfill obligations to a covered entity. For example, a vendor needs access to data that might contain e-PHI to research a bug that needs to be fixed with the next update to an IS.

> **business associate agreement (BAA)**—A contract used between healthcare entities and third parties to establish a mutual understanding of safeguards of e-PHI.

Access allowed to business associates must be limited to the minimum amount of access required to perform necessary functions and activities of the job. This access is controlled by role-based access. This access must have the ability to be audited for activity of the business associates, the same as how auditing abilities are required for internal e-PHI activity.

For example, third parties need a BAA to access e-PHI data to perform the following functions:

- Insurance claims processing
- Data analysis
- Quality assurance
- Private practice office management

Covered entities often require third-party assistance with operations; for example, a software vendor might be contracted to support software and provide regular updates and bug fixes. It is recommended to have a **service-level agreement (SLA)**. An SLA, much like a BAA, establishes how information is to be shared and used. It also sets expectations for service provided so everyone is on the same page and understanding.

> **service-level agreement (SLA)**—Contracts used between healthcare entities and third parties to establish how e-PHI is shared and used. An SLA also establishes expectations of service provided.

In the previous example, a covered entity might use an IS vendor to support that IS and provide updates for bug fixes. The covered entity needs an SLA with the vendor. The SLA establishes the security protocols for the electronic transfer of e-PHI to the company as needed to resolve problems. The SLA also covers the protocol to reset passwords to access the software. The SLA establishes the support protocol, such as if users should call the vendor directly when an issue arises or if the users at a covered entity must go through the IT department to receive support from the vendor.

However, sometimes covered entities need to ensure that personnel and departments within their facility understand the rules regarding access to sensitive information. A **memorandum of understanding (MOU)** establishes a mutual understanding with personnel or departments that wouldn't normally have access to sensitive information. For example, cafeteria workers might see PHI occasionally as they prepare meals for patients with special dietary needs. An MOU is needed to make sure the cafeteria workers understand the HIPAA rules about patient privacy.

> **memorandum of understanding (MOU)**—Contracts are sometimes necessary within an organization between departments or personnel for mutual understanding of the safeguards of e-PHI.

HIT in the Real World

Even though healthcare IT technicians are not healthcare providers, we still are exposed to PHI. We are exposed to PHI even when working remotely. Actually, HIT technicians often have god-like access to data in a hospital because we must have the capability to troubleshoot all systems at any given time. For example, when you troubleshoot problems in the information systems at a hospital, you often encounter problems that require you to ask for a patient's name, MRN, procedure ordered, or test results. All this information is protected by HIPAA. HIPAA enables healthcare IT technicians to access this information as long as you use the information only in the performance of your job duties.

Having family members in the medical field, I was already familiar with HIPAA and how privately patient information should be respected. When I started my job in the healthcare entity, I was required to complete a short HIPAA study course, pass a test to verify I had read the information, and sign contracts that I would not divulge PHI outside of necessary work duties. Even though I knew the rules, I was still surprised at how many times I needed to obtain patient data while working.

In one specific case, I was troubleshooting the perioperative IS at a facility in Georgia. A nurse was explaining to me that a printed report was not showing information about patients that should have been on the printed document, and we couldn't quite communicate properly on the phone what she was talking about. So the nurse faxed to me the printed document with a note written showing what she was trying to explain. I remember I was pleased with my colleague because she had taken the time to black out as much PHI as she could and still allow me to see the information I needed to do my job. Even though she knew that I was privileged to the information, she couldn't fax that much information and risk hitting the wrong number on the fax machine and having it go to the wrong person.

It's these careful efforts that we make in our daily jobs that prove we are honorable professionals who take e-PHI seriously. People notice and appreciate these efforts. It's worth it to do your best to honor your obligations even if you are not noticed by someone who might reward your efforts.

Chapter Summary

Identifying Standard Agencies, Laws, and Regulations

- Covered entities are health plans, health clearinghouses, and healthcare providers.

- The U.S. Department of Health and Human Services (HHS) is tasked with protecting the health of Americans and providing a means to access healthcare by Americans who are least able to help themselves, containing and treating any national health emergencies, and testing and regulating food and drug supplies.

- The Centers for Medicare & Medicaid Services (CMS) is responsible for administrating Medicare and Medicaid, as well as regulating standards of electronic transactions of claims, provider, and diagnostic codes.

- Version 5010 is the most recent standard format for electronic claims transactions.

- ICD-10 is the most recent standard format for electronic provider and diagnostic codes.

- The Office of the National Coordinator for HIT (ONC) is responsible for certifying EMR/EHR solutions as HIPAA-compliant.

- The National Institute of Standards and Technology (NIST) advances HIT security and usefulness of remote healthcare.

- Medicare is a social insurance program to provide hospital and medical care for elderly and certain disabled citizens.

- Medicaid is a social welfare program to provide health and medical services for certain citizens and families with low incomes and few resources. Medicaid participation by states is voluntary. Medicaid is administrated by states.

- Health Insurance Portability and Accountability Act (HIPAA) is a set of rules for protecting e-PHI (electronic protected health information).

- The Office of Civil Rights (OCR) enforces the HIPAA rules.

- HIPAA has four primary rules: Privacy Rule, Security Rule, Breach Notification Rule, and Enforcement Rule.

- The American Recovery and Reinvestment Act (ARRA), called the Recovery Act, aims to help citizens through the economic recession. In healthcare, the Recovery Act provides funding to HHS branches to help preserve and improve affordable healthcare in the United States.

- The Health Information Technology for Economic and Clinical Health (HI-TECH) Act creates incentive and opportunity for the advancement of HIT through the ONC.

- Meaningful use is the demonstration by healthcare entities to use HIT in a meaningful way.

- Participants in the incentive programs are called eligible providers.

Learning HIPAA Controls and Compliance Issues

- HIPAA aims to ensure confidentiality, integrity, and availability of e-PHI.

- In the event of a violation, or breach, of HIPAA rules, fines may be imposed by the OCR.

- Covered entities are required to ensure confidentiality, integrity, and availability of e-PHI they create, receive, maintain, or transmit; identify and address risks to e-PHI; and ensure compliance by their workforce.

- Written permission must be obtained before e-PHI may be released or distributed to anyone HIPAA does not allow.

- Covered entities must use role-based access control to restrict access to e-PHI by its personnel.

Learning Rules of Record Retention and Disposal

- The three types of health records are public, private, and legal.

- The public health record is used for the collection of public health data to be analyzed by researchers.

- The private health record is the health record created and maintained by an individual.

- The legal health record is collected and retained for use by the patient or legal services.

- Health records must be retained for a minimum of six years. States may add to the length of time for record retention.

- Disposed records must be unreadable, indecipherable, and unable to be reconstructed.

Learning Legal Best Practices and Documentation

- Waivers of liability are forms used by healthcare entities to be protected from being inappropriately responsible for harm or debt.

- Business associate agreements (BAA) are used to ensure a mutual understanding of safeguards of e-PHI between a covered entity and a contracted third party.

- Service-level agreements (SLA) are used to establish how e-PHI is shared and used, as well as expectations of service provided.

- Memoranda of understanding (MOU) are used within a covered entity to ensure understanding of the safeguards of e-PHI among departments or personnel who may not normally be exposed to sensitive information.

Key Terms

- breach notification rule
- business associate agreement (BAA)
- covered entity
- electronic protected health information (e-PHI)
- eligible provider
- enforcement rule
- Health Insurance Portability and Accountability Act (HIPAA)
- healthcare clearinghouse
- ICD 9
- ICD 10
- legal health record
- meaningful use
- memorandum of understanding (MOU)
- privacy rule
- private health record
- public health record
- service-level agreement (SLA)
- Version 5010
- waiver of liability

Acronym Drill

Acronyms sometimes get confusing, especially when a single sentence can have four or five. As an HIT professional, you must know the acronyms and what they stand for. Fill in the blank with the correct acronym for the sentence.

1. The divisions of the _____ involved in healthcare are the _____, the _____, and the _____.

   Answer: _____

2. The new standard of medical diagnosis and inpatient procedure coding, called _____, is required to be adopted by October 1, 2013, by _____-compliant facilities.

   Answer: _____

3. The _____ tests and certifies all _____ solutions to be _____-compliant.

   Answer: _____

4. The _____ enforces _____ rules to protect _____.

   Answer: _____

5. An _____ is used to establish how information is shared and to set expectations for service provided.

   Answer: _____

Review Questions

1. Which branch of the HHS controls the electronic standards of transaction for an insurance claim? And what is the current standard?

   Answer: _____

2. Which HHS division is responsible for enforcing HIPAA rules?

   Answer: _____

3. Do federal or state agencies administrate Medicare? Medicaid?

   Answer: _____

4. What does the HIPAA Enforcement Rule determine?

   Answer: _____

   _____

   _____

5. What are the goals of the meaningful use of technology in healthcare?

   Answer: _____

   _____

6. Why would an eligible provider want to demonstrate the meaningful use of technology?

   Answer: _____

   _____

7. What are possible breaches of e-PHI?

   Answer: _____

   _____

8. What is the purpose of a public health record?

   Answer: _____

   _____

9. What is the basic rule of thumb of record disposal?

   Answer: _____

   _____

10. Why are SLAs important and what do they establish?

    Answer: _____

    _____

Practical Application

1. The .gov websites are a great resource for HIT professionals. Suppose your boss asks you to develop a contract to be used to establish the SLA with a software vendor to support the software and provide fixes to bugs discovered. Rather than reinventing the wheel by making up your own contract, use an Internet search engine to find templates for contracts and checklists. Find a template on the http://www.hhs.gov website for an SLA/MOU document. Write down the websites where you found the documents.

   Answer: _____

   _____

   _____

2. Search online for two case examples and resolution agreements to HIPAA violations. You can find several in news articles, and the http://www.hhs.gov website gives some examples where acceptable resolutions agreements were reached. What was the cause of the breach? What were the consequences of the breach? What was the resolution agreement reached? Were policies implemented to prevent the violation from happening again?

   Answer: _____

   _____

   _____

   _____

   _____

   _____

3. While in the waiting room at the free clinic with three other patients, Nurse Jack calls out, "Patti Patient." Patti Patient begins to walk to Nurse Jack. Before leaving the waiting room, Nurse Jack asks Patti Patient, "Has the herpes cleared up yet?" Is this a HIPAA violation? Why?

   Answer: _____

   _____

   _____

CHAPTER 4
Organizational Behavior

In this chapter you learn about:

- **The best practices for safeguarding protected health information (PHI) through physical and technical means and while using electronic communication**

- **The different roles of hospital staff and their needs to access PHI in the information systems**

- **The different organizational structures among healthcare facilities**

- **How to go about executing your daily activities as an HIT technician in a hospital**

As a healthcare IT technician, one of your goals is to safeguard patient information against violations of patient privacy. Imagine you are writing a script for a movie where a thief sneaks into a hospital to steal medical information about someone famous who is a patient in the hospital. Think of all the ways the villain will try to steal the PHI. For example, he might casually walk by a printer and pick up a printout of the patient's lab work. He might stand near a nurse while she enters information about the patient into the HIS and read the information as she types. Outlining possible breaches of privacy helps to pinpoint potential weaknesses. With this knowledge, you can install physical and technical measures to prevent violations.

The best place to start is to learn how to handle PHI in the workplace.

Handling PHI

HI001 Objectives:

2.1 Use best practices for handling PHI in the workplace.

PC placement, privacy screens, printer placement, screensavers, time lockout

Remember that PHI is protected health information as defined by Health Insurance Portability and Accountability Act (HIPAA). The goal of HIPAA regulations is to protect PHI from being seen or accessed by an individual who does not have authority to access it. HIPAA enables access to PHI on a need-to-know basis. If a hospital staff member doesn't need to know certain PHI to fulfill her job duties, that person should not have access to that PHI.

HIT personnel in a hospital are expected to protect PHI using both physical and technical safeguards. The HHS offers suggestions on how to successfully integrate safeguards for healthcare environments on its website, as shown in Figure 4-1.

The section that follows covers some physical safeguards you can use in a healthcare facility to protect PHI.

Figure 4-1 The http://www.healthit.hhs.gov website offers suggestions to successfully protect e-PHI.

Physical Safeguards

PHI is viewable on computer screens throughout the hospital. For example, computers can access PHI in the patient rooms, nurses' stations, lab, pharmacy, registration, visitor information desk, or even waiting rooms. Visitors and certain personnel, such as cleaning staff, do not need access to PHI. These people are all over the hospital, in and out of rooms, down hallways, and talking to nurses at the nurses' station. If computers are carelessly placed, anyone could see whatever is displayed on the monitors, including PHI. For this reason, computers must be placed so that they are protected from theft and so screens are not viewable by anyone but the computer user. For example, computers should be behind the desk at the nurses' station, so a visitor standing at the nurses' station cannot view the screen, as illustrated in Figure 4-2.

Figure 4-2 When possible place computers so visitors and patients cannot see the screen.

Photo credit: Lisa F. Young

EXAM TIP For the Healthcare IT exam, you need to be familiar with using physical safeguards to protect PHI from accidental and intentional breaches.

Computers that have access to PHI should not be placed without extra safeguards in common areas for visitors. For example, the tracking board in the ED is a big screen monitor mounted to the wall with patient information easily viewed by staff for quick reference for patient status. Information that identifies patients on the tracking board must be written in code so only those who need to know who a patient can identify the patient and his status. Another example is the waiting room for the **operating room (OR)**. A display board is placed in the OR waiting room for loved ones of patients to monitor the progress of a patient through surgery and recovery. The patient's name must not be viewable. Instead, the patient is assigned a code, which is given to the patients' visitors. Visitors use this code to identify patients and their information.

operating room (OR)—A room in a hospital equipped for performing surgical procedures.

If it is not possible to place a computer in a location so that the monitor is not viewable to others, a **privacy screen** filter can be used. A privacy screen is a clear film or acrylic filter placed in front of a monitor's screen, as shown in Figure 4-3. A privacy screen makes the screen viewable only to the person sitting directly in front of the screen. The privacy screen makes the monitor screen appear blurred or darkened when the screen is viewed from an angle. Make sure the privacy screen fits the monitor properly. To assist the antiglare feature of privacy screens, install louvers, or "egg crates," in overhead lighting fixtures to diffuse light to reduce glare, as shown in Figure 4-4.

> **privacy screen**—A clear film or acrylic filter placed in front of a monitor to decrease the viewing angle of the monitor.

Figure 4-3   Privacy screens prevent prying eyes from viewing computer screens.

In addition to physical safeguards, keep these tips in mind when placing a computer in a hospital:

- Encourage staff to use ergonomically correct posture at their desks, as illustrated in Figure 4-5.

Figure 4-4   Louvers in overhead lighting fixtures diffuse light to reduce glare.

Photo credit: Tyler Olson

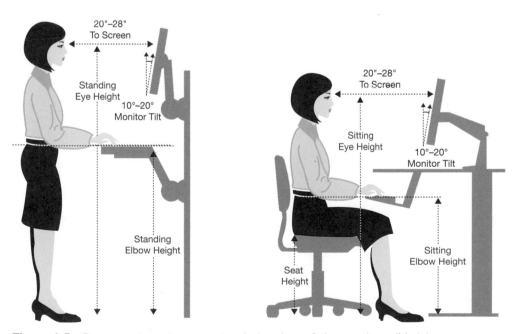

Figure 4-5   Proper posture at a computer desk reduces fatigue and possible injury.

- Place the monitor directly in front of the user at least 20 inches away.

- Don't put a computer on the floor.

- Make it clear to users that food and drinks are not allowed near the computer.

- Install cables and wires out of the traffic pathway, making sure cables and wires are tied up and secured to the power outlet.

- Install an **uninterrupted power supply (UPS)** (see Figure 4-6) and, in clinical areas, connect the UPS to the generator at the facility if available.

- Install at least one UPS on one computer in nonclinical areas.

> **uninterrupted power supply (UPS)**—A device connected to a computer to provide power for a few minutes in case the power to the facility goes out. These few minutes give the user enough time to save work and log out.

Figure 4-6   A UPS provides a few minutes of power to a computer when a power outage occurs at a facility.

Photo credit: amorphis

Printers produce many of the physical PHI documents used in a hospital. For example, the lab IS might automatically send a report to the printer at the nurses' station when a lab analysis is completed. These printouts might sit on the printer for a while until they're noticed and picked up. In the meantime, they are vulnerable to anyone who can grab them and walk away. For this reason, printers should never be placed where visitors or a patient can easily retrieve a printed document or view the information on the document.

Not everyone who works in a hospital is allowed to view PHI. Two departments should not share a printer if users in one of those departments do not have proper access to see the PHI printed by the other department. As a general rule, no matter where a document is printed, all employees must be careful not to leave printed documents or faxes on remote machines. The documents must be picked up immediately after printing or faxing.

In addition to securing PHI, consider the following when placing a printer in the hospital:

- Don't place a printer on the floor.
- Install cables and wires out of traffic pathway, making sure cables and wires are tied up and secured to the power outlet.
- Install a UPS and, in clinical areas, connect the UPS to a generator.

Now that you know about physical safeguards, the following section describes some technical safeguards that also help protect PHI.

Technical Safeguards

EXAM TIP   For the Healthcare IT exam, you need to be familiar with using technical safeguards to protect PHI. Technical safeguards reinforce physical safeguards and serve as a backup when physical safeguards fail.

For best practice, whenever a user logs into a computer to look up or enter information about a patient, she must use a unique Windows user account. When she is finished using the computer for that moment, she must log off or **lock** the computer before walking away. If available, also use the option to suspend a session on the application that locks the application and saves any progress. Occasionally, users forget to lock or log off a computer, which leaves PHI vulnerable to anyone who might use the computer next or walk by. **Screensavers** should be set to activate after a period of inactivity on the computer. Screensavers are especially needed on computers in high-traffic and vulnerable locations. The screensaver should require a password to unlock.

lock—When a Windows user is logged on to a computer, but needs to walk away for a moment and does not want to close all programs running to log off, the user can simply lock the computer pressing the Windows key+L. This user's password or a computer administrator's username and password is required to unlock the computer.

screensaver—When a computer is idle for a set time, an image appears on the screen until the mouse is moved or a key is pressed on the keyboard.

Length of time for screensavers to activate can vary. If a computer is in a restricted room with a door that is kept locked, the timer might be set for a longer period to reduce frustration from users who are being required to log in frequently. If a computer is located in a high-traffic area accessible to visitors or patients, the screensaver should activate more quickly to increase protection from possible violations.

Windows has a force log off option available in case the user who is logged in, but locked the computer, is not available to unlock the computer for the next user to use. This option automatically logs off a user after a set period of time. Some **single sign-on (SSO)** programs provide an option for a force log off button that does not require the user or a computer administrator to log off a locked computer. This option does not require a timed force log off. The user remains logged in and locked until another user walks up to the computer and clicks the force log off button, so she may log in to the computer.

single sign-on (SSO)—A program that enables a user to enter a username and password once to log in to multiple information systems.

Time lockout is another way to safeguard against unauthorized access to PHI. Time lockout limits the hours that users are allowed to log in. Some software enables administrators to limit the hours of the day when certain users are allowed to log in. For example, personnel who should be in the office only Monday through Friday from 8 a.m. until 5 p.m. can be limited to log in only during those hours. Time lockout is not practical for all employees because some have flexible hours and cannot limit their access to only certain hours.

time lockout—The capability of software to limit to certain hours of the day and week when users can log in.

The technical safeguards are a bit of a sore spot between computer administrators and healthcare providers. For better security, timers for lockout and screensavers should be set for a short time interval. Healthcare providers become irritated when they get locked out quickly or blocked from logging in because a previous user locked the computer. The best way to offset this frustration is to create a culture of being security conscious in the facility. As HIT technicians, we educate users about the importance and practicality of data security. For example, we can explain to personnel the importance of logging off a computer when they walk away or not leaving printouts on the printer for a long time. One of our goals is to have health-care providers as conscious about the security of e-PHI as they are about infection control.

The next section focuses on how to secure e-PHI when it is communicated using various methods.

Applying Proper Communication Methods

HI001 Objectives:

2.3   Apply proper communication methods in the workplace.

E-mail, IM vs. secure chat, EMR system, fax, secure FTP, phone, VoIP

Just as in personal lives, healthcare providers have a variety of ways to communicate electronically. HIT technicians must secure these forms of communication when e-PHI is transferred. You need to be concerned with HIPAA violations, the threat of **hackers**, and the misuse of communication. In this section, you learn best practices for securing e-PHI in various methods of communication.

hacker—An individual who maliciously attempts to access electronic information he is not authorized to view.

EXAM TIP   For the Healthcare IT exam, you need to know proper methods of communication in the workplace. Pay attention to whether the communication is secure and how to make communication more secure.

E-Mail

One of the most common forms of communication in HIT is e-mail. E-mail is quick and easy; however, e-mail comes with security risks. Whenever e-PHI is sent through an e-mail, the e-mail must be encrypted. Some healthcare facilities choose to encrypt all e-mails to ensure that e-PHI is secured. Other healthcare facilities use software that scans all e-mails for key words or length of numbers (such as a number with 9 digits that might be a SSN). When an e-mail is flagged, it is encrypted.

User training helps to secure e-mail. As an HIT technician, you might get requests through e-mail to reset passwords. A username and password should never be sent in the same e-mail. Healthcare providers understand that they cannot send e-PHI to just anyone. The recipients must be authorized to access the e-PHI they are receiving.

IM Versus Secure Chat

Instant messaging (IM) is not a secure method of electronic communication. IMs are sent in plain text without any encryption in real time. All a hacker needs to do is intercept an IM to access the content of the message. The hacker doesn't even need to decipher the message because it is in plain text. Because IMs are not secured, they should never be used in a healthcare facility.

> **instant messaging (IM)**—A method to communicate over a network electronically in real time. Typed messages are immediately viewable by the recipient. IMs are not secured and are sent as plain text.

secure chat functions much like IMs in real time but provides encryption. Some EHR/EMR or hospital information systems offer secure chat as part of the application suite. Secure chat programs are still developing, so it is up to the **security officer** at the facility to decide if there is a secure chat program secure enough to prevent HIPAA violations.

> **secure chat**—A method to communicate over a network electronically in real time. Typed messages are immediately viewable by the recipient. Secure chat sessions are encrypted.
>
> **security officer**—The hospital employee responsible for determining policies necessary to ensure security of PHI. The security officer is also responsible for ensuring that the hospital staff complies with these policies.

If secure chat is used in a hospital, users need to understand that the chat session might become part of a patient's legal health record. Users often use abbreviations and shorthand while chatting that might be inappropriate for a legal health record.

EMR/EHR System

Some EMR/EHR or hospital information systems offer a messaging portion to the software. Figure 4-7 shows a messaging system integrated with an EHR IS. The messages enable healthcare providers to communicate about patients with other departments, support staff, or the next shift of healthcare providers. Because this messaging system is integrated with the EMR/EHR IS, it is easily saved to a patient's EMR/EHR. Another benefit to using the EMR/EHR messaging system is that the messaging system is designed specifically for use by healthcare providers. The messaging system can have message templates that make sending messages fast and easy. The messaging system also has the added security that the EMR/EHR IS provides. A full **audit trail** is created for tracking messages.

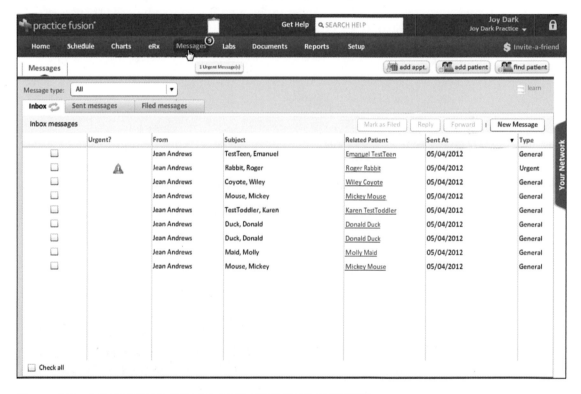

Figure 4-7   A messaging system can be integrated with an EHR IS.

http://www.practicefusion.com

> **audit trail**—A record of activity in an IS. Audit trails typically record the activity along with a time and date stamp and the username performing the activity.

Fax

The fax system is commonly integrated into the information systems in hospitals. Faxing is by default not encrypted for security. Because faxing is not secure, extra precautions must be taken to avoid HIPAA violations. Consider the following when using faxes to communicate PHI:

- Ensure that the recipient is authorized to view the PHI.
- Always use a cover sheet.
- Keep a log for all PHI fax transmissions for at least 90 days.
- Frequently audit programmed speed dial numbers on the fax machine.

Using a programmed phone number in the speed dial can reduce the chances of misdialing a number. It is a HIPAA violation if a user misdials a fax number and the fax containing PHI is received at an incorrect number. A violation happens if the fax is received by someone outside of the facility. It is also a HIPAA violation if the fax is received by the wrong department in a hospital and that department doesn't have privileges to view PHI.

Secure FTP

Healthcare facilities frequently use **file transfer protocol (FTP)** to transfer data. FTP is a **communications protocol** used to transfer data across the Internet. FTP uses client-server architecture. Data sent using FTP needs to be secured because of the sensitive nature of the data a healthcare facility might transfer. Two methods are used to secure FTP:

- Requirement of usernames and passwords
- Encryption of FTP transmissions

Users are required to use their username and password and not use the anonymous login option. Logging in is needed to create the audit trail of which user has uploaded or downloaded files. Anonymous login must be disabled on FTP servers. The system administrator can scan the network to ensure the anonymous login option has been disabled.

> **file transfer protocol (FTP)**—A method to communicate over a network electronically. This communication method enables documents to be placed on and copied from a remote server. FTP is great for sharing large files with other people who also have access to the FTP server.
>
> **communications protocol**—The format and rules for exchanging digital messages between information systems.

Secure FTP uses the Secure Shell (SSH) protocol to transfer files securely. This protocol encrypts both commands and data to prevent passwords and other secure data from being transferred in plain text. For secure FTP to work, both the FTP server and the FTP client must use the secure protocol. Secure FTP is different from FTP. A secure FTP server cannot communicate with a client that supports only FTP, and a secure FTP client cannot communicate with an FTP server.

> **NOTE**   Chapter 5 covers SSH in more detail.

> **secure FTP**—A secure form of FTP that encrypts both commands and data. Sometimes called SSH FTP because secure FTP uses SSH to secure the transfer.

Phone

When managing a phone system in a hospital, consider the following guidelines:

- Disable speakerphones in patient care areas.
- Use software to track records and store history of phone numbers dialed and received.
- To keep costs down, block long distance calling from phones in areas that are accessible to patients or visitors. Personnel can be assigned long distance access codes to make a long distance phone call.
- Routinely check voicemail greetings for out-of-office greetings, change of staff, or change of extension.
- Make analog phones available in case the digital phone systems go offline. Fax lines are great for this use.
- Use business phone etiquette when recording voicemail or systemwide messages or greetings.

Many healthcare facilities use a **private branch exchange (PBX)** infrastructure. The PBX infrastructure uses a **phone switch** within the facility, so the facility has more control over the phone systems (see Figure 4-8). A facility using PBX can assign extensions to each phone in the hospital. Having the phone switch within the facility reduces the risk of eavesdropping from outside the facility.

> **private branch exchange (PBX)**—A private telephone system. Switches are housed within a facility to provide greater control over the phone system. With a switch, the facility can customize phone routing and assign extensions.
>
> **phone switch**—A server used to route telephone calls in a facility.

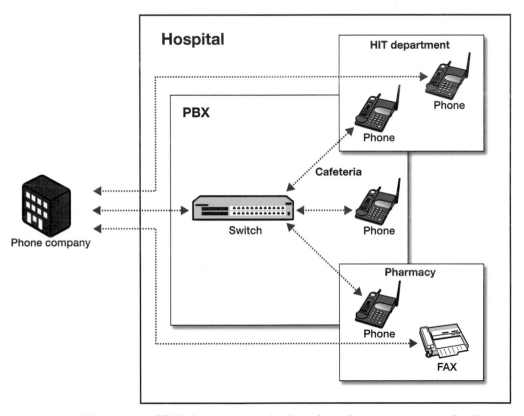

Figure 4-8   When using a PBX infrastructure, redundant phone lines must connect directly to the phone company in case the PBX switch goes offline.

Healthcare facilities usually prefer to have control over their phone extensions. When a facility manages its own phone system, it controls where extensions are assigned, how phones are routed, the phone menu when someone dials into the main line, and voicemail systems.

> **NOTE**   A PBX makes a phone system more flexible. For example, when I was at a hospital while new computer systems were implemented, we set up a miniature help desk in an office. The helpdesk support phone number was rerouted to the room where we were all camped out, so we could resolve all issues with the implementation as quickly and as efficiently as possible. Without the PBX infrastructure, this would not have been possible to configure for just a temporary situation.

VoIP

Voice over Internet Protocol (VoIP) is a communication protocol used to communicate voice over the Internet. VoIP is usually used as a more capable replacement of the older analog phone systems. VoIP phone systems are digital and use the network infrastructure in a facility for internal calls and the Internet for calls outside the facility. Because VoIP uses the Internet, a facility's Internet security protects the phone systems from being hacked (see Figure 4-9).

> **voice over Internet protocol (VoIP)**—A method of communication using IP networks such as the Internet. VoIP operates at the application or seventh layer of the OSI reference model.

VoIP relies on the Internet service to function. If the Internet goes out, so does the phone system. For this reason, it is necessary to have redundant access to phones for communication in case the Internet service fails. Fax lines are ideal for providing this redundancy. A facility can have all VoIP phones and then have several fax machines connected to analog phones that are connected directly to the phone company.

Now that you have learned how to protect PHI, the next section outlines who accesses the PHI.

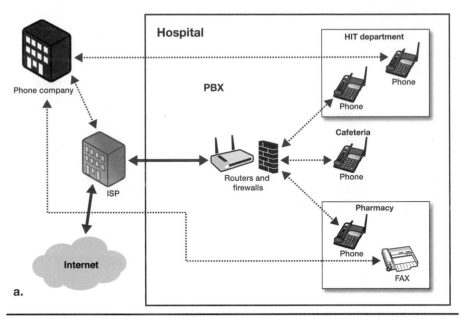

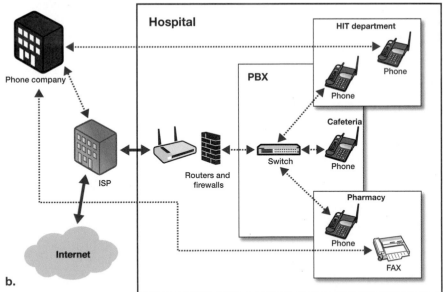

Figure 4-9 Because VoIP communication relies on the Internet, it is protected by the network security already in place. Figure A shows a VoIP system configured without a PBX infrastructure. Figure B shows a VoIP system configured with a PBX infrastructure.

Identifying EHR/EMR Access Roles and Responsibilities

> **HI001 Objectives:**
>
> **2.2   Identify EHR/EMR access roles and responsibilities.**
>
> Medical roles, technical roles, business associate access and contractor access, access limitations based on role and exceptions, access based on sensitive patient data

HIT technicians need to know who works in a hospital and where to find personnel in the hospital when they need support. For example, did you know a phlebotomist works with blood and is likely working in the lab? Hospitals have politics, same as many other industries, so you must know the role of the person you might be speaking with. However, regardless of the job role a person has, make sure in your role as a support personnel that you treat everyone with respect and urgency.

The level of access a person gets to a system is determined by his job role. Figure 4-10 shows how all job role classifications have some level of access to practically every system. To know specifically what level of access a job position should have, ask the chief financial officer (CFO) or security administrator at your facility. The CFO is responsible for approving initial role-based access levels and any exceptions. As you read through this section, keep in mind that an HIT technician needs to know access roles and responsibilities of personnel in all systems, but the CompTIA HIT objectives focus on just the EMR/EHR information systems.

EXAM TIP   For the Healthcare IT exam, you need to know about the job roles of those who work in a hospital including both medical and technical job roles.

Now learn about the roles of the personnel in the healthcare facilities.

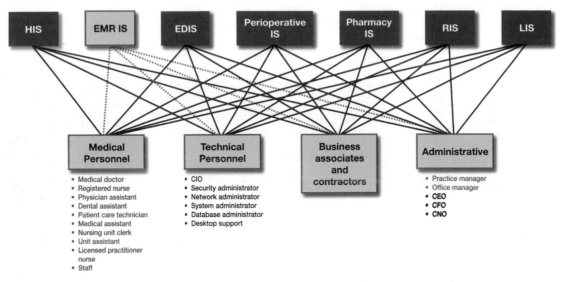

Figure 4-10 The HIT technician exam focuses on access roles and responsibilities for the EMR/EHR systems, even though on the job, you must be concerned about access to all systems.

Medical and Medical Support Roles

A **medical doctor (MD)** is a physician who is licensed and trained to practice medicine without supervision. MDs promote, maintain, and restore health through treating, diagnosing, studying, and advising patients about healthcare. Specialist medical practitioners are MDs who focus their practice on a certain type of medicine, such as surgery or emergency medicine. General practitioners provide continuing and comprehensive medical care to individuals, families, and communities.

> **medical doctor (MD)**—A physician who is licensed and trained to practice medicine without supervision.

Because the MD is ultimately responsible for the medical actions performed for a patient, he must have full access to the patient's information he is treating. Sometime physicians work in groups and might cover the patients of another physician in their group. When setting up access, make sure the physician can access all the patients' information he might need to treat so that he can cover for another physician. Because physicians sometimes have access to more patients than just their own, an audit trail is required in case there is a legal issue with a patient's record. The audit trail records which physician did what for the patient.

A **physician assistant (PA)** is a healthcare provider who is licensed and trained to practice medicine under the direct supervision of a physician. PAs are trained using the same training model that physicians use. Because a PA performs the same tasks as a physician, he must have full access to the patient's information he is treating.

> **physician assistant (PA)**—A healthcare provider who is licensed and trained to practice medicine under the direct supervision of a physician.

A **nurse practitioner (NP)** is a healthcare provider who is a registered nurse who has graduate-level education and training. NPs can see patients as a primary healthcare provider. NPs can diagnose and treat patients, much like a physician. NPs can also specialize in a field of medicine, like a physician. Depending on state laws, some NPs can work independent of a physician. Because an NP can be a primary healthcare provider, she needs full access to the patient's information for the patient she is treating.

> **nurse practitioner (NP)**—A healthcare provider who is a registered nurse who has completed graduate-level education and training. Dependent on state laws, some NPs can work without the supervision of a physician.

A **registered nurse (RN)** is a healthcare provider who has completed a nursing school program and passed the national licensing exam. RNs treat and educate patients and communities about medical conditions. RNs advise and provide emotional support for patients and their families. Much like physicians, an RN might specialize in certain areas of medicine, such as a perioperative nurse or **dermatology** nurse.

RNs perform the following tasks in the hospital:

- Record patient history and symptoms.
- Perform diagnostic tests and analyze results.
- Operate medical equipment.
- Administer treatment.
- Help with following up with patients and rehabilitation.

> **registered nurse (RN)**—A healthcare provider who has completed a nursing school program and passed the national licensing exam.
>
> **dermatology**—The study of the skin and its conditions, including scalp, hair, and nails.

Because an RN has the most contact with a patient and enters the most information in to an IS about a patient, he needs to have full access to the patient's information he is treating.

A **licensed practical nurse (LPN)** is a healthcare provider who completed an LPN program in a school, typically one year, and passed a state exam. An LPN assists nurses much like a medical assistant assists physicians. An LPN works under the direct supervision of a licensed healthcare provider, such as an RN. An LPN usually provides bedside care, collects specimens for labs, and records patient data. Because an LPN might be tasked by a licensed healthcare provider to record patient information, he needs access to a patient's information.

> **licensed practical nurse (LPN)**—A healthcare provider who completed an LPN program and passed a state exam. An LPN typically assists an RN and provides bedside care. Sometimes called a licensed vocational nurse (LVN).

A **medical assistant (MA)** is a healthcare provider or administrator who is not certified. An MA works under direct supervision of a licensed healthcare provider or office manager. An MA performs both administrative and clinical tasks. Most MAs have a high school diploma and are trained on the job; although, it is preferred that an MA complete a 1- or 2-year training program. Because an MA might be tasked by a licensed healthcare provider to update patient records, fill out insurance forms, or arrange for healthcare services, she needs to have access to the patient information for the patient she is caring for.

> **medical assistant (MA)**—A healthcare provider or administrator who is not certified and works under direct supervision of a licensed healthcare provider or office manager.

A **dental assistant (DA)** helps a dentist perform procedures and prepare patients for dental procedures. A DA might take X-rays, make molds of teeth, or assist a dentist during a dental procedure.

> **dental assistant (DA)**—A healthcare provider who helps a dentist perform procedures and prepare patients for dental procedures.

A **patient care technician (PCT)** is a healthcare provider who works directly under the supervision of a licensed healthcare provider. A PCT might be trained through on-the-job training, formal education, or apprenticeship. A PCT provides basic bedside care. A PCT might assist moving patients, taking vitals, or assist patients with personal hygiene. Because a PCT might record patient information, he needs to have access to patient information for the patient he cares for.

> **patient care technician (PCT)**—A healthcare provider who works directly under the supervision of a licensed healthcare provider.

A **nursing unit clerk (NUC)** is an employee of a hospital who assists the healthcare providers in an area of the hospital, or a unit of the hospital. A NUC does not perform medical actions but may assist with recording into an IS the medical information about patients and patient demographics. An NUC helps with paperwork that the hospital processes. An NUC facilitates communication for the unit. Because an NUC might assist with typing information into an IS about patients, she needs access to patient information.

> **nursing unit clerk (NUC)**—An employee of a hospital who assists the healthcare providers in a unit with clerical work. Sometimes called a health unit coordinator (HUC).

A **unit assistant (UA)** is an employee of the hospital who facilitates the function of a unit in a hospital. A UA performs general receptionist duties, as well as maintains paperwork that the unit processes and other clerical functions. A UA rarely needs access to patient information, so check with your security officer or security administrator for hospital policy before granting access to UAs.

> **unit assistant (UA)**—An employee of the hospital who facilitates the function of a unit in a hospital.

A **practice manager (PM)** in a medical environment is the employee of a medical practice who facilitates the operations of the practice. A PM is responsible for the flow of patients and finances in the practice. PMs perform the following tasks:

- Hire and train staff.
- Supervise staff.

- Ensure compliance with current regulations.
- Assist with billing issues.
- Coordinate with other departments or facilities.

> **practice manager (PM)**—An employee of a medical practice who facilitates the operations of the practice.

Because a PM is responsible for improving or verifying quality of financial performance or patient care, she needs access to the reporting features in the information systems used in the practice. These reports pull information from public health records and provide statistics on the performance of the practice and lets the PM know where improvements need to be made. In most cases, she does not need access to individual PHI.

An **office manager** in a medical environment is the employee of a physician's office and performs many of the same functions of a PM. The office manager is responsible for financial performance and quality of patient care in a physician's office. The office manager maintains the flow of the business side of patient care, which can be affected by the quality of patient care. Because the office manager is responsible for the quality of financial performance and patient care, he needs access to the reporting features in the information systems used in the physician's office. In most cases, he does not need access to individual PHI.

> **office manager**—An employee of a physician's office who facilitates the operations of the office.

The rest of the staff in healthcare facilities are the employees who help run the facility. This staff ensures that the healthcare providers have the supplies and environment necessary to provide excellent patient care. The staff can be, but are not limited to, social workers, janitorial staff, and cafeteria workers. The staff may need access to patient census information, but rarely any more information than that.

Now that you know the key players who provide medical care and support staff of a hospital, the next section helps you to understand the technical support staff who support and maintain the tools that healthcare providers use to care for patients.

Technical Roles

The personnel in the HIT department are crucial to the smooth operation of hospital functions. An HIT department requires multiple job roles necessary to perform all the tasks given to the department.

The medical field has a better developed and more mature group of certifications and training standards than does the IT industry. For example, the MD, RN, or LPN degree or certification is legally required before a person can function in these job roles. The IT industry has been developing standards over the past 30 years, but these standards are currently recommended standards and not legal requirements to do a job. As you read about the different IT job roles described next, the generally recommended background or certification is noted. These certifications demonstrate to potential employers that you are prepared to perform the tasks required of the job position.

Because of the nature of the jobs HIT personnel have, most HIT personnel have a level of god-like access to the information systems. If an HIT technician needs to reset only passwords, some information systems enable security access to the system to reset passwords but not to reassign access to usernames. HIT technicians have authority to view PHI if it is required to troubleshoot or resolve an issue with an IS. Because it is harder to limit HIT personnel access to PHI, it is best to just understand that access to PHI is on a need-to-know basis only. Only view PHI if it is absolutely necessary to resolve an issue.

Some hospitals are large enough to have help desk staff. This staff receives support requests and assigns the issues to the appropriate support personnel. The help desk staff helps facilitate communication between support staff and users until a resolution to the issue is reached. In smaller hospitals, all HIT personnel share the responsibility of receiving support requests and following through with those requests until a resolution is reached.

Now review these job roles and their responsibilities. Not all hospitals require all these job roles, and IT personnel might perform multiple roles.

System Administrator

The **system administrator** in a healthcare facility is the HIT personnel responsible for the overall health of the information systems in the facility. The system administrator is the jack-of-all-trades of the HIT department, which makes him the consult whenever support personnel encounter a problem they cannot resolve.

> **system administrator**—The HIT personnel responsible for the overall health of the information systems in the facility.

Because a system administrator tends to be the jack-of-all-trades person in an IT organization, he has likely attained his job status by acquiring a variety of IT certifications and experience. For Windows-based systems, typical certifications a system administrator might have include the Microsoft Certified IT Professional (MCITP) certifications, the older Microsoft Certified Systems Administrator (MCSA) certification, and the Microsoft Certified Technology Specialist (MCTS) certification. For UNIX-based systems, a system administrator might have a Certified System Administrator (CSA) certification from a UNIX vendor.

The system administrator performs the following tasks and possibly more:

- Configure, install, support, monitor, and maintain computers, servers, or network devices.
- Create and maintain backups of the information systems and the IS data.
- Plan for and respond to system outages.
- Manage projects involving information systems.
- Supervise or train computer users.

Security Administrator

The **security administrator** in a healthcare facility is the HIT personnel responsible for securing data in the facility. The security administrator consults with the security officer at the facility to create policies for standards of security. The security administrator is likely to have the foundational CompTIA Security+ certification and other more vendor-specific security certifications such as the Cisco VPN Specialist certification.

> **security administrator**—The HIT personnel responsible for securing data in the facility.

To maintain the security of the data in the facility, the security administrator performs the following tasks:

- Applies updates and patches to all computers and servers connecting to the network

- Ensures network hardware is configured to best protect the network from hackers

- Applies policies and settings to all servers and computers to best prevent hacking

- Grants access in information systems to personnel based on the minimum access required

- Monitors the network, computers, servers, and information systems for security breaches

- Resolves vulnerabilities to the security of the data when issues arise or when normal monitoring shows a risk, such as unnecessary open ports

Network Administrator

The **network administrator** in a healthcare facility is the HIT personnel responsible for maintaining the integrity of the network. The network administrator is responsible for setup, deployment, monitoring, and maintenance of network devices. These tasks might include managing routing tables, DNS servers, or static IP address assignments. Certifications a network administrator might have include one or more Cisco certifications including the Cisco Certified Network Associate (CCNA) certification.

network administrator—The HIT personnel responsible for maintaining the integrity of the network.

NOTE   A routing table is a data table stored on a router or computer connected to the network that indicates where network traffic should be directed.

NOTE   The domain name system (DNS) is a hierarchy for distributing names for computers and devices on a network. A DNS assigns hostnames that identify a source to their IP address.

Database Administrator

The **database administrator (DBA)** in a healthcare facility is the HIT personnel responsible for the management of the databases in the information systems used in a facility. A DBA is likely to be certified by the company that provides the database software. This software is called a database management system (DBMS). The two most popular examples of a large-scale DBMS are SQL Server by Microsoft and Oracle by Oracle Corporation. For these database solutions, a DBA is likely to have Microsoft or Oracle certifications for database administration. The DBA directly accesses the database tables through the DBMS. Users access the database tables through an IS, which uses interface software between the DBMS and the user, as shown in Figure 4-11. The IS limits the kinds of changes or additions to the data tables a user in the IS such as a nurse can make, which protects the integrity of the data from user mistakes. For example, the HIS accesses the tables in the database to provide fields that users use to enter data, which will be added to the database tables, such as heart rate and blood pressure records. The DBA must be familiar with this interface and able to support it, and might have a vendor certification that applies to the interface.

> **database administrator (DBA)**—The HIT personnel responsible for the management of the databases in the information systems used in a facility.

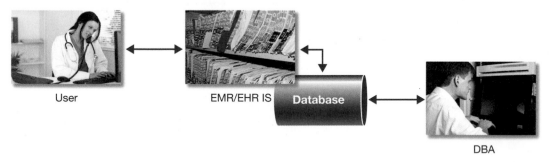

User   EMR/EHR IS   Database   DBA

Figure 4-11   Although a DBA accesses database tables directly using a DBMS, users must use an information system to enter data to the database tables.

Photo credits: andreiorlov, WavebreakmediaMicro, and hoboton

The DBA's tasks include the following responsibilities:

- Design, implement, maintain, and repair databases.
- Troubleshoot issues as they arise.

- Monitor storage capacity and cleanup and backup databases as necessary to ensure data integrity and availability.

A DBA is the sole responsible party for the databases who typically does not like sharing this responsibility. If someone changes a database structure or table without knowing what they are doing, the damage can significantly affect users and cause hours of work for the DBA to correct the mistakes. Anyone other than a DBA must ask the DBA for access to directly change a database structure in an IS because the DBA is usually the only person who can grant this access. The DBA might give temporary access to the database design tools so that the changes can be made.

Desktop Support Technician

The **desktop support technician** in a healthcare facility is the HIT personnel responsible for the support of computers and certain peripheral devices in the facility. Desktop support technicians usually assist users when they encounter a problem and are generally not responsible for preventative measures. A desktop support technician might be A+ certified.

> **desktop support technician**—The HIT personnel responsible for the support of computers and certain peripheral devices in the facility.

The desktop support technician might support the following devices:

- Desktop computers
- Laptop computers
- Tablet computers
- Mobile phones (smartphones that can connect to the hospital network)
- Printers
- Fax machines
- Televisions

Third-Party Access

Healthcare facilities often use business associates and contractors to assist with functions of the facility. For example, a facility might use a business partner or a contractor for technical support, reporting, billing, or analyzing data. As you remember from Chapter 3, "Regulatory Requirements," a BAA and an SLA are required for e-PHI to be shared with business associates and contractors. Before third-party access to an IS can be granted to a business associate or contractor, a BAA and an SLA must be in place.

The security administrator is responsible for creating a username and password for the third party to use to access the information systems necessary. Having an audit trail is important for ensuring the business associate or contractor is accessing the information required to perform only agreed-upon tasks. The network administrator and system administrator are responsible for creating the means for the third party to connect to the IS, usually remotely, but occasionally a third party comes on site to offer services.

Role-Based Access and Exceptions

The security officer and the security administrator at a facility are responsible for creating the policies used at the facility for how much access personnel and third parties have. The CFO is responsible for approving security policies. Rather than deciding the level of access for each individual, a policy determines the level of access a job title requires to perform duties of the job. This policy establishes rules called **role-based access control (RBAC)**. These RBAC policies determine the access assigned to individuals based on their job title.

> **role-based access control (RBAC)**—The assignment of access to information systems based on job title and not individual evaluation for need of access.

When an employee is hired, that employee is given a unique username and password to log in to workstations and the information systems. The username is assigned access based on the employee's job title. The access assigned to each job title is the minimal access necessary to perform the job duties. Because personnel often blur job responsibilities to other job titles, occasionally an exception is required to allow a user additional access to an IS. When this happens, the employee's manager, or supervisor, fills out a role-based exception (RBE) form, and submits it to the security administrator. The RBE form lists the access the user already has, lists the access requested, gives reason why the user needs additional access, and is signed with approval by the chief financial officer (CFO) of the facility. When the request is approved by the CFO, the security administrator will grant the user the additional access.

Mandatory access control (MAC) is much stricter than RBAC. MAC requires a security or system administrator to grant a user access to a resource in an IS or on the network. Although MAC is more secure than RBAC, it requires each user of the entire facility to be individually granted access, which is not practical in the real world. RBAC is a more practical real-world approach that is still secure. In practice, RBAC might be used in HIT for granting most access, and MAC might be used on rare occasions in specific situations such as when an employee is given the right to remotely log into a network.

> **mandatory access control (MAC)**—A security mechanism where a user can only gain access to a resource if the security or system administrator grants the access.

Discretionary access control (DAC) is not as secure as RBAC. DAC enables users to control access to the resources they own, meaning when a user has access to a resource, he can grant access to another user to that resource as well. Windows user accounts typically use DAC enforcement. DAC can be used in HIT for a shared file server. For example, each user has a personal folder on the file server, and the user has the ability to grant access to this folder to another user.

> **discretionary access control (DAC)**—A security mechanism where a user has control to grant access to resources owned by the user account.

Occasionally, the assigned access might malfunction and prevent a user from accessing an IS. This can cause a critical emergency in patient care. Even though HIPAA is strict with the attitude that granting access should be minimal, HIPAA allows one exception to never have access issues cause a delay in patient care. The security administrator has a username and password on reserve for occasions when a patient is in need of emergent care and access to the IS is crucial to giving the patient proper care. This emergency access is called **break the glass access**. Whenever break the glass access is used, the event must be thoroughly documented and reported according to hospital policy.

> **break the glass access**—A username and password reserved for emergency use to access patient information.

Access Based on Sensitive Patient Data

Although the PHI of all patients is to be protected through great efforts, a classification of patients requires even stricter rules for privacy, called a **sensitivity label**. These patients, for example, could be in the behavioral health unit, HIV positive patients, or at the patient's request. When patients have a more taboo condition, their presence in a hospital receives extra protection. Sensitive patients are flagged in the information systems as having different sensitivity levels. The EMR/EHR information systems have the capability to block the majority of users from viewing a patient's name if a patient is flagged as sensitive.

> **sensitivity label**—A classification of how confidential a patient's information is above and beyond HIPAA regulations.

For sensitive patients, even the patient's presence in the hospital is protected. For example, patients in the behavioral health unit are highly sensitive. Because dietary personnel cannot view anything about these patients, the behavioral health NUC collects the dietary requirements for the entire unit and sends the information to the dietary personnel. This way the dietary personnel know only the number of patients in the behavioral health unit and know the dietary orders but are unaware of any PHI. Another example is the phone operator at the hospital. The operators can usually look up patient names in the hospital and room assignments to redirect phone calls to patient rooms. Sensitive patients do not show on the operator's patient census, so the operator does not know the room or unit assignment of a sensitive patient or even that the patient is in the hospital.

Levels of Access and Audit Trails

The lowest level of patient sensitivity label gives clearance to access patient information to most personnel. An example of low-level access is the dietary personnel. The dietary user might have the lowest level of clearance because she does not need to access all patient data to bring food to the patient. The dietary user might have access to the patient census and dietary orders at all units in the hospital, except the behavioral health unit, to know how many food trays to prepare for each unit and any special dietary orders.

The highest level of patient sensitivity label and clearance to access for patient information is one that few personnel have access to. An example of a high-level access is the EHR/EMR system analyst in the HIT department. The analyst must have access to everything in the EHR/EMR system to troubleshoot an issue no matter which patient is affected in the IS.

Although a user might have high-level access, there is a control system in place to help ensure the user doesn't just go looking at any patient information whenever he wants. If someone questions what has been accessed about a particular patient, an audit trail can be viewed of who has viewed any patient's information. This ensures that even though a user may have full access to any patient information, he can view only that information if necessary to fulfill his job duties.

Now that you are familiar with the personnel in healthcare facilities, the following section takes a closer look at the different kinds of facilities and how they might be organized.

Identifying Organizational Structures and Different Methods of Operation

HI001 Objectives:

2.4   Identify organizational structures and different methods of operation.

Organization structures: hospital, private practice, nursing homes, assisted living facilities, home healthcare, hospice, surgical centers

Methods: differences in scope of work, availability of resources, formality of procedures

All organizations have a structure or hierarchy of management. Healthcare facilities use management levels to have a chain of command to ensure compliance with all the rules and regulations required by HIPAA. The larger the facility, the more complex the organization structure the healthcare facility uses.

The next section begins with the hospital because it is the most complex, and then you learn about other healthcare organizations and their scope of work. As you learn about each facility, pay close attention to what is expected of HIT personnel at each facility.

Hospitals

The hospital is the largest and most complex of healthcare facilities. Figure 4-12 shows an organizational structure of a hospital. Organizational structures can vary slightly from facility to facility. The hierarchy begins with the board of directors, which has the final say about the policies and finances of a hospital as matters are presented to them to vote on. They are also responsible for hiring the CEO.

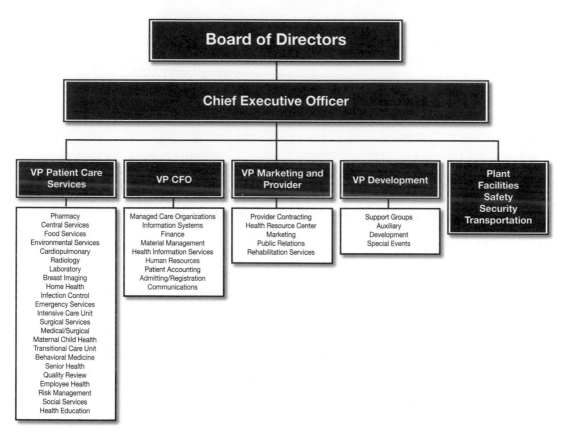

Figure 4-12 A hospital is organized by grouping similar functions together under vice presidents

Photo credit: Image content derived from Figure 2.3 in *Being a Health Unit Coordinator*, 5th edition by Kay Cox-Stevens. Prentice Hall [ISBN 0-13-091612-9]

After the board comes the chief executive officer (CEO). The CEO is in charge of the hospital and acts much like the president of a company. The CEO has vice presidents (VPs) to help run the hospital administration. The VPs oversee specialized functions of the hospital; for example the chief financial officer (CFO) oversees hospital finances and the HIT department. The administrative staff includes business-minded leaders whose goals are to make the hospital successful in both the medical field and in finances, which can lead to further successes. Administrators, like the security officer, establish hospital policies and procedures. The administrative staff is also responsible for public relations within the community.

The rest of the hospital personnel are grouped under a VP based on the similarity of the job duties and services provided by a department. Following is a summary of common VP positions and the departments they typically oversee:

- The VP of Patient Care Services might oversee all clinical areas, quality review, **risk management**, social services, and health education.

> **risk management**—The proactive approach to preventing lawsuits and liability issues due to medical errors.

- The CFO is a VP who oversees all the financial aspects of the hospital as well as information management.
- The VP of Marketing and Provider Contracts handles public relations and is responsible for attracting healthcare providers to work at the hospital.
- The VP of Development handles special events, support groups, auxiliary services (such as fundraising and volunteers), and development within the hospital.
- The CEO might have the responsibility to oversee Support Services or there might be a VP of Support Services. The CEO or this VP oversees the unsung heroes of the hospital. These employees ensure the hospital is stocked with supplies, are responsible for cleaning, and make sure equipment functions. Also the security, safety, and transportation departments report to the CEO or the VP of Support Services.

A hospital has more available resources than any of the other healthcare facilities. The bigger the hospital, the more resources should be available. Because a hospital is open 24 hours a day, 7 days a week, 365 days a year, all resources are available at all times, even if, for example, medical help must be called in at 3 a.m. The HIT department is also required to be available at all hours.

Private Practices

Private practices are organizations in which one or more doctors practice medicine without being employed by a hospital. Many different specialists might be organized as a private practice and can vary in size. Even though a doctor might be in private practice, she still serves a hospital's needs. For example, all the **anesthesiologists** might work for a group practice, rather than employed directly by the hospital. For just about every area of medicine, there can be a private practice, such as **gastro-enterology**, dental, family medicine, sports medicine, or **ophthalmology**. A private practice can be for just one doctor or a group of doctors. A medical group practice is when three or more physicians share business management, facilities, records, and personnel. Because a private practice generally runs only during business hours, the HIT support staff needs to be available only during hours of operation.

anesthesiologist—A physician who is trained in anesthesia and perioperative medicine. Anesthesia means to block sensation to prevent a patient from feeling pain; for example, during a surgery.

gastroenterology—The study of the digestive system and its disorders.

ophthalmology—The study of the eye and its diseases.

A private practice that works outside of the hospital has the medical equipment and staff necessary to function in the specialty of care they offer. However, some medical equipment, such as a magnetic resonance imaging (MRI) machine, is too expensive for a private practice to own and maintain, so private practice patients might be sent to the hospital for certain procedures or treatments.

The number of private practices is decreasing. The expense and responsibility of running a private practice are becoming more and more problematic for doctors due to government regulations on healthcare to push all practices to start using EHR/EMR systems. Many physicians leave practices to be employed by healthcare organizations because the responsibility and expense for compliance with facility resources and information systems is then shifted from their private practice to the facility. A doctor's salary might decrease with this change, but shifting compliance responsibilities and expenses from the doctor to the facility helps compensate for the decrease of salary.

Nursing Homes

Nursing homes are healthcare facilities that provide inpatient care for elderly, permanently disabled, or mentally incapacitated patients. These patients who need around the clock care might not be able to afford to pay for private care at their home, so they go to a nursing home. The patient care needs of nursing home patients are not as intensive as in a hospital, but this care is more than what they receive at home. When a nursing home patient's healthcare needs become more acute, the patient is transported to the hospital for treatment.

Because a nursing home is open 24 hours a day, 7 days a week, 365 days a year, all resources are available at all times, even if, for example, medical help must be called in at 3 a.m. The HIT department is also required to be available at all hours.

Assisted Living Facilities

Assisted living facilities are healthcare facilities that provide limited care for elderly, permanently disabled, or mentally incapacitated individuals. Assisted living facilities offer limited nursing care, but focus on simple assistance with daily life skills such as cooking and cleaning. For example, an assisted living facility might offer meals and rooms for individuals. When an assisted living facility resident's need for care becomes more acute, the resident is transported to the hospital for treatment.

Because an assisted living home is open 24 hours a day, 7 days a week, 365 days a year, all resources are available at all times, even if, for example, medical help must be called in at 3 a.m. The HIT department is also required to be available at all hours.

Surgical Centers

Surgical centers are healthcare facilities that offer surgical services on an outpatient basis. Surgical center patients arrive for surgery and go home to recover all in the same day. Due to advancement in medicine, surgeries are often less intrusive than they used to be, so patients have the ability to recover at home. Having a surgical procedure done at a surgical center is usually less expensive to the patient than at a hospital because the patient does not need to stay overnight. Surgical centers usually offer only surgeries that are unlikely to require admittance to a hospital in case there are complications during the surgery. If the surgery is high risk but can still be done as an outpatient procedure, the patient will likely have the procedure done at the hospital in an ambulatory surgery unit to have easy access to emergency hospital resources.

Because surgical centers generally run only during business hours, the HIT support staff needs to be available only during hours of operation as well.

Home Healthcare

Advances in healthcare technology have made medical services more mobile. Some patients require regular medical attention, but not intense enough to warrant admittance to a hospital or nursing home. Home healthcare providers travel to the patient's home and offer medical services, such as nursing, therapies, or physical rehabilitation.

Because home healthcare providers generally offer services during business hours, the HIT support staff needs to be available only during hours of operation as well. Because providers travel to a patient's home, HIT staff focuses on remotely supporting these providers.

Hospice

When a patient becomes terminally ill with a prognosis of 6 months or less, hospice offers its services to the patient and her family. To receive hospice care, a patient must agree to not receive treatment to try to cure the illness. Hospice programs assist with medical, emotional, spiritual, and financial needs of a patient or her family. Hospice programs offer comfort care and symptom management to the patient, as well as bereavement services to the family after a patient's death. Most often services are provided in the home of the patient, but hospice care is also available in hospice residences, nursing homes, assisted living facilities, or hospitals.

Because hospice generally offers services during business hours, the HIT support staff needs to be available only during hours of operation as well. A few hospice employees might work overnight, but do not usually require emergency IT support. If healthcare providers travel to a patient's home, HIT staff focuses on remotely supporting these providers.

Now that you know how to handle PHI, who works in healthcare facilities, and different types of facilities, the following section covers how HIT technicians work in the healthcare environment.

Executing Daily Activities

> **HI001 Objectives:**
>
> **2.5   Given a scenario, execute daily activities while following a code of conduct.**
>
> Communicate in a professional fashion, adapt procedural behavior according to different situations and environments, imaging room, adapt social behavior based on sensitivity of the environment, use proper sanitation steps—follow medical precautionary guidelines, conform to requirements set forth by project manager

While working in a hospital as an HIT technician, you might go to almost any room of the hospital speaking with almost every kind of personnel. All IT technicians need to conduct themselves in a professional manner, but healthcare IT technicians need special knowledge of how to behave in a healthcare environment.

Communication

As an HIT technician, you need to communicate in a professional manner. Behaving professionally keeps potentially tense situations calm and helps users feel comfortable coming to you for help with their technical problems. Clinical users are under a lot of stress in their jobs, and technical issues add to that stress. Realize that when you speak with a user in the hospital, the user, for example, might be in the middle of or just experienced a trauma in the ED or a patient **coding** in the intensive care unit (ICU). Use the following tips to help you communicate with ease:

> **coding**—When a patient goes into cardiac arrest where the heart stops beating. Sometimes referred to as code blue.

- Look at the person as you speak with him.
- Don't cross your arms, which is body language that you are resisting the other person.
- Don't use inappropriate language.
- Smile occasionally, and try not to use negative facial expressions.
- Speak in a normal tone. Don't get excited.
- Be a good listener, and allow the user to fully explain the issue they are experiencing before trying to resolve the issue.
- Be aware that even though it might appear to be a minor issue to you, it might be affecting the user in a significant way.
- Explain the situation and the technology involved using common language, and avoid using terminology of the IT profession. You want the user to understand what you're saying.
- Put important details on paper to give to the user and explain the document to the user.
- Ask for feedback and follow up.

> **EXAM TIP**   For the Healthcare IT exam, you need to know how to interact successfully with other employees and to be a good communicator.

IT Functions in a Healthcare Environment

HIT technicians must adapt procedural behavior according to different situations and environments. For example, downtime is often required when servicing, backing up, or updating computers, servers, or information systems. During downtime, users are greatly affected. HIT technicians should aim to schedule downtime so that it interferes with as few users as possible. This usually means scheduled downtimes should occur during after hours at night or over a weekend.

You should always get permission before making any changes on a computer or server. In a healthcare environment, computers and servers perform critical tasks. For example, a computer used during a critical surgery or running a **fetal monitor** or sleep study cannot have any interruptions. When possible, think ahead, plan, and get permission to schedule downtime.

> **fetal monitor**—A device used to monitor a baby before birth, usually recording the baby's heartbeat.

When implementing any new systems or applying updates, it is critical to thoroughly test the change before implementing or deploying it to the entire facility. Not testing an update or new system and applying or implementing it blindly can potentially bring down an entire IS in the hospital. Instead of deploying an update or implementing a new system blindly, test the change on a small number of noncritical workstations. Then test on a few more workstations. When you have thoroughly tested and worked out any issues with the change, you should safely implement or apply the change to the entire facility without disruption.

When implementing a new EHR/EMR IS in a healthcare facility, a **project manager (PM)** directs and ensures deadlines are met with the implementation staff. The PM focuses on meeting the deadlines set by the HHS to meet the requirements to receive the financial incentives. As an HIT technician, you are responsible for complying with the requirements set by the PM. The PM knows how to best implement the new EHR/EMR IS while considering the overall goal to ensure the users have the least amount of interruption to their job performance. The implementation is a long process and must be handled appropriately so users will be more willing to give the new EHR/EMR IS a chance and not resist the change.

> **project manager (PM)**—The individual who oversees an implementation project, such as installing an EHR/EMR IS in a hospital.

HIT Technician Presence in the Hospital

HIT technicians might need to go in any room of the hospital where there is a computer, printer, or even a phone. Basically, as an HIT technician, you need to know how to enter rooms where patients are present or where staff is working so that you can be respectful, follow established protocols, and not interfere with what is going on and yet still accomplish your task.

In every room where a patient is present, always ask permission before entering by knocking, announcing yourself, and waiting a moment for a reply. Never barge into a patient's room. It is always helpful to get assistance from a clinical employee to know if it is okay to go in to a room to service a computer. You are encouraged to make verbal contact with a patient when you enter her room to let her know who you are and why you are there. For example, most healthcare facilities have a way to indicate in the women's center whether a patient has just had a miscarriage. When you greet the patient, you need to know whether there is a sensitive condition you need to be considerate about and not make comments about.

Some of the rooms in a hospital that require special considerations are as follows:

- **Recovery room**: When you enter a recovery room, a patient will likely be resting after undergoing a medical procedure. Be quiet and let the patient rest as much as possible.

- **Holding or float room**: When you enter a holding room, also called a float room, a patient is usually there temporarily waiting to be moved to another room or unit for a procedure. Patients are sometimes tense or anxious about having a procedure done, so be certain to not add to any tension in the room.

- **Procedural room**: Be aware of any clothing requirements for each procedure room you enter. Some procedural rooms require a gown to cover your clothes, booties to cover your shoes, a cap to cover your hair, or a mask to cover your face. This is to protect the patient and you. Any clinical employee in that unit can assist you.

- **Imaging room**: When you enter any imaging room, make certain you ask an imaging staff member in that unit when you should enter. Radiology technicians wear a lead-lined apron or stand behind a wall during an X-ray to reduce exposure to radiation. You should never walk into an imaging room when an image is in progress, so you are not exposed to radiation. The MRI imaging room is special because no metal objects are allowed to enter the room. The MRI machine has a strong magnet that will pull any metal object to it, such as keys. Remember you cannot bring any HIT equipment that contains metal into this room. The MRI machine is always on, so the magnetic force is always present and can be extremely dangerous.

- **Examination room**: When you enter an examination room, a patient may be in a vulnerable state during an exam. If at all possible, wait until the exam is finished and the patient has left the room before you enter unless what you are working on is necessary for the exam or patient.

- **ED room**: When you enter an ED room, ED personnel might be working diligently to treat a very sick or injured patient. Be considerate at all times to not interfere with the work of the healthcare providers assisting the patient.

HIT technicians work in an environment unlike most other typical environments in which IT technicians work. Because HIT technicians work in a hospital, there are guidelines for proper sanitation to follow. You must be aware of these guidelines, so when an emergency arises, you are aware of the guidelines necessary to ensure sanitation and protect yourself and patients from infections.

Always follow these guidelines when working in a healthcare facility:

- Make sure clinical areas have washable keyboards and mice.
- Always wash your hands before entering and after leaving a patient's room.
- Be aware of your surroundings; never enter where you are uncomfortable.
- Wear a mask to cover your nose and mouth if you have a cold or other contagious illness, as shown in Figure 4-13.

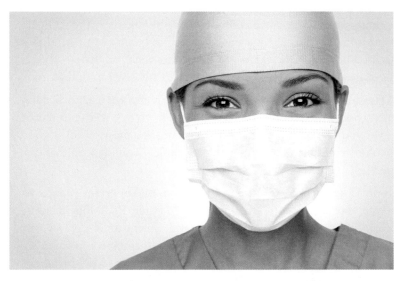

Figure 4-13   A mask that covers your nose and mouth can help prevent spreading a cold.

Photo credit: Maridav

- Wear a gown when entering surgical or lab areas, as shown in Figure 4-14.

Figure 4-14   Wear a gown when entering a surgical or lab area of a healthcare facility.

Photo credit: Yuri Arcurs

HIT in the Real World

We were installing all new computer systems in a hospital in Texas. When a corporate company acquires a new facility, we switch the new facility's information systems to one of the information systems that we know how to support. The implementation analysts compare the database tables to the same database tables at a similar facility that is already using the information systems we're implementing to make sure the tables are correctly set up. Not all the tables match exactly because the facilities are still a little different.

We were getting close to the "go live" date when every IS officially switches from the old systems to the new systems. All the different information systems were ready to go except for one portion of the lab information system (LIS): the microbiology lab IS. The project manager decided that this portion of the LIS would not delay the go live, and the microbiology lab IS would have to catch up later. In the meantime, the microbiology lab IS would be used in a makeshift version to limp along until it caught up. The go live went smoothly until the second night. I got a call from the hospital saying that the microbiology lab IS was broken. Orders were not available; results were not coming through; nothing was working. I called the LIS analyst and asked her if she knew what was going on, but she had not touched the LIS since earlier that afternoon and didn't know of any changes that would cause this. She did remember giving another LIS analyst (who had just arrived to help during the go live) access to the LIS databases to help her get caught up, though. I called him to find out if he was working on the microbiology lab IS, and sure enough he was.

He had tried to pull a query to show the LIS analyst that some files were missing information. Somehow he accidentally copied the tables from a different facility to the one that was going live. After we determined what had happened, the tables had to be removed and replaced with a backup of the tables. Something as simple as looking for information directly in the database tables caused a major problem.

In this one story you can see several lessons to learn. Work diligently with your project manager to keep on schedule so that you're not scrambling at the last minute to catch up. Make sure that when you grant access directly into the database tables of your IS that the person knows exactly what he's doing; otherwise, the whole system might come crashing down. And finally, always make regular backups and especially before making any changes to an IS or database.

Chapter Summary

Handling PHI

- PHI is protected by physical and technical safeguards.
- Place computers where only personnel can view the screen and use privacy screens when you can't place the computer in a restricted location.
- Place printers and fax machines out of public areas.
- Ask users to quickly pick up printed documents containing PHI.
- Activate the locking screensaver on a computer.
- When staff schedules permit, use a time lockout on user accounts.

Applying Proper Communication Methods

- Ensure email containing PHI is encrypted.
- Never use IM in a healthcare environment. Secure chat might be approved for use by the security officer. EHR/EMR information systems sometimes have a messaging system that might be secure enough for use.
- When using fax machines, educate your users to make sure only the intended recipient receives the fax and use a coversheet.
- Use secure FTP to transfer data rather than regular FTP that is not secured.
- Phones should be managed and monitored to prevent breaches of PHI.
- VoIP phone systems offer the extra security provided by using the network security.
- Train clinical personnel to be as conscious about protecting e-PHI as they are about infection control.

Identifying EHR/EMR Access Roles and Responsibilities

- A medical doctor (MD) is a physician who is licensed and trained to practice medicine without supervision. MDs need full access to patient information.
- A physician assistant (PA) is licensed and trained to practice medicine under supervision of a physician. PAs need full access to patient information.
- A nurse practitioner (NP) is a healthcare provider who is a registered nurse who has additional education at a graduate level. In some states NPs are allowed to work without a physician supervising them and can be a patient's primary care provider.

- A registered nurse (RN) has completed a nursing school program and passed the national licensing exam. RNs need full access to patient information.

- A licensed practical nurse (LPN) has completed a LPN program in a school and passed a state exam. LPNs need access to patient information as assigned by the security administrator and approved by the CFO.

- A medical assistant (MA) is a healthcare provider or administrator who is not certified and works under supervision of a licensed healthcare provider or office manager. MAs need access to patient information as assigned by the security administrator and approved by the CFO.

- A dental assistant (DA) helps a dentist perform procedures or prepare patients for dental procedures. DAs need access to patient information as assigned by the security administrator and approved by the CFO.

- A patient care technician (PCT) works under supervision of a licensed healthcare provider, typically providing basic bedside care. PCTs need access to patient information as assigned by the security administrator and approved by the CFO.

- A nursing unit clerk (NUC) assists the healthcare providers in a unit with general receptionist duties. NUCs need limited access to patient information.

- A unit assistant (UA) facilitates the function of a unit. UAs rarely need access to patient information, so verify with hospital policy if a UA requests access.

- A practice manager (PM) facilitates the business operations of a private practice. PMs need access to reporting features in information systems.

- An office manager facilitates the business operations of a physician's office. Office managers need access to reporting features in information systems.

- The staff at a healthcare facility ensures healthcare providers have supplies and clean environments necessary to provide proper patient care. Staff may need access to patient census data.

- The system administrator is the HIT personnel responsible for the overall health of the information systems.

- The security administrator is the HIT personnel responsible for the security of e-PHI.

- The network administrator is the HIT personnel responsible for maintaining the network and its integrity.

- The database administrator (DBA) is the HIT personnel responsible for maintaining the integrity of the data.

- The desktop support technician is responsible for supporting computers and certain peripheral devices, such as printers and mobile phones.

- Before a business associate or contractor is given a username and password to access an IS, a BAA and an SLA needs to be in place.

- Using role-based access control (RBAC), access to information systems is based on job titles rather than individual assessment.

- Break the glass access is an emergency username and password to be used when a user's normal username is malfunctioning and patient care requires immediate access to the information system.

- Patients with sensitive data, such as patients in the behavioral health unit, have strict confidentiality and the patient's presence in the hospital is treated discreetly.

Identifying Organizational Structures and Different Methods of Operation

- A hospital is organized by grouping similar functions together under vice presidents. The CEO is the administrator of the hospital. A board of directors approves budgets and policies and hires the CEO.

- A private practice is a physician or group of physicians who practice medicine but are not employed by a hospital.

- A nursing home offers patient care for elderly, permanently disabled, or mentally incapacitated patients.

- An assisted living home offers limited care for elderly, permanently disabled, or mentally incapacitated patients.

- Surgical centers offer surgical services on an outpatient basis.

- Home healthcare brings limited healthcare services to a patient's home.

- Hospice offers services to terminally ill patients and their families with a prognosis of six months or less to live.

Executing Daily Activities

- Communicate with users in a professional manner that encourages users to ask for help again and helps to keep tense situations calm.

- Conform to the requirements of a project manager (PM) to ensure deadlines are met and users are satisfied with the changes in the information systems.

- Whenever you enter a room where a patient is present, ask permission before entering. Check with a clinical employee if you are uncertain if you should enter. Let the patient know who you are and why you're there.

- Be aware of clothing requirements for any specialized rooms you enter.

- Ask an imaging staff before entering an imaging room. Do not bring any metal into a room containing an MRI machine.

- Be respectful of patients in exam rooms because they may be feeling vulnerable while being examined. If possible, wait until the exam is over and the patient has left before entering.

- When in the ED, be certain to stay out of the way of the healthcare providers as they treat a patient who is likely very sick or injured.

- Be aware of sanitation requirements for special rooms in the hospital. For example, a surgical gown is required to enter an operating room or lab.

- Know sanitation rules of the hospital, such as always washing your hands when entering or leaving a patient room.

Key Terms

- anesthesiologist
- audit trail
- break the glass access
- coding
- communications protocol
- database administrator (DBA)
- dental assistant (DA)
- dermatology
- desktop support technician
- discretionary access control (DAC)
- fetal monitor
- file transfer protocol (FTP)
- gastroenterology
- hacker
- instant messaging (IM)
- licensed practical nurse (LPN)
- lock
- mandatory access control (MAC)

- medical assistant (MA)
- medical doctor (MD)
- network administrator
- nurse practitioner (NP)
- nursing unit clerk (NUC)
- office manager
- operating room (OR)
- ophthalmology
- patient care technician (PCT)
- phone switch
- physician assistant (PA)
- practice manager (PM)
- privacy screen
- private branch exchange (PBX)
- project manager (PM)
- registered nurse (RN)
- risk management
- role-based access control (RBAC)
- screensaver
- secure chat
- secure FTP
- security administrator
- security officer
- sensitivity label
- single sign-on (SSO)
- system administrator
- time lockout
- uninterrupted power supply (UPS)
- unit assistant (UA)
- voice over Internet protocol (VoIP)

Acronym Drill

Acronyms sometimes get confusing, especially when a single sentence can have four or five. As an HIT professional, you must know the acronyms and what they stand for. Fill in the blank with the correct acronym for the sentence.

1. A _____ is a device connected to a computer to provide power for a few minutes in case the power to the facility goes out.

    Answer: _____

2. One of our goals is to have healthcare providers as conscious about the security of _____ as they are about infection control.

    Answer: _____

3. An _____ is trained and licensed to practice medicine without supervision, however a _____ is trained and licensed to practice medicine but requires supervision of a physician.

    Answer: _____

4. A _____ provides basic bedside care.

    Answer: _____

5. A _____, sometimes called a _____, assists the healthcare providers in a unit by doing clerical work.

    Answer: _____

6. A _____ is an employee of a medical practice who facilitates the operations of the practice. A _____ is the individual who oversees an implementation project, such as installing an EHR/EMR IS in a hospital.

    Answer: _____

Review Questions

1. What physical safeguard can you install on a computer monitor if a computer cannot be placed in a restricted area?'

    Answer: _____

2. Why should two departments in a hospital not share a printer?

    Answer: _____

    _____

    _____

3. What should a user do before walking away from a computer she is logged into?

   Answer: _____

4. When is time lockout not feasible to apply to a user?

   Answer: _____

   _____

5. Why should instant messaging never be used in a healthcare environment?

   Answer: _____

6. Why is a VoIP phone system more secure than a regular phone system?

   Answer: _____

   _____

7. Why should a physician have full access to his patient's information?

   Answer: _____

8. Which HIT personnel is responsible for the overall health of the information systems in a healthcare facility?

   Answer: _____

9. Which HIT personnel has access to make changes directly to an IS database design or structure?

   Answer: _____

10. What types of devices might a desktop support technician support?

    Answer: _____

    _____

11. Why does HIPAA allow for break the glass access?

    Answer: _____

    _____

12. Who is responsible for hiring the CEO at a hospital?

    Answer: _____

13. Why are surgical centers typically less expensive for patients than having surgery at a hospital?

    Answer: _____

    _____

    _____

14. Why should HIT technicians behave in a professional manner?

Answer: _____

_____

15. What is a special rule to remember before entering an MRI imaging room?

Answer: _____

_____

Practical Application

1. Find a privacy screen for sale online. What is the website and price? Check the reviews of the product online. Why did some privacy screens receive good reviews, and why did some receive poor reviews?

Answer: _____

_____

_____

_____

_____

_____

2. Configure a Windows computer to go to Screen saver after 1 minute of inactivity and require a logon to use it again. List the steps to do that.

Answer: _____

_____

_____

_____

_____

_____

_____

3. You work at a hospital that uses Windows XP workstations. List the steps to set an XP workstation to automatically log off a user after being idle for 5 minutes.

Answer: _____

_____

_____

_____

_____

_____

_____

_____

CHAPTER 5
IT Operations

In this chapter you learn about:

- **How the Internet or an intranet works**
- **How a network works**
- **Managing network resources**
- **Configuring a workstation and peripheral devices**

No matter what your job role consists of as an HIT technician, you need to understand the basic concepts of IT operations that happen in a hospital. Even if IT operations are not directly related to your job role, your job responsibilities can be indirectly affected.

NOTE Because most HIT technicians come from an IT background, this chapter is intended as a review of IT operations. CompTIA designates the HIT technician certificate to follow the A+ certification. The A+ certification covers most of the content in this chapter in much greater detail.

The first section reviews IT operations by showing how the Internet or an intranet works.

How the Internet or an Intranet Works

HI001 Objectives:

3.1   Identify commonly used IT terms and technologies.

Protocol terms: TCP/IP, DNS, DHCP, FTP, wireless (802.11x), RDP

Devices: domain controller, printer server

Industry terms: ASP, ISP, client-server model, mainframe, cloud computing, virtualization, terminal services, fiber, APIs

Languages: XML, SQL, HTML, Flash, PHP, ASP

All HIT technicians need to have a fundamental understanding of how the Internet and intranet works. The HIT department in a hospital routinely receives support calls because data is not getting across the network. As an HIT technician, you need to interpret what a user tells you so that you can decide where and how the problem is occurring as it relates to the Internet or an intranet.

The Internet is a network infrastructure made up of many computers and networking devices all over the globe. This global network supports many types of communication. The most common type of communication on the Internet is called the World Wide Web (WWW) or the web. The web is made up of many web servers that serve up web pages to client computers using client software called a browser. Internet Explorer (IE) is the most common browser program and is integrated into the Windows operating system. Even though other browsers are available for personal computers, usually healthcare facilities limit computers in the facility to only IE for consistency and support.

An **Internet service provider (ISP)** is a company or an organization that offers individuals and companies an entry point to the Internet through a **wide area network (WAN)**. An ISP might offer several types of connections for accessing the Internet: for example, DSL, cable Internet, or T-lines.

Internet service provider (ISP)—An organization that provides access to the Internet.

wide area network (WAN)—A network that covers a large area. WANs are used to connect networks together such as when facilities or doctor's offices connect to the Internet.

There are many ways to connect to the Internet; however, the typical access method for a hospital is to use a **T-line** because T-lines can handle large volumes of data. T-lines carry data over **fiber optic** lines or copper wire. Fiber optic lines are currently considered the fastest and most reliable for accessing the Internet and have greatly replaced copper wire. Fiber optic lines are strings of glass where data is sent as pulses of light through the fiber (see Figure 5-1). Glass is used to transmit data because glass experiences little interference from other data transfer media nearby. Fiber is also extremely fast; however, fiber is more expensive than other solutions.

> **T-line**—A type of data transmission technology that uses fiber optic cabling. A T1-line transmits up to 1.544 mbps (megabits per second). A T3-line transmits up to 45 mbps.
>
> **fiber optic**—Strings of glass or plastic in a cable where data is sent as pulses of light. Also called fiber.

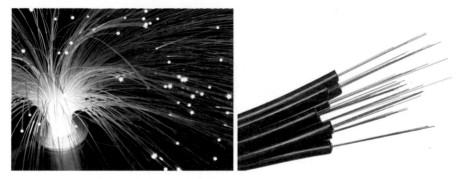

Figure 5-1   Fiber optic cabling uses strings of glass for transmitting light.

Photo credits: Sigurd and Witold Krasowski

An **intranet** is the private network secured within a facility. Access to an intranet is limited, and the intranet is likely to have its own websites and homepage. Intranets are a great avenue for providing resources to healthcare providers and employees that should not be accessed by the general public. For example, a hospital intranet might provide access to an entire library of online medical books, reference books, and medical calculators.

> **intranet**—The private network that is secured within a facility. All intranets use the TCP/IP suite of protocols also used on the Internet.

The OSI Model

The Internet and all intranets use a group or suite of protocols for communication called **TCP/IP**. This common format assures that all devices and software on the network can communicate correctly.

> **TCP/IP**—A suite of protocols used for communication on the Internet or an intranet.

All communication on a TCP/IP network can be assigned to one of seven layers of communication as described by the **Open Systems Interconnection model (OSI model)**. The purpose of the OSI model is to identify the type of communication on a network. For example, an application must communicate with another application on the network. This communication must pass through the operating systems on each computer and the firmware on the network adapter of each computer. What might appear as a simple communication between two applications are actually several layers of communication through the OS and firmware.

> **Open Systems Interconnection model (OSI model)**—A description of all communication on a network expressed as seven layers.

The OSI model explains the seven layers of communication that data goes through as it is prepared to be sent across the network. When the data arrives at the remote computer, the data goes through the seven layers again in reverse order. Each layer has a function, as described in Figure 5-2. The top five layers are handled by the operating system, and the bottom two layers are handled by firmware on the network adapter.

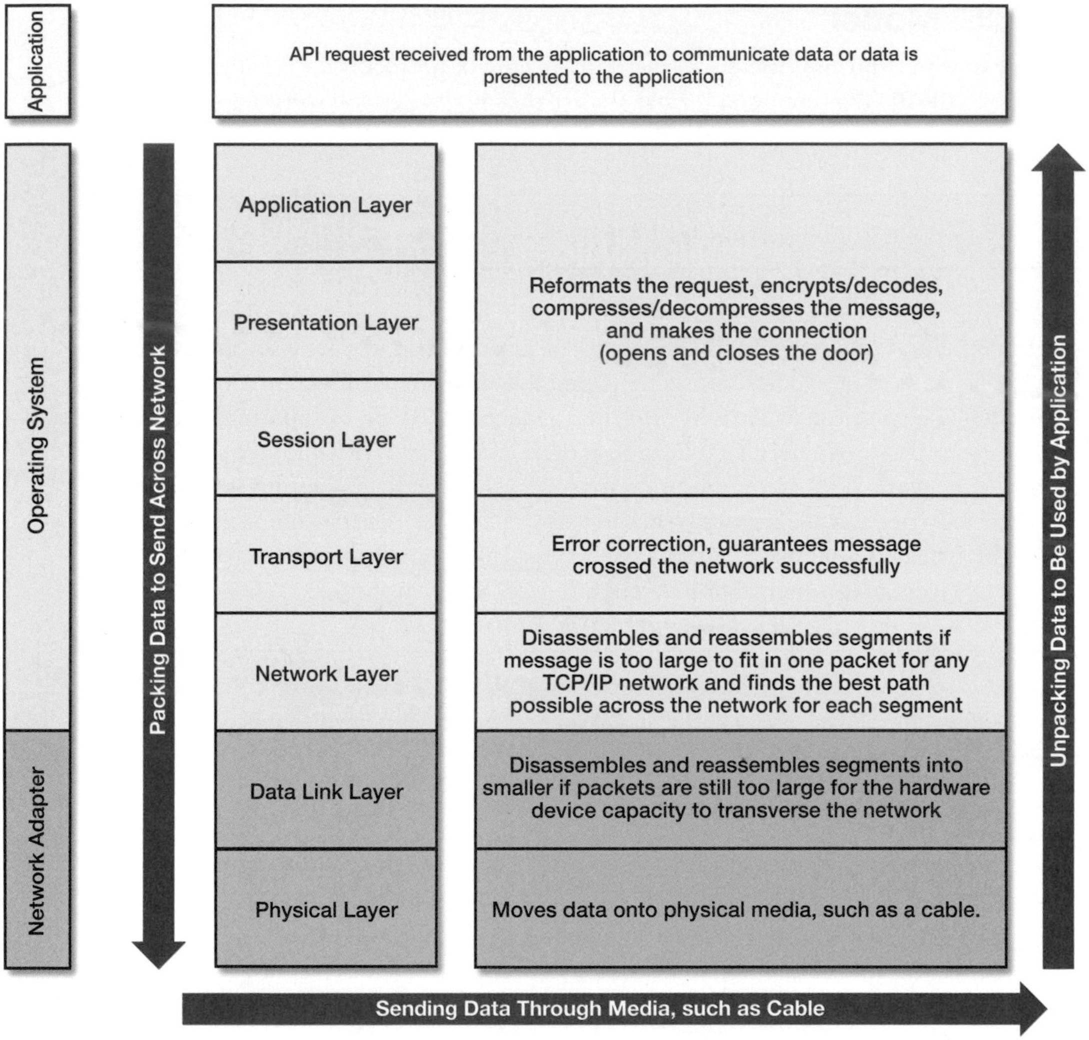

Figure 5-2   The OSI model describes network communication in seven layers.

Protocols within the TCP/IP suite are used in the top five layers of the OSI model. The operating system uses these protocols to manage the application, presentation, session, transport, and network layers of the OSI model. The following sections look at several of the more common TCP/IP protocols used at each of these layers, as shown in Figure 5-3.

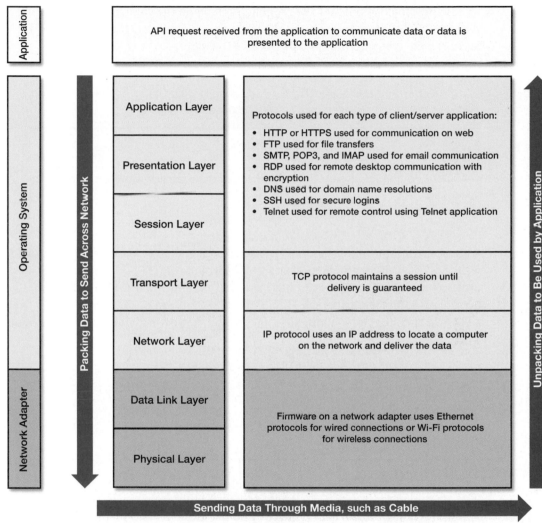

Figure 5-3 The TCP/IP protocols are used in the top five layers of the OSI model.

Application, Presentation, and Session Layer Protocols

The application protocols discussed in this section are Hypertext Transfer Protocol (HTTP), Hypertext Transfer Protocol Secure (HTTPS), File Transfer Protocol (FTP), and Remote Desktop Protocol (RDP). All these protocols use a **client-server architecture**. Using a client-server architecture, one computer or program, called the client, makes a request for data or services from another computer or program, called the server. Technical people often use the terms "client" and "server" to mean either the computer or the program running on the computer. For example, the term "web server" might mean the web server software such as Apache HTTP Server or the computer running the Apache software.

> **client-server architecture**—A network architecture in which client computers rely on services or resources provided by a server computer.

> **EXAM TIP**   For the Healthcare IT exam, you need to be familiar with the client-server architecture.

The most common use of the Internet or an intranet is to serve up web pages for a website. The web uses the **hypertext transfer protocol (HTTP)** or **hypertext transfer protocol secure (HTTPS)** protocol to manage communication at the application, presentation, and session layers. HTTP or HTTPS is responsible for receiving from a browser the request for a web page, formatting the request, and initiating a session with a web server.

> **hypertext transfer protocol (HTTP)**—An application protocol that defines how data is sent to and from a web server on the web.
>
> **hypertext transfer protocol secure (HTTPS)**—A secure version of HTTP that encrypts data sent to and from a web server.

The **file transfer protocol (FTP)** is used to transfer files from one host device to another host device. A browser, such as Internet Explorer, can use the FTP protocol to download a large file from an FTP server. Sometimes a login to the server is required before resources on the FTP server can be accessed. When a login ID and password are not required, the login is said to be anonymous. Internet Explorer and other browsers provide limited use of the FTP protocol. To take full advantage of FTP functions, use an FTP client software such as SmartFTP or CuteFTP, as shown in Figure 5-4.

> **file transfer protocol (FTP)**—A protocol standard for exchanging files over the Internet or an intranet.

Files and folders on local computer   Files and folders on remote computer

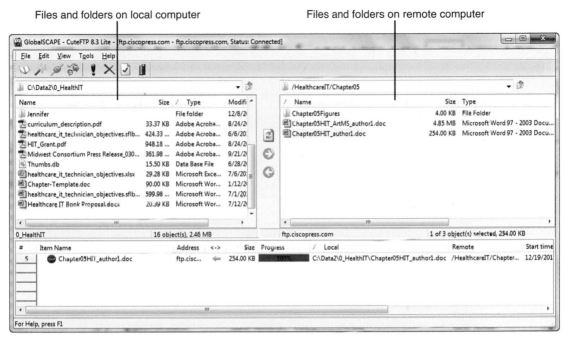

Figure 5-4   FTP client software offers more FTP functionality than a browser does.

Sometimes as an HIT technician you need to access a computer remotely. Rather than sitting directly in front of a computer, you can remotely access that computer using Microsoft's remote desktop connection. This utility provides a window to view the desktop of another computer, as shown in Figure 5-5. The protocol used by the technician's computer and the remote computer is **remote desktop protocol (RDP)**. Remote desktop connection is particularly useful for HIT technicians when it is difficult to understand a user trying to describe what she sees on her screen. Instead of struggling to get a complete description from the user, you can simply remote into her computer and view the screen in a window on your computer. When you have connected, you can use your mouse and keyboard to control her computer as if you were sitting right in front of it.

remote desktop protocol (RDP)—A protocol developed by Microsoft and used with the Remote Desktop Connection utility that allows a user to connect to a remote computer over a network.

Window shows desktop of computer connected through Remote Desktop Connection

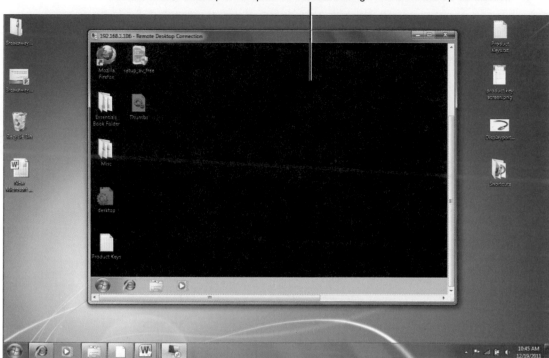

Figure 5-5   Microsoft Remote Desktop Connection utility enables you to remotely access another computer and use the RDP protocol.

Transport and Network Layers

HTTP, FTP, and Remote Desktop are all examples of client-server applications. When a client or server application runs on a computer, it is assigned a port number at the transport layer of the OSI model. This **port** is used to identify the application when multiple applications run on the same computer. Table 5-1 shows some of the more commonly used port number assignments.

> **port**—A number assigned to a client or server application that serves as an address to the application, which the OS uses to get network communication to the correct application. Common port assignments are designated by TCP/IP. Also called a port number or port address.

Table 5-1 Common TCP/IP Port Assignments

Port	Protocol	Service	Description
20	FTP	FTP	Data transfer
21	FTP	FTP	Data control information transfer
22	SSH	Secure Shell	Encryption login information and data used to remote control a computer on the network
23	Telnet	Telnet	Control a computer on the network remotely without encryption
25	SMTP	Email	Simple Mail Transfer Protocol; Outgoing e-mail
53	DNS	DNS server	Domain Name Service; Translates name to IP address
80	HTTP	Web server	World Wide Web protocol
110	POP3	Email	Post Office Protocol, version 3; Incoming e-mail
143	IMAP	Email	Internet Message Access Protocol; a newer protocol for incoming e-mail
443	HTTPS	Web server	HTTP including authentication and encryption
3389	RDP	Remote Desktop	Remote Desktop Protocol; Control a computer on the network remotely using encryption

The **transmission control protocol (TCP)** is used at the transport layer of the OSI model. TCP is responsible for guaranteeing the data is received after traversing the network. If the application requires guaranteed delivery of the data, the TCP protocol is called on to do the job.

> **transmission control protocol (TCP)**—A protocol used in TCP/IP networks at the transport layer of the OSI model. TCP is responsible for guaranteeing data is received and in the correct order.

The **Internet protocol (IP)** is used at the network layer of the OSI model and is responsible for breaking down messages into packets small enough to travel through the network. IP is also responsible for reassembling those packets at the receiving end. In addition, IP is responsible for finding the path to use to get the packets across the network.

> **Internet protocol (IP)**—A protocol used in TCP/IP networks at the network layer of the OSI model. IP is responsible for finding the best path to a destination and breaking down messages into packets small enough to travel through the network and reassembling the packets when received.

The network layer uses **IP addresses** to locate a computer or other device on the network. IP addresses function much like mailbox addresses used by the postal service. Every host or connection point on a network has its own unique IP address.

> **IP address**—The address used to identify a computer or other device on a TCP/IP network. A TCP/IP version 4 IP address has 32 bits, and a TCP/IP version 6 address has 128 bits.

Two versions of IP addresses are used today. IP version 4 (IPv4) uses 32 bits in an address, which is divided into 4 octets of 8 bits each. An example IPv4 IP address is 192.168.1.109. Because an octet cannot exceed 8 bits, the octet cannot exceed the number 255. The newer version of IP addresses is IP version 6 (IPv6). IPv6 uses 128 bits. These bits are divided into blocks of 16 bits each. An example of an IPv6 address is fe80::1914:d755:770c:44a6. The blocks are written as hexadecimal numbers separated by colons. Two colons together indicate one or more blocks filled with zeroes. IPv6 became necessary because of the increasing demand for unique IP addresses, and IPv4 addresses ran scarce.

IP addresses can be difficult to remember. Words are easier to remember than a series of numbers. A name, called a domain name, that makes sense to humans can be assigned to one or more IP addresses. Computer users need to remember only a domain name to access the IP address they want to visit on the Internet. For example, you can remember one of the IP addresses for the Google website, or you can just remember www.google.com, where google.com is the domain name.

The service that controls the translation from words to numbers is called the **domain name service (DNS)**. The DNS resolves domain names into the IP address that the network understands to reach the correct computer on the intranet or Internet. The DNS runs in the background on a computer, and a user does not need to be aware that it is running.

domain name service (DNS)—A service that resolves domain names into the IP address that the network uses to reach the correct computer on the network.

EXAM TIP   For the Healthcare IT exam, you need to be familiar with DNS and symptoms that might indicate a problem with the DNS.

Now learn how the data traverses the network.

Data Link and Physical Layers

Computers connect to a **local area network (LAN)** using either an Ethernet wired network connection or they connect wirelessly to the network. Computers using a wired connection get faster network speeds than computers using wireless connections. Ethernet cables can transmit up to 10 Gbps.

local area network (LAN)—A small network of computers or other connected devices covering a small area such as a home, business, school, or airport.

Running network cables can be difficult or expensive when computers are in remote locations of a hospital or in the middle of a large room. Sometimes it's easier to connect mobile devices, tablet computers, or a computer-on-wheels using a wireless connection. Wireless connections to a local network use the **wireless fidelity (Wi-Fi)** technology. The group of Wi-Fi standards for local networks is IEEE 802.11. Table 5-2 lists the different versions of Wi-Fi standards.

wireless fidelity (Wi-Fi)—The wireless standards used for local networks as defined by the IEEE 802.11 specifications.

Table 5-2   IEEE 802.11 Wi-Fi Standards

IEEE 802.11 Standard	Frequency	Maximum Speed	Description
802.11a	3.7 GHz or 5.0 GHz	54 Mbps	Not widely used now. Because it does not work in the 2.4-GHz frequency, it is not compatible with 802.11g/b. Can be used at distances up to approximately 50 meters.
802.11g 802.11b	2.4 GHz	54 Mbps 11 Mbps	Disadvantaged by using the same frequency as most cordless phones, which causes interference. Can be used at distances up to approximately 100 meters.
802.11n	2.4 GHz or 5.0 GHz	600 Mbps	Latest Wi-Fi standard released. Uses multiple input/multiple output (MIMO) technology, which increases data throughput by using multiple antennas.

When wireless devices detect more than one **wireless access point (WAP or AP)**, the device connects to the AP with the strongest signal. The 802.11k and 802.11r standards were developed to balance the load among APs so the strongest doesn't have to bear most of the wireless network traffic. The 802.11k standard distributes wireless network traffic among several APs, so the AP with the strongest signal does not become overloaded. The 802.11r standard defines how mobile devices transition from one AP to the next as the mobile device moves out of range for one AP and into the range of another AP.

> **wireless access point (WAP or AP)**—A device that enables a wireless computer, printer, or other device to connect to a network.

Now that you know how the data transmits over the network, the next section covers the servers that control the data and control access to the data.

Servers on the Network

A **mainframe** computer (see Figure 5-7) is a large-scale server used by corporations and the government. A mainframe supports multiple computers as they access and use it simultaneously. A mainframe computer has greater memory capacity and processing capability than regular servers. Because so many users access a mainframe, it needs to be available at all times.

> **mainframe**—A large-scale computer that supports many users and client computers.

Figure 5-7   A mainframe is designed to provide resources for multiple users and to run for long periods of time without interruption.

Photo credit: Petr Ivanov

Mainframes have many parts that are redundant and are hot swappable. A **hot swappable** part does not require the computer to be shut down to exchange or service the part. This capability enables the mainframe to run for long periods of time while regular maintenance and repairs occur. Because mainframes are so reliable and provide heavy resources, government and corporations choose to use mainframes rather than regular servers.

> **hot swappable**—A device or piece of equipment that does not require a reboot to establish a connection and function.

A large network with many users requires complex methods to manage all these users. A hospital might have hundreds of employees who require specific access to computer resources. This specific access is determined by job role rather than by individual needs. When a new employee is hired, her job role, therefore, determines what access to resources she is given. Administering large groups of usernames with similar permissions is easier than individually addressing each username.

Rather than configuring user permissions at each individual computer in the facility, a domain is set up that controls the permissions for all users on all computers in the domain. Using a domain, when a user logs onto the network, the domain determines what resources he has permission to access (see Figure 5-8).

The **domain controller** is the server that administers the user account information, authenticates usernames and passwords, and enforces security policies. **Active directory (AD)** is the Microsoft database that the domain controller uses to house all the information needed to manage access to the domain. Active Directory is included in Windows Server operating systems, such as Windows Server 2008.

> **domain controller**—The server that administers the user account information, authenticates usernames and passwords, and enforces security policy.
>
> **active directory (AD)**—The Microsoft database managed by the domain controller that system administrators use to control access to the Windows domain. Active directory contains information about users, groups of users, computers on the domain, organizational units, and configuration data.

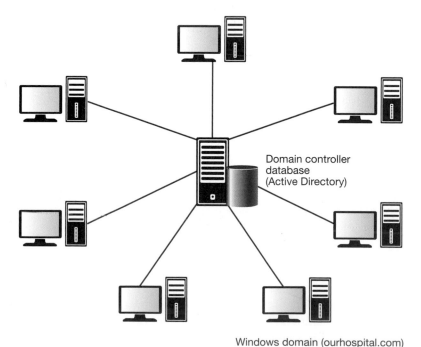

Domain controller database (Active Directory)

Windows domain (ourhospital.com)

Figure 5-8   A domain is used to control access to all resources on a network.

A **print server**, or printer server, connects computers on a network with printers on the same network. A print server receives print jobs from computers into a print queue and sends the print jobs to the requested printer on the network. Print servers are especially useful in a healthcare facility because information systems from one department might need to print needed information directly to the printer at a different department. This saves the time of having to walk documents between departments.

> **print server**—A server that connects computers and other devices on a network with printers on the same network. Also called printer server.

Cloud Computing and Virtualization

Some healthcare facilities do not have the room or finances to house all the servers needed to run health information systems. Cloud computing and virtualization are two techniques designed to reduce the overall costs of these systems.

Using **cloud computing**, a healthcare facility delegates to another organization a degree of responsibility to provide a hospital information system (HIS). Using this option, the HIS company provides the computer storage and processing services needed by the healthcare facility. The facility accesses the storage and services by way of the Internet. When using cloud-based services, a user at the healthcare facility might have no idea where the equipment providing the service is physically located on the globe, as shown in Figure 5-9.

> **cloud computing**—Applications and data stored on remote computers on the Internet made available through a browser.

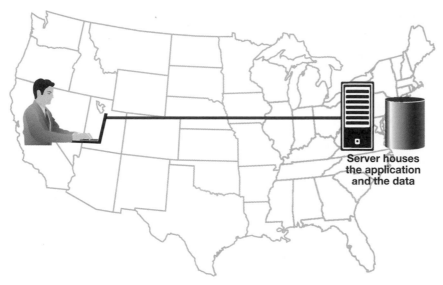

Figure 5-9   With cloud computing, the application and the data can be far away from the user.

The degree of responsibility the hospital might delegate to the cloud computing service varies, as shown in Figure 5-10.

The three levels illustrated are described as follows:

- **Infrastructure as a Service (IaaS):** The cloud computing service provides the hardware including servers, virtual machines, storage devices, networks, and load balancing on that network. The hospital is responsible for the operating systems and applications installed on these machines.

- **Platform as a Service (PaaS):** The cloud computing service provides the hardware and operating systems, including keeping each OS updated and optimized. The hospital is responsible for the applications running on these platforms.

- **Software as a Service (SaaS):** The cloud computing service provides the hardware, the platform, and the applications needed for the hospital information system (HIS), including updates and support for the applications.

Using SaaS, the cloud computing service is provided by an HIS company that offers full services to maintain and house the hardware, operating systems, and HIS applications.

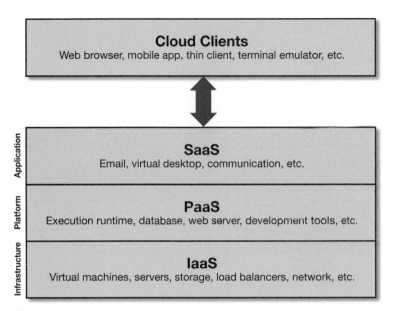

Figure 5-10 One implementation of virtualization is for multiple server applications to run on one computer.

Infrastructure-as-a-Service (IaaS)—A service that hosts hardware remotely, that is needed for cloud computing. Organizations are allowed to use the hardware to host operating systems and software belonging to the organization.

Platform-as-a-Service (PaaS)—A service that hosts hardware and operating systems remotely that is needed for cloud computing. Organizations are allowed to use the hardware and operating system to host the software belonging to the organization.

Software-as-a-Service (SaaS)—A software delivery method where the hardware hosting the software is housed remotely and organizations are allowed to access the software and functions as a web-based service.

A concern about using cloud-based services in healthcare is the security of the data. When the healthcare facility isn't housing the equipment, it has less control of the data. When using cloud-based services, make sure that the security of the data and e-PHI is sufficient and compliant with the same HIPAA regulations as if the equipment were housed onsite. Another consideration of using cloud-based services is access to the service. Because cloud-based services rely on the Internet to provide the services, always make sure there is redundant Internet access.

To help keep the cost down for machines and maintenance for each information system, many facilities are starting to move toward virtualization. Generally, **virtualization** means that one physical machine hosts multiple activities normally performed by individual machines. For example, several information system server applications can run on a single computer (see Figure 5-11). Using several virtual servers on one physical server usually reduces cost. This physical server must be more robust with greater power and memory, however. The downside to using virtualization is if the physical components of the one machine break, then all the server applications running on this one server also fail.

> **virtualization**—One physical machine hosts multiple activities normally implemented on individual machines.

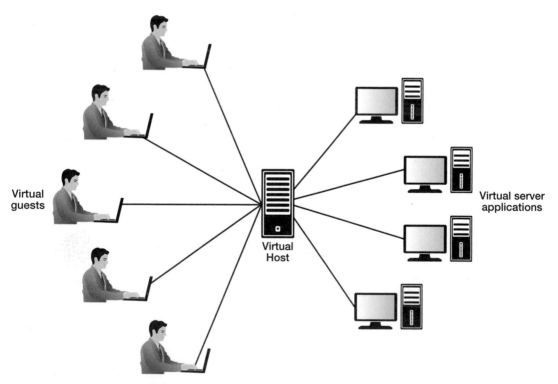

Figure 5-11   One implementation of virtualization is for multiple server applications to run on one computer.

Another implementation of virtualization is when one physical machine hosts multiple virtual machines (VM). Software such as VMware (www.vmware.com) or Microsoft Virtual PC (www.microsoft.com) manages the VMs. Each VM has its own operating system and applications installed. For example, Figure 5-12 shows a Windows desktop with two VMs, each open in its own window.

Figure 5-12   A VM has its own OS installed and provides a Windows desktop complete with taskbar and installed applications.

Virtualization can be taken a step further if these VMs are accessed by remote users. Some facilities structure their information systems using this method called **terminal services** or remote desktop services. A VM, complete with an OS and application, is installed on a central server. The user accesses the VM remotely. To the user, it appears that the Windows desktop is on the machine in front of her when actually it could be many miles away. Keystrokes and mouse action by the user are passed to the server, and the server processes this activity with the OS and application installed there. If the access is over the Internet or an intranet, the protocol used is RDP. Because the software is only on one machine, software management and troubleshooting is simpler.

> **terminal services**—Applications or even the entire desktop are made available to a user from a remote server. Only user interaction is presented at the client machine and all other processing takes place at the server. Also called remote desktop service.

The main advantage of using terminal services (also called remote desktop services) is that the client machine can be thin, which means it does not require much computing power. The client machine might be a simple terminal that boots up to find its operating system on a server and allows for the user's monitor, keyboard, and mouse to connect to the network.

Programming Languages

As you work with information systems in healthcare and websites made available to users of a hospital intranet, you are likely to encounter several programming languages used to support or build these resources. A few common programming languages are explained next.

Structured query language (SQL) is a programming language used to manage data stored in databases. SQL commands can be used to insert new data, query existing data, delete and modify existing data, and control access to data. Historically SQL is a commonly used query language for database management systems. However, many vendors have modified and adapted SQL command structures to fit their own databases management systems. Therefore, compatibility among different SQL vendors can be a problem. Figure 5-13 shows some SQL commands that query a database.

> **structured query language (SQL)**—A programming language used to manage data stored in databases.

```
SELECT [ALL | DISTINCT] [TOP nExpr [PERCENT]] Select_List_Item [, ...]
    FROM [FORCE] Table_List_Item [, ...]
        [[JoinType] JOIN DatabaseName!]Table [[AS] Local_Alias]
        [ON JoinCondition [AND | OR [JoinCondition | FilterCondition] ...]
    [WITH (BUFFERING = lExpr)]
    [WHERE JoinCondition | FilterCondition [AND | OR JoinCondition | FilterCondition] ...]
    [GROUP BY Column_List_Item [, ...]] [HAVING FilterCondition [AND | OR ...]]
    [UNION [ALL] SELECTCommand]
    [ORDER BY Order_Item [ASC | DESC] [, ...]]
    [INTO StorageDestination | TO DisplayDestination]
    [PREFERENCE PreferenceName] [NOCONSOLE] [PLAIN] [NOWAIT]
```

Figure 5-13   SQL is a command programming language used to manage data in a database.

Hypertext markup language (HTML) is the most common language used for developing web pages. A markup language is a programming language that inserts commands in a file that also contains text to be displayed. The commands are distinguished from the text by enclosing them in special characters. HTML uses angle brackets to separate the commands (called tags) from text. The tags describe to the program how to display the text. A web page sent from the web server contains HTML tags and text. A web browser interprets the HTML document and creates the web page on the screen. Figure 5-14 shows a web page with HTML tags.

> **hypertext markup language (HTML)**—A common markup language used for developing web pages.

HTML tags used to build the web page

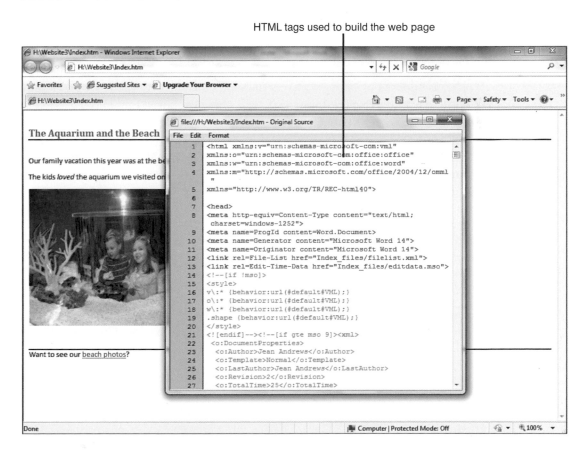

Figure 5-14   A web page sent to a browser contains text and HTML tags.

Extensible markup language (XML) is a language used to write a new markup language. Using XML, you can create your own HTML tags. The author defines the new HTML tags in an XML document. Open XML is an XML standard first developed by Microsoft that is designed to be used in word processing documents, presentations, and spreadsheets and can be interpreted by multiple applications including Microsoft Office and used with various operating systems.

> **extensible markup language (XML)**—A markup language used to write a new markup language. Using XML, you can create your own HTML tags.

Hypertext preprocessor (PHP) is a scripting language, which is a short program segment that is not intended to be used as a stand-alone program. The short PHP program or script is embedded into the HTML document. A web server reads the HTML document and follows the directions in the PHP script to create a customized web page for each individual viewing. This web page is said to be a dynamic web page, as opposed to static web pages that don't change with each viewing. For example, a dynamic web page for an SaaS for a physician portal can update the web browser with the doctor's patients and the patients' up-to-date information. Because the web server executes the script before the web page is sent to the browser, PHP is called a server-side scripting language. By contrast, a client-side scripting language is executed by the browser; JavaScript is an example of a client-side scripting language.

> **hypertext preprocessor (PHP)**—An open source, server-side, HTML embedded scripting language used to create dynamic web pages.

Active server pages (ASP or ASP.NET) is another server-side scripting language used to create dynamic web pages. ASP is by Microsoft and is free with Windows Server.

> **active server pages (ASP or ASP.NET)**—A server-side, HTML embedded scripting language used to create dynamic web pages. ASP is provided by Microsoft.

Many developers reuse the same coding in different programs to do the same thing. An **application program interface (API)** is a segment of programming code that can be used by many programs. An API is a shortcut for programmers so they do not have to rewrite the same code many times. APIs use a common format so programs can easily interface with them. For use on the Internet, an API can be used to embed content from one website onto another site. In this situation, if the source content changes, the destination content automatically updates.

> **application program interface (API)**—A segment of programming code that can be used by many programs. An API can be a routine, protocol, or tool used to build a software application.

Adobe Flash is a plug-in or add-on to a browser and is used to add multimedia graphics to web pages. Flash can add animation, video, and interactivity, such as when playing a game on a website. Animation created with Adobe Flash is stored in a file with a .swf file extension. The .swf file is downloaded from the website along with the web page that uses the animation. Flash can be used on many devices, including a computer, mobile phone, or tablet so long as the Flash software is installed.

> **Adobe Flash**—A plug-in or add-on to a browser used to add multimedia graphics to web pages.

Most browsers come with Adobe Flash already installed; however, some animations require the latest version of Flash be installed. In this case, you need to download and install the latest version of Flash from the Adobe website (adobe.com). You can also download and install the stand-alone Flash Player. To find out which version of Flash is installed as a browser add-on, open the Internet Options box for Internet Explorer and then navigate to the list of add-ons installed. For example, in Figure 5-15, you can see the list of add-ons and see which version of Flash is installed.

Now you know how the Internet and an intranet work and a bit about the programming languages they use. The next section focuses on learning about the network in a facility.

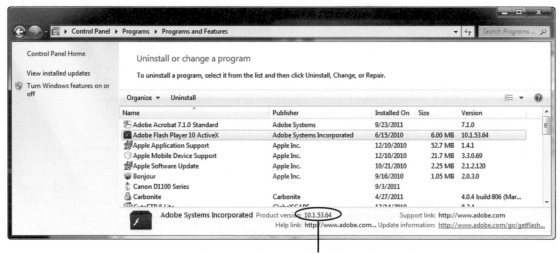

Version number of installed Flash add-on software

Figure 5-15   Some Flash animation requires the latest version of Flash be installed.

How a Network Works

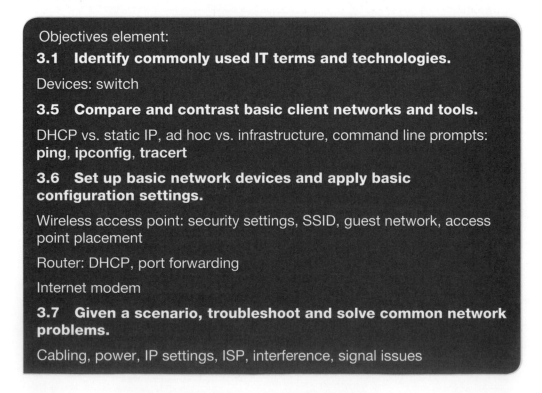

Objectives element:

3.1   Identify commonly used IT terms and technologies.

Devices: switch

3.5   Compare and contrast basic client networks and tools.

DHCP vs. static IP, ad hoc vs. infrastructure, command line prompts: **ping**, **ipconfig**, **tracert**

3.6   Set up basic network devices and apply basic configuration settings.

Wireless access point: security settings, SSID, guest network, access point placement

Router: DHCP, port forwarding

Internet modem

3.7   Given a scenario, troubleshoot and solve common network problems.

Cabling, power, IP settings, ISP, interference, signal issues

All HIT technicians need to have a basic understanding of how a network works. When the HIT department receives a support call that data is not getting across the network, know that the symptom can be caused by a variety of problems including problems with hardware, software, the network configuration, or other sources. When you understand the network, you can better pinpoint the source of the problem.

A network can be simple or complex. When just a small group of devices need to connect to share resources, an **ad hoc** network is the simplest solution. An ad hoc network is a wireless, decentralized, temporary, and peer-to-peer connection (see Figure 5-16). All devices are directly connected to the others without using a centralized AP. Performance diminishes as more devices are added to an ad hoc network, so ad hoc networks should be used only for a small group of devices. Also ad hoc has issues with interference because all devices are connected on the same channel, which is another reason why ad hoc should be considered as only a temporary solution.

> **ad hoc**—A network that is a wireless, decentralized, temporary, and peer-to-peer connection.

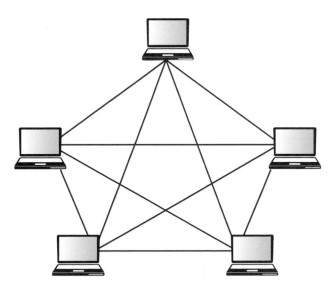

Figure 5-16   An ad hoc wireless network has no centralized device.

EXAM TIP Even though in the real world a hospital's IT infrastructure would not be based on an ad hoc network, you still need to know about an ad hoc network for the Healthcare IT exam to understand how it contrasts with an infrastructure setting.

A more complex and powerful network uses an **infrastructure** of one or more network devices that provide connectivity. An infrastructure is useful when setting up a large group of computers or a permanent network. The devices of an infrastructure provide organization and services for large groups of computers to be networked together. The infrastructure includes all the hardware and devices needed to connect devices, such as a wireless access point, to create a network. Figure 5-17 shows a small wireless infrastructure network built using a single wireless access point or AP.

infrastructure— A centralized network. Devices connect to an access point to join the network.

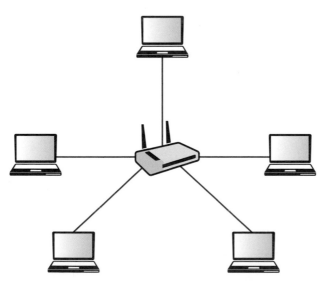

Figure 5-17 A wireless infrastructure network requires a centralized wireless access point.

A wireless infrastructure is more expensive than an ad hoc network because of the additional network devices needed. When designing an infrastructure network, a site survey should be performed to discover the needs of the infrastructure devices and any possible complications that may exist.

Basic Network Devices and Hardware

Network devices used to support a local network include wireless access points, routers, switches, and Internet modems. All these devices are discussed next.

Wireless Access Point

When using a wireless infrastructure, wireless APs provide access for wireless devices to the wired network. Figure 5-18 shows an AP that could be mounted to the ceiling in a facility. APs should be placed as determined by a wireless site survey. The survey considers the following possible obstacles:

- Signal strength of each AP
- Shape of the building
- Types of materials used in the building, such as concrete walls, wooden walls, sheetrock, and lead-lined rooms in the Radiology department
- Elevators
- Number of floors

Figure 5-18   Mount an AP to the ceiling to make the device unobtrusive.

Wireless networks broadcast information through the air, which makes the data susceptible to theft. The AP secures the transmission of data by using encryption at the data link layer of the OSI model (refer to Figure 5-2). The three main standards for wireless encryption are as follows:

- **Wired equivalent privacy (WEP)** secures data using an encryption key. WEP is a weak encryption because the encryption key is static (does not change), which makes it easy to be hacked.

- Because of the weakness of WEP, **Wi-Fi protected access (WPA)** was created to replace WEP. WPA uses temporal key integrity protocol (TKIP), which changes the encryption key periodically. A flaw was discovered in TKIP because it reused weak designs from WEP to make it backward compatible. This weakness enables hackers to spoof data, or to falsify data on the network.

- **Wi-Fi protected access 2 (WPA2)** is the most current and secure encryption available for wireless networks. WPA2 uses **advanced encryption standard (AES)**.

Another type of encryption standard is **remote authentication dial-in user service (RADIUS)**, which uses an authentication server to control access to the wireless network.

---

wired equivalent privacy (WEP)—A security protocol used on a wireless LAN that uses a static encryption key.

Wi-Fi protected access (WPA)—A security protocol used on a wireless LAN that uses TKIP for encryption.

Wi-Fi protected access 2 (WPA2)—A security protocol used on a wireless LAN that uses AES for encryption. WPA2 is currently the preferred encryption standard for a wireless LAN.

advanced encryption standard (AES)—An encryption cipher that uses a block length of 128 bits. The National Institute of Standards and Technology (NIST) adopted AES as an encryption standard.

remote authentication dial-in user service (RADIUS)—A protocol and system used to authenticate access to a network. User passwords to the network are sent over the network encrypted using the RADIUS encryption standard.

The **service set identifier (SSID)** is the name assigned to the AP. On encrypted wireless networks, the SSID is normally broadcasted so wireless devices can detect the wireless network. When SSID broadcasting is disabled, only devices that know the SSID can detect and connect to the network. This is just one more layer of security for a wireless network.

---

service set identifier (SSID)—The name assigned to a wireless access point.

Facilities usually have two wireless networks. One network is used by the employees and information systems that share e-PHI. This wireless network usually has disabled broadcasting the SSID. The second network is the guest network. This wireless network is used by visitors and patients in the hospital for accessing the Internet. The guest wireless network should have a firewall to prevent visitors from accessing the secured wireless network that hosts sensitive data.

> **EXAM TIP**   For the Healthcare IT exam, you need to understand wireless security and possible causes of interference and how to fix it.

Router

A **router** is a device that separates one network from another and enables traffic to flow between them (see Figure 5-19). The router connects to both networks and has two distinct IP addresses. One IP address works on one network, and the other IP address works on the other network. A large hospital might be divided into more than one local network with routers standing as the gateway to each network. If the hospital has only a single local network, a router stands between the network and the Internet. A router can serve many purposes. Besides allowing communication between networks, a router's second most important purpose is to stand as a firewall between the network it is protecting and another network or the Internet to make sure that unwanted traffic does not pass through.

> **router**—A network device that separates one network from another. The router logically and physically belongs to both networks.

Figure 5-19   This router can support a local network of up to 1,000 sessions, or connections.

One way a router serves as a firewall is to act like a middle man to prevent the detection of devices on the LAN by devices outside the LAN. This process is called **network address translation (NAT)**. When a device inside the network initiates communication with a device outside the network, the router substitutes its own IP address for the IP address of the device inside the network, as shown in Figure 5-20.

NAT is responsible for passing the communication from the remote device back to the correct device on the LAN.

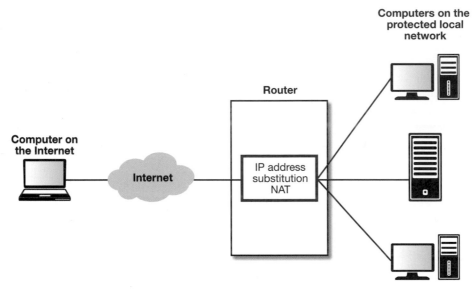

Figure 5-20 Networks using NAT hide the names and IP addresses of devices on the network from outside devices.

> **network address translation (NAT)**—A router or other gateway device substitutes its own IP address for the IP address of computers behind the firewall that it is protecting.

For best security, a firewall does not allow communication initiated from outside the LAN to a computer inside the LAN. However, exceptions might need to be allowed such as when the LAN hosts a web server that serves up web pages to computers anywhere on the Internet. In this situation, **port forwarding** is used to allow for the exception. The web server behind the firewall is assigned a static IP address that will not change and a port number. (Recall from Table 5-1 the default port number for a web server is port 80.) This IP address and port are entered into a table kept by firmware on the router. The router then allows communication initiated from the Internet only to this particular IP address and port, as shown in Figure 5-21. The network administrator is responsible for doing all manual configurations on the network, including port forwarding.

port forwarding—Communication from outside the network is allowed past the firewall only to a specific computer and port.

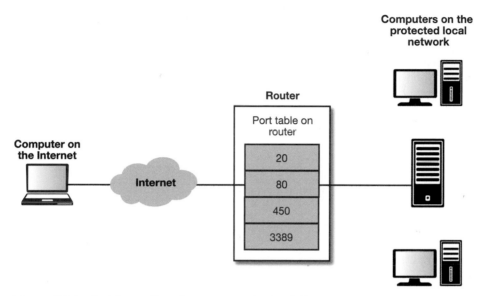

Figure 5-21 Port forwarding allows communication initiated outside the LAN only to a certain computer and port.

A router might also function as a server to serve up IP addresses to devices on the network it supports. Recall that every device on a network requires an IP address, which must be unique from every other IP address on the same IP network. An IP address called a **static IP address** can be manually assigned by the network administrator. Alternatively, the static IP address can be automatically assigned by a device such as a router.

static IP address—An IP address manually assigned to a computer or device. A static IP address does not change automatically.

The service running on the router or other network device that automatically assigns the IP address uses the **dynamic host configuration protocol (DHCP)**. Whenever a device connects to a network, the DHCP assigns it a new IP address that is not currently being used. The IP address comes from a range of IP addresses given to the router. So if a user reboots his computer, the IP address might change on the network. IP addresses assigned by a DHCP server are called **dynamic IP**

addresses. Static IP addresses can be used in a DHCP environment so long as the DHCP service is configured to restrict the use of IP addresses assigned statically. Static IP addresses are usually assigned to servers, network printers, or any medical equipment that connects directly to the network. User computers are usually configured to receive a dynamic IP address from a DHCP server.

> **dynamic host configuration protocol (DHCP)**—The service running on a router or other network device that automatically assigns an IP address to a computer or device when it joins the network.
>
> **dynamic IP address**—An IP address assigned by DHCP.

In large facilities, DHCP is handled by a server computer rather than a router. If the DHCP server fails, new devices cannot connect to the network. When a computer does not receive an IP address from a DHCP service, automatic private IP addressing (APIPA) assigns a temporary IP address. APIPA continues to search for an IP address from a DHCP service every five minutes. Devices already on the network can access the network so long as the device does not lose connection and needs to reconnect before the DHCP server is fixed. Often facilities divide the available IP addresses and use two DHCP servers, so if one fails, half of the IP addresses are still be available to join devices to the network until the other DHCP server is repaired.

> **EXAM TIP**   For the Healthcare IT exam, you need to be familiar with the DHCP service and the symptoms that might indicate a problem with the DHCP service.

At the time a device is assigned an IP address, the device must also receive a subnet mask and default gateway. The **subnet mask** is a series of 1s and 0s that determine which part of an IP address identifies the local network and which part identifies the host. When a data packet arrives at a router, it examines its subnet mask and decides if the packet is destined for a computer on its local network or must be sent on its way to another network. The **default gateway** is the IP address of a router, which should receive all requests for communication with computers outside the local network.

subnet mask—A series of 1s and 0s that determine which part of an IP address identifies the local network and which part identifies the host.

default gateway—The IP address of a router that should receive all requests for communication with computers outside the local network.

The subnet mask and default gateway are configured during the installation of the router or DHCP server. These values are then passed on to any device it assigns an IP address. For static IP addresses, it is the responsibility of the person manually entering the IP address to also enter the subnet mask and default gateway. Figure 5-22 shows the configuration window where these values can be manually assigned. When configuring a workstation with a static IP address, ask the network administrator for the subnet mask and default gateway.

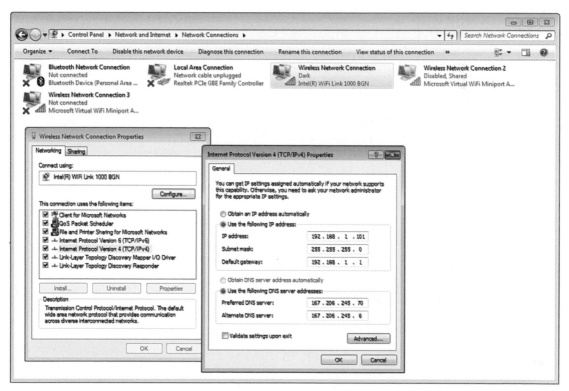

Figure 5-22 Manually assign the IP address, subnet mask, and default gateway to a computer.

A static IP address, subnet mask, and default gateway remain assigned to a computer until the network administrator changes it, even if the computer is rebooted. This method provides stability on the network if it is properly managed by the network administrator, so no two devices have the same static IP address.

In the event a router fails, the network needs a redundant way to access other networks or the Internet. For this reason, a network is likely to have multiple routers. The router that is the fastest or has the fastest access to the Internet is likely to be designated as the default gateway. If it fails, other routers on the network are used until it is restored.

Switch

On a LAN, a **switch** (see Figure 5-23) is a physical device with multiple network ports for connecting devices such as computers, printers, or servers. When a switch receives a data packet, the switch can determine where the packet is intended to go and send it only to that device, rather than broadcasting all packets to all devices connected to it.

> **switch**—A device with multiple network ports for connecting devices such as computers, printers, or servers.

Figure 5-23   A switch contains tables on its firmware that help it route data to the correct device to reduce overall network traffic.

Internet Modem

An ISP brings the Internet to the facility and an Internet modem stands between the ISP and a router connected to the local network, as shown in Figure 5-24. A modem is a device that converts one type of transmission to another. For example, if access to the Internet is through a DSL connection, an **Internet modem** is used to convert the DSL signal on the phone line to Ethernet used by the router and local network. Figure 5-25 shows a DSL modem.

> **Internet modem**—A device used to convert the signal from the ISP to Ethernet used by the router and local network.

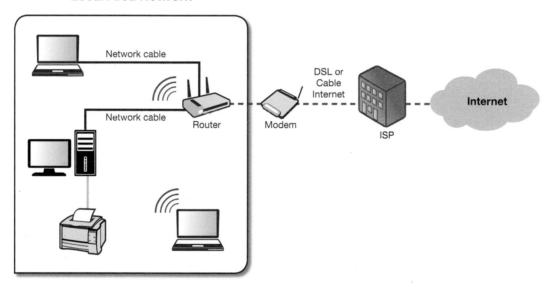

Figure 5-24   An Internet modem stands between the ISP and a router connected to the LAN.

Figure 5-25   A DSL modem converts DSL transmission over phone lines to Ethernet on a LAN.

Photo credit: Petr Ivanov

Next, learn about the tools for troubleshooting failures on a network.

Network Tools

An HIT technician is often the first person involved when troubleshooting technical issues with a network. One of the first things the technician needs to do to isolate the problem is to check for a network connection. An important tool used when testing network connections is the command prompt. The command prompt is accessed from the Windows Start menu. Three commonly used commands for testing the network connection are **ipconfig**, **ping**, and **tracert**.

ipconfig Command

The first step to determine if a computer has network connectivity is to find out the IP address of the computer. Use the **ipconfig** command to display the TCP/IP network configuration values, which includes the computer's IP address.

> **ipconfig**—A command used in the command prompt window to display the TCP/IP network configuration values.

To use the **ipconfig** command, follow these steps:

1. Using the computer that is having a connectivity problem, open the command prompt window.

2. Type **ipconfig** and press **Enter**. The IP address, subnet mask, and default gateway settings are displayed.

> **NOTE**   If you want more information about the TCP/IP network configuration values, use the **/all** switch by typing **ipconfig /all**.

To use the DHCP services to assign a new IP address, follow these steps:

1. Open the command prompt window.

2. Type **ipconfig** and press **Enter** to view the current IP address.

3. Type **ipconfig /release** and press **Enter**.

4. Type **ipconfig /renew** and press **Enter**.

5. Type **ipconfig** and press **Enter** to verify the computer has been assigned a new IP address.

ping Command

Now that you know the computer can communicate with the DHCP server on the network, use the **ping** command to send a request to another device to find out if the two devices can communicate on the network. If a ping fails, the remote device is not connected to the network. The ping results also give the round-trip time that it takes for the message to be received by the target host and response received back.

> **ping**—A command used in the command prompt window to send a request to another device to find out if the two devices can communicate on the network.

Both IP addresses and website URLs can be pinged. Figure 5-26 shows the results from pinging google.com. When a URL is pinged, the IP address for that website displays.

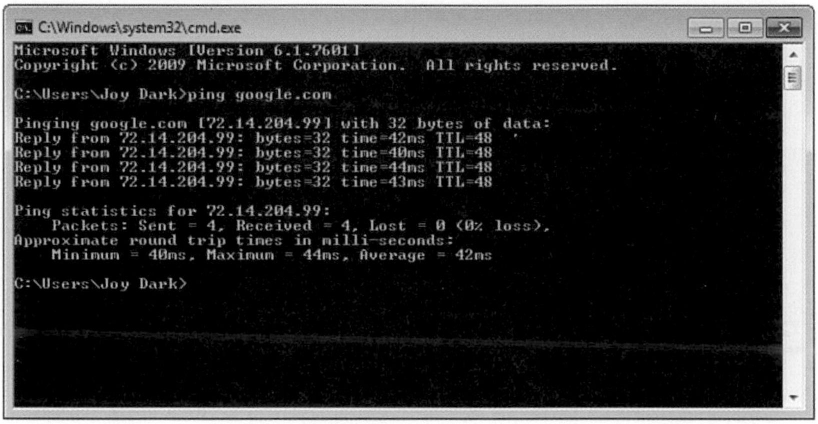

Figure 5-26   The ping to google.com is successful and shows the IP address of a Google web server.

> **NOTE**   Pinging a URL and verifying if the IP address displays is a great tool for knowing if the DNS service is functioning.

To use the **ping** command, follow these steps.

1. Open the command prompt window.

2. Type **ping**, followed by a space, and then the IP address of the target host or URL of the website, as shown in Figure 5-26. Press **Enter**. The results from the ping are displayed.

tracert Command

When a network connection becomes slow or unreachable, the **tracert** command can display the path a connection takes to reach a target host and how long the wait times are for each hop, or jump from one router to the next. If an HIT technician receives a support call that a connection has been lost to a machine, the technician should first try pinging the target host. If the **ping** times out or takes a long time to complete, the network administrator needs to be engaged. Most network administrators want to see the **tracert** report taken at the time of the request for support to document the connection failure.

> **tracert**—The **trace route** command is used to trace the path a connection takes to reach a target host.

To use the **tracert** command, follow these steps.

1. Open the command prompt window.

2. Type **tracert**, followed by a space, and then the IP address of the target host or the URL of the website, as shown in Figure 5-27. Press **Enter**. The results start to display.

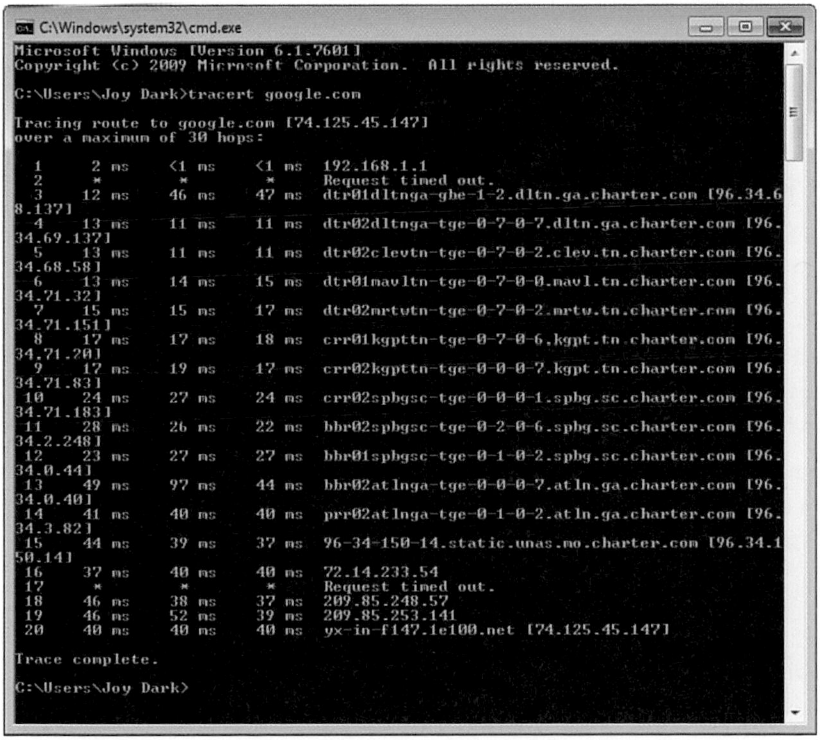

Figure 5-27   The tracert command reports the path taken to a target host.

If the **tracert** starts to time out repeatedly, the command prompt displays an asterisk. You can wait for the maximum number of hops to be reached or you can cancel the **tracert** by pressing the control key (Ctrl) and the letter C at the same time (written in documentation as Ctrl+C).

After you have the information from a **tracert**, you might need to save the data to document any network connection issues. Two ways to save the information are to take a snip or screen shot of the screen or to redirect the output of the **tracert** command to a text file.

If you can see all the information on the screen, use the Windows Snipping Tool to take a screen shot. Follow these steps:

1. With the command prompt window and the **tracert** results showing in it, open the Snipping Tool in the Accessories group on the Windows Start menu.

2. In the Snipping Tool dialog box, select a snip of a window.

3. Select the command prompt window.

4. The command prompt window snip appears in the Snipping Tool window. Save the snip to a file. You can then open the file and copy and paste the image into an email message to the network administrator or into a trouble ticket.

To redirect the results of the **tracert** command to a text file, follow these steps:

1. Type the **tracert** command as you normally would and complete it with the redirect symbol and the name of the file where you want the results to be saved. For example, use this command: **tracert google.com > myfile.txt**. Be sure to use the .txt file extension.

2. When the **tracert** command has finished or you have used **Ctrl+C** to cancel the command, use Windows Explorer to locate the newly created file. By default the file is saved in your user folder, for example, C:\Users\Joy Dark.

3. Double-click the file to open it. By default, the file opens using Notepad. You can then copy and paste the text into an email message to the network administrator or into a trouble ticket.

> **EXAM TIP**   For the Healthcare IT exam, you need to identify network troubleshooting commands (**ipconfig**, **ping**, and **tracert**) and how/when to use them.

Now that you know about some network troubleshooting tools, the following section covers some common problems you might face and how to solve them.

Solving Network Problems

Experienced technicians realize many connectivity problems that might appear to be network problems are actually caused by applications failing, user error, or other sources. However, sometimes the breakdown in communication actually is due to a network problem. Some network problems are more common than others. In this section you learn some of the more common network problems, how to identify them, and what to do about them.

Duplicate IP Address

A duplicate IP address on the network can cause one device to stop working or give intermittent errors while using the network. If one of the devices is a printer, it might not print any print jobs, or it might present an error to the device sending the print request.

The network administrator is responsible for keeping a list of IP addresses designated for static IP address assignments. When one of these IP addresses is used, the network administrator documents on the list that this IP address is unavailable. Usually duplicate IP addresses occur because a static IP address was not documented properly and possibly given out to another device. To prevent accidentally assigning a static IP address to two devices at the same time, always properly document whenever a static IP address is assigned.

Another less effective option is to use a network scanner to report all IP addresses currently in use. The report is not always a complete list of IP addresses currently assigned because a device with a static IP address might be powered down at the time of the scan.

Another reason for a duplicate IP address is when a device has been manually assigned a static IP address that is within the range of IP addresses that the DHCP server regulates. The DHCP server never assigns the same IP address twice, and it does not ask if an IP address is being used before assigning it to a device. It bases the availability only on its records.

To figure out if this conflict is the cause of a duplicate IP address, disconnect the device with the static IP address from the network. Ping the IP address that was assigned to this device. If the ping is successful, you know you need to find the other device with the same IP address and correct the static IP address.

Another reason for a duplicate IP address is that two DHCP servers might be regulating the same IP addresses. Normally two DHCP servers do not regulate the same IP address ranges on the same network. When two DHCP servers are assigning the same IP address ranges, having duplicate IP addresses on the same network is bound to happen. When adding new network equipment to the network, for example a new router, check to make sure it does not contain a DHCP service or the DHCP service is deactivated.

Broken Cables and Crosstalk

Network cables are vulnerable to breaking. The cable or fiber might bend and break, or the connectors at the end of the cables might break. Bending a fiber cable can break the glass inside the cable.

When running cables through a building, copper network cables should never run side by side to electrical wiring because this causes crosstalk, or interference due to electro-magnetic interference (EMI). Whenever network cables and electrical wiring need to cross paths, you can avoid crosstalk by crossing the cables, making a + to limit the proximity of the two wires as much as possible.

Interference with Wireless Networks

Wireless networks share the airspace and frequencies used to transmit data. Because of sharing, interference might be caused by competition between devices. For example, the 802.11g network uses the 2.4-GHz frequency. Many cordless phones use this same frequency, which might cause interference. Also the structure of the building might cause interference. For example, in the radiology department, the walls are lined with lead to prevent spreading radiation. This lead might also prevent wireless signals from passing through to the wireless devices inside the procedure rooms. Another example of this type of interference is the steel elevator shafts. A site survey can show the best placement for APs to avoid interference. Using a device with a stronger signal or placing APs closer together can create a signal strong enough to overcome interference.

Poor AP Placement

Do not place APs close together so that the signals overlap. When a wireless device, such as a computer on wheels, is in range of two signals, the device might continuously switch back and forth between the two APs. This causes a brief drop of network connection as the device switches to the other AP. A drop in network connection is problematic because a healthcare provider might be entering patient information into a chart when the connection is dropped, resulting in the loss of all typed information since the last save. Another problem is a wireless IP phone in range of two APs may drop the call when the network connection is dropped. On the other hand, not enough APs can cause a weak signal, which might also cause loss of connection intermittently.

The range of an AP's reach is determined by the device and any interference. Because this can be complicated to configure, a site survey is performed to design the placement of APs. The radio power of an AP can be adjusted so as not to cause interference with other nearby APs. To avoid interference from nearby APs, you can also configure the AP to use a different channel other than the channel another device uses. In the United States and Canada, 11 channels are allowed (Channels 1 through 11). For best results, don't use a channel close to another device. For example, use channels 1, 6, and 11 rather than channels 1, 2, and 3 for three APs in a close geographical area.

Lost Connectivity to the ISP

Occasionally the ISP cannot provide Internet service or connectivity to the ISP WAN fails. For example, this failure may happen when a construction crew accidentally cuts a fiber line or maybe a storm disrupts the service. For this reason it is a good idea to have a redundant ISP providing a secondary connection. The second connection doesn't need to be the same speed as the primary connection. If the primary ISP service is disrupted, the facility has a backup plan to avoid total downtime until the primary ISP service is restored.

When the ISP service is down, the internal network still functions, but any IS that depends on remote connections outside the facility will be down, as well. For example, if a facility uses cloud computing, connectivity to the remote IS is lost. Also, most healthcare facilities use satellite facilities, such as an offsite outpatient surgery center. HIT support covers the facility and the satellite facilities. A satellite facility often depends on the ISP service to connect to the main campus. When the ISP service is disrupted, a satellite facility cannot use any IS on a server located at the main campus.

> **NOTE**   As an HIT technician, you might be called on to help with researching to find a secondary ISP. Be sure to consider their source for service. It's not uncommon for several ISPs in a town in a remote area to share a single fiber line running through the entire town. If this is the case, a secondary ISP might not be useful if the fiber fails.

Power Failure, Blackouts, and Brownouts

Every facility is susceptible to power failures or blackouts. This vulnerability is unacceptable for a network that services a healthcare facility. The facility's management personnel are responsible for providing generator power in case the power goes out. HIT personnel are responsible for making sure necessary devices are plugged into a UPS that supplies power until the generator kicks in. Facilities usually have three different types of power outlets to plug in devices:

- **Regular outlet**: These outlets lose power completely if the power goes out in the facility. These outlets are typically white, ivory, or brown.

- **Hospital-grade outlet**: These outlets are designed for use by sensitive medical equipment. These outlets are typically orange.

- **Emergency generator outlet**: Red outlets usually mean the outlet is connected to the emergency generator in the event of a power outage. A device plugged into a red outlet will lose power only for a few seconds.

When the power at a facility flickers for just an instant, routers and switches shut down completely. These sophisticated devices can take several minutes to power back up. This time of unavailability for connection can cause problems and frustration for healthcare providers. Remember one of your goals as HIT personnel is to ensure that patient health information is ready and available to healthcare personnel. Having these devices on an uninterruptible power supply (UPS) can prevent this downtime. The UPS needs to have sufficient wattage to provide the temporary power needed to avoid network downtime during a brownout.

Now that you know how the network works and some of the problems that you might encounter, the following section covers how to manage the resources on the network.

Managing Network Resources

Objectives elements:

3.8   Explain the features of different backup configurations and the associated maintenance practices.

Daily, differential, incremental, archive flags

3.9   Classify different server types, environments, features, and limitations.

Database server, application server, interfaces, physical connections, server load and utilization, application services, OS and application interoperability, storage space limitations based on application usage and electronic record storage

3.10   Compare and contrast EHR/EMR technologies and how each is implemented.

ASP/Cloud vs. client-server (locally hosted), browser vs. installed application vs. terminal/remote access, hardware requirements

Many different vendors offer electronic health record (EHR) and electronic medical record (EMR) information systems. Each vendor offers the IS in a variety of configurations. You need to understand the possible configurations and the benefits and problems with each. Recall that many facilities are in the process of implementing EHR and EMR information systems because of the HITECH Act. HIT personnel have valuable input into the process of deciding which vendor to choose. During this process, we can offer knowledge about the pros and cons of each system configuration and how it can affect the healthcare providers.

Locally Hosted or Remote EHR and EMR Information Systems

When the EHR/EMR IS server is located at the healthcare facility, it is said to be locally hosted. A vendor provides the software while the facility is responsible for providing the hardware to meet the vendor's specifications. Usually the server and client computers are on the same LAN. The application used to access the IS is provided as one of the following:

- **Thick client**: A thick client, also called a fat client, is used when an application is installed on the client computer. The client application communicates with the server to access the application resources. As much processing of data as possible is done on the client computer. A desktop, all-in-one, or laptop computer is required when using a thick client.

- **Thin client**: A thin client is used when an application is accessed by a computer, but not installed on the computer. The thin client application is hosted on a remote server and the application is usually accessed using a web browser. A thin client requires only maintenance of the application to be performed on the server, and not on the client computer. The only requirement of the client computer is to meet performance specifications and an updated browser. Most vendors are moving toward using a thin client. A thin client computer can be a low-end desktop, all-in-one, or laptop that does not have as much computing power or storage capacity as does a thick client computer.

- **Terminal services**: Terminal services (also called remote desktop services) are when the application and the client's operating system are installed on a terminal server that allows for multiple clients to simultaneously log in to access the software. The client machine does not require it to have an OS installed and can be as light as a simple device that can boot up to find its OS on the server. All processing of data is done on the server. Terminal services require only the application to be installed and maintained on the server.

A problem with hosting the hardware and software locally is that it is more difficult for vendors to support their software. When using a locally hosted IS and a vendor's application, the vendor either has to remote into the system or travel to the facility to offer support. A locally hosted IS is more expensive upfront because the facility must purchase both software and hardware, but the ongoing costs are considerably cheaper to pay the vendor for only the software. Another consideration is the expense to keep the hardware up to the vendor's specifications as the vendor updates its software.

An **application service provider (ASP)** is a vendor that offers an IS provided remotely. The server of an ASP is located at the vendor site. Both ASPs and cloud solutions are offered as Software as a Service (SaaS). The vendor maintains and houses the hardware used to host the IS. Healthcare providers access the IS using the thin client model. Usually the thin client accesses the IS through a web browser, but sometimes it is accessed through a VPN connection or a direct connection to the vendor. An obvious downside to using a SaaS is if there is ever a failure with the WAN connection, the EHR/EMR IS will be completely unavailable. When using a SaaS, the upfront costs are lower because the facility does not have to purchase the hardware to host the IS, but the ongoing costs are higher.

> **application service provider (ASP)**—A vendor that offers an IS provided remotely.

EHR/EMR information systems rely on servers to hold the data and possibly to run the application. The section that follows describes what to consider regarding implementing and supporting servers for an EHR/EMR IS.

Considerations for Servers on a Network

Two purposes for servers in a typical EHR/EMR IS are a database server and an application server (see Figure 5-28). The database server stores data used by the applications. The database server runs a DBMS, such as SQL Server or Oracle. The database server is constantly updated with EHR/EMR information. For this reason, the database server should be backed up regularly. The vendor is responsible for implementing the DBMS and the databases, but the HIT technicians at the facility are responsible for limited maintenance such as OS updates, backups, or rebooting. An application server runs the application when using a thin client or provides resources when using thick clients.

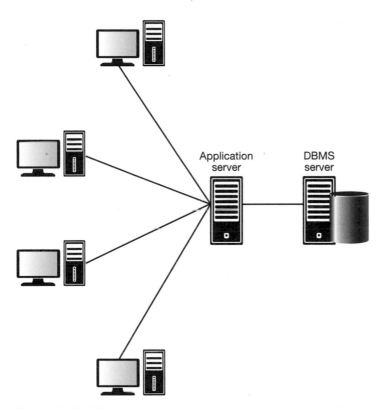

Figure 5-28   The database server holds the data and the application server holds the application used by thin clients.

The sections that follow cover several issues to consider when supporting servers and the data and software they hold and maintain.

Security Risks

The application server uses the resources on the database server. A security risk might occur when a user has access to an application. He might use this access to gain entry to another application that connects to a different database. This risk is heightened if an application connects to more than one database. To lessen this security risk, facilities often use an interface engine in order to prevent direct connections between information systems. Because an interface engine has the capability to filter data as it passes through, it is much harder for data to be accidentally transferred through the network to the wrong application.

High Traffic and Load Balancing

Because of high traffic and volume, servers should be connected to a fast switch or router. Sometimes servers are connected using fiber cabling directly to the core of the network to provide faster response times for users. A demanding process can sometimes result in unbalanced server processing. To limit diminished capabilities, restrict certain processes to take up only a set percentage of the server processor capacity. Also, the server load can be balanced between multiple servers if one server cannot handle the utilization load. Even virtual servers can provide this load balancing.

Hardware and Software Specifications Required by Vendors

Vendors not only have hardware specifications, but also have software specifications required to run their applications in an optimal environment. Vendors require certain OS and Service Packs to be installed on the computers running or accessing their applications. This specification is not always the one most recently released by the OS vendor, such as Microsoft.

If an EHR or EMR solution is purchased and expected to be interfaced with other information systems in the facility, the HIT technicians need to ensure that the information systems are compatible with each other. For example, the radiology IS (RIS) vendor might require the thin client to use Internet Explorer 7.0 while the EHR/EMR IS requires the thin client to use Internet Explorer 8.0. However, both information systems might need to be accessed on the same computer.

Purging Old Logs

When a server runs an application, the application creates logs from the activity of the application. These logs are for auditing the user activity and for logging the interface messages as they are sent and received. These archives continue to grow unless a threshold set deletes old logs after a set number of days.

Maintain Backups and Downtime Procedures

Creating backups is one of the most important tasks of an HIT technician. When a backup is made, the media should be stored in a protected and safe location. Based on facility policy, a backup copy should be taken to an offsite location as an extra precaution in case a catastrophic event occurs at the facility that destroys the backups at the facility.

Backups are usually done after hours when information systems are not used as heavily. When a file is backed up, depending on the type of backup, it is flagged as being backed up or needing to be backed up. This mark is called an archive flag. Following are three kinds of backups:

- The daily backup is performed every 24 hours. With the daily backup, only the files that have changed are backed up, and the files are not marked as having been backed up.

- A differential backup backs up new and changed files, and does not mark the files as having been backed up.

- An incremental backup backs up the files that have been created or changed since the last incremental backup and marks the files as having been backed up.

> **EXAM TIP**   For the Healthcare IT exam, you need to be familiar with the different kinds of backups.

In case there is a failure in the HIT information systems, all employees should know the downtime procedures. Downtime might be caused by a scheduled maintenance or due to an unexpected outage. Having downtime procedures available to all employees means that patient care will be the less affected when IS resources are limited. This means having paper charts available to continue documenting patient information when the IS is not immediately available. When downtime can be scheduled, be sure to schedule downtime during a time of day or night when the fewest users will be affected. If downtime is scheduled after hours, make sure that technical support is available in case something goes wrong. This means someone from the HIT department needs to be on call and always available. Usually the HIT staff rotates the responsibility of being on call.

HIT technicians need to understand the Internet, intranet, and network and the servers and devices that run them. At the other end of the cables and wires are the computers that the users stand in front of and the peripheral devices used to manage and facilitate healthcare. The following section covers these workstations and devices.

Configuring a Workstation and Peripherals

Objectives elements:

3.2 Demonstrate the ability to set up a basic PC workstation within an EHR/EMR environment.

Basic installation, configuration and maintenance procedures, basics of operating systems, mouse, keyboard, monitor and applications

3.3 Given a scenario, troubleshoot and solve common PC problems.

Malfunctioning hardware: mouse, printer, power, monitor, cables

Software patches/hotfixes/updates, documentation

3.4 Install and configure hardware drivers and devices.

Imaging devices: barcode scanner, document scanner, card/badge scanner, fax printer, camera, signature pads

Physical interfaces: USB, IEEE 1394, SCSI, serial, Bluetooth

Mobile storage devices: flash drives, external hard drives, DVDs, CDs, tapes, SD cards

Mobile devices: tablet PCs, smart phones, portable media players

A significant part of the job of an HIT technician is working with workstations, or computers, and the peripheral devices. A good deal of support calls received by the HIT department are because something is not working with a workstation. Today many facilities consider computers to be disposable and would rather replace them than fix the more complicated repairs. Some of the more simple repairs, such as replacing a video card, are quick and easy, and HIT technicians are still expected to do these repairs on occasion.

The following section covers the proper deployment of a workstation or personal computer.

Deploy a Workstation

When a new workstation is needed, first make sure the specifications for a new computer are still sufficient. Perhaps these specifications need to be updated. If examination determines the current machines are not sufficient for new uses, upgrade the standards for all new machine purchases. New machines set a standard for the facility, so as new machines are purchased, they should all be the same brand and model.

All devices, such as computers, printers, or servers, should be documented for reference in the event the device fails. The document about each device should record the following information:

- Brand
- Model
- Name on network
- Serial number
- OS version
- Static or DHCP IP address (If static, record the IP address used.)
- MAC address for wired and wireless connections
- Applications installed
- Printers installed

When deploying a standard computer in the facility, use the same brand and model if possible throughout the facility, satellite offices, and at the corporate headquarters. The consistency of computer hardware makes it easy for technicians to troubleshoot and to find replacement parts.

Set the configuration of all computers the same, such as virus protection, desktop background, screensaver, standard toolbars, browser version, and applications. The easiest way to do this is to set up one computer with the configuration that is the most widely used across the facility. Make a **disk image** of this computer and then copy that image to all other computers as they are deployed. If a computer needs to be customized, it is easier to individually configure a small number of computers from the image rather than build each and every computer. For example, if only one out of every ten computers needs an email thick client, configure the image without the email client and then install it on the one computer. If a computer has problems in the future, an easy resolution is to reimage the computer rather than rebuilding the configuration from scratch.

disk image—The contents of a hard drive, including configuration settings and applications stored so the contents can be replicated to another computer.

The naming convention for all computers on the network should be consistent. The name of the computer should indicate where the computer is physically located; for example, ICU01 to indicate this computer is in the Intensive Care Unit, computer number one. If the facility is located in multiple buildings or campuses, then that should be indicated in the name as well. The computer's name should be clearly labeled on the computer or the monitor attached to it so whoever is standing in front of it can easily find out the name of the computer for reference when calling in a support request.

Data should never be stored on a workstation. Map a drive letter to a file server on the network so that the users can save documents and files to a remote server rather than locally on the computer. Users can easily retrieve the same files from multiple workstations. The file server should be backed up regularly. If one of these files is accidentally deleted, it is easily restored from the latest backup. If the personal computer crashes, the HIT technician does not have to spend time salvaging data that might not be recoverable. When a computer crashes, the HIT technician needs to spend only the time it takes to reimage the computer rather than troubleshooting and rebuilding the computer configuration and data.

Even with the best of firewalls, all computers and servers are susceptible to viruses. All computers and servers should always have antivirus software installed. The antivirus software should have up-to-date **virus definitions** because new viruses are deployed daily. Virus definition updates should be done on a daily basis and be configured to be updated automatically. The most vulnerable computer on the network is the weakness of the entire network. One entrance into the network provides a hacker the ability to access sensitive information on the network.

virus definitions—The unique identifiers of a computer virus that antivirus software uses to detect threats and eliminate them. Also called virus signature.

An application should be installed on a computer only if the application is needed. For example, a computer in the pharmacy would not need the RIS installed. When deploying a computer, ask the supervisor in the department which applications need to be installed. Do not install applications that are not needed so that computer resources are not used unnecessarily.

When choosing a computer to deploy, consider the external ports and connection types needed to connect with peripheral devices for interfacing with information systems. **Parallel communication** sends data through several streams simultaneously. Parallel communication requires several wires or strands to send data bits simultaneously. **Serial communication** sends data through a single stream. Serial communication may seem slower because data is sent on smaller media, but it can be sent at faster speeds.

> **parallel communication**—A process of sending data several bits at a time through several streams simultaneously.
>
> **serial communication**—A process of sending data one bit at a time through a single stream.

The list that follows describes the different types of communication standards.

- **Universal serial bus (USB)** is a standard for a hot swappable port. Up to 127 USB devices can be connected to a single USB port using up to 4 hubs daisy-chained together. The maximum length of a USB cable is 5 meters. Most USB devices are plug-and-play, meaning you do not have to find and install a driver for them to work. USB is versatile and can be used to connect several different kinds of devices to a computer, such as a mouse or a printer. Figure 5-29 shows a USB cable.

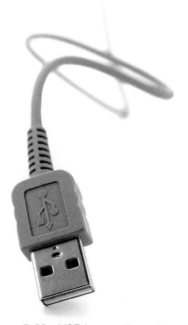

Figure 5-29 USB is versatile and can be used to connect several types of devices to a computer.

Photo credit: Yahia LOUKKAL

■ **IEEE 1394**, or Firewire, is a standard for a hot swappable port. Up to 63 devices can be connected to a single IEEE 1394 port. The maximum length of an IEEE 1394 cable is 4.5 meters. IEEE 1394 offers a faster data transfer rate than USB 1.1, but not 2.0. IEEE 1394 is usually used for transferring multimedia data. Figure 5-30 shows an IEEE 1394 cable.

Figure 5-30   IEEE 1394, or Firewire, is usually used for transferring multimedia data.

Photo credit: F.A.Y.

■ **Small computer system interface (SCSI)**, pronounced "skuzee," is hot swappable. SCSI can be daisy-chained but requires terminators at each end of the cables or software termination. A SCSI chain can have up to 7 or 15 devices. Although SCSI connections are reasonably fast, they can be more complicated to configure than other more common interface standards such as SATA. SCSI connections are usually found on servers and are used by hard drives and optical drives. Figure 5-31 shows a SCSI ribbon cable.

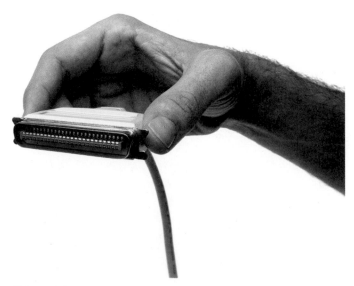

Figure 5-31   SCSI connections are usually found on servers for hard drives and optical drives.

Photo credit: pixel

- **Bluetooth** is a wireless communication protocol used to connect devices over short distances. Bluetooth is used to transmit both voice and data signals. Bluetooth uses radio frequency 2.4 to 2.48 GHz to connect a mouse, a keyboard, or other wireless devices. Bluetooth is an ad hoc connection that can reach up to 100 meters.

---

universal serial bus (USB)—A standard for a hot swappable port. USB standard 2.0 (Hi-Speed USB) is approximately 40 times faster than original USB. USB standard 3.0 (SuperSpeed USB) is approximately 10 times faster than USB 2.0.

IEEE 1394—A standard for a hot swappable port generally used for transferring multimedia data. Also called Firewire.

small computer system interface (SCSI)—A standard for a hot swappable port and storage devices that use these ports. SCSI connections are usually found on servers and are used by hard drives and optical drives.

Bluetooth—A wireless communication protocol used to connect personal devices over short distances.

EXAM TIP   For the Healthcare IT exam, you need to be familiar with the different kinds of communication standards.

The mouse and keyboard should have Universal Serial Bus (USB) connections. · Monitors are mostly flat screen, usually LCD, but occasionally LED or plasma monitors are used. Occasionally older machines are still used and have PS/2 mice and CRT monitors. When these older technologies break, replace them with newer equipment.

Monitors usually use a VGA connection, but certain departments require higher quality or resolution and need a DVI connection. For example, picture archiving and communication system (PACS) requires a larger monitor with higher resolution and quality to view the details of a medical image, such as an MRI.

Maintain Operating System Updates

Most facilities use Microsoft Windows on the computers. Operating System (OS) updates should not be set to update automatically. Many of the vendors' applications are only compatible with a certain service pack or update to the OS. When a new OS update becomes available, install the update on a test computer on the network. This test computer should have all applications used in the facility installed.

Thoroughly test the applications on the updated computer to make sure there are no problems with compatibility. After this testing is complete and approved, install the update on about 10 percent of the workstations to provide one more level of testing for any problems. The group in the 10 percent should be representative of all the different configurations used in the facility. After the test group of computers approves the update, install the update on all computers in the facility.

After a computer has been deployed, problems show up eventually. Now learn about some of the common problems computers experience and how to resolve them.

Troubleshoot Common Problems

Keep a reserve of replacement hardware in case one malfunctions and you cannot repair it quickly. This includes mice, keyboards, monitors, printers, and cables. Also keep replacement computers on hand to use as loaners until the repair is completed or a replacement purchase has been fulfilled.

Problems with a Mouse

If you receive a support call saying the mouse is not working, try the following to resolve the issue. If none of these work, replace the mouse.

- For mice using a trackball
  - Verify the ball is not missing or dirty.
  - Take out the ball and clean the rollers.
- For optical mice
  - Verify the light is on under the mouse.
  - Unplug and replug the mouse.
  - Reboot the computer.
  - Try plugging into a different USB port.
  - Try the mouse on a different computer.

If you discover the problem to be a bad mouse or port, document the problem for future reference.

> **NOTE**   PS/2 mice are typically not hot-swappable. If a PS/2 mouse is unplugged, plug it back in, and reboot the computer to verify the mouse works. USB mice are hot-swappable and do not require you to reboot the computer.

> **EXAM TIP**   For the Healthcare IT exam, you need to know the next step in trouble-shooting when given a scenario of an issue. Always start with the fastest and easiest solutions before moving to the more complicated or expensive solutions.

Problems with a Monitor

If you receive a support call saying the monitor does not work, try the following to resolve the issue. If none of these work, replace the monitor.

- Check to make sure the monitor is receiving power.

- Make sure all connections are secure and not loose.

- If the image is weird, try adjusting the settings on the monitor. Available settings are position, contrast, and brightness. Usually these settings are automatically set by the computer.

- Try the monitor with its cables on a different computer. If it works, it is possible the problem is with the video card in the original computer. If you have another video card available, replace the video card.

- Use Device Manager to check the video system for reported errors and to update or rollback the video driver. Try uninstalling and reinstalling the video driver.

- If the monitor does not work on another computer, try using a different video cable and then a different power cable to verify whether either cable is bad.

If you discover the problem to be a bad monitor, port, or cable, document the problem for future reference.

Problems with a Printer

If you receive a support call saying the printer does not work, try the following steps to resolve the issue. If none of these work, replace the printer.

- Verify the printer has paper and ink or toner.

- Verify the printer has power.

- Check for a paper jam. If there is a paper jam, clear the jam before trying to print a test document.

- Verify the printer driver is installed on the computer. Most printers come with a disk that has the driver on it, or you can find the driver file for downloading on the manufacturer's website.

- If the printer is connected directly to the computer, verify the driver is installed and the printer is listed as an option for that computer.

- Power off and on the printer.

- If it's a network printer, ping the printer's IP address. If unsuccessful, make sure the network cable is securely connected and not loose.

- Clear the printer queue and reboot the computer.

If you discover the problem to be a bad printer, port, or cable, document the problem for future reference.

Power Problems

If you receive a support call saying a device does not power on, try the following steps to resolve the issue. If none of these work, replace the device.

- Try plugging the device into a different outlet that is known to work while bypassing the power strip, surge protector, power outlet, or UPS.

- If troubleshooting reveals the problem is the power cable, the power cable is easily replaced.

The power supply is one of the most often replaced parts of a computer or server. Although this is a common failure, power supplies can be expensive to replace because of the size and power requirements of servers. Servers often have redundant power supplies to avoid downtime. The power supplies need to be checked regularly because the server might not exhibit the problem because it runs on the secondary power supply.

Software Patches, Hotfixes, and Updates

Software or operating systems often require a patch, a hotfix, a service pack, an update, or an upgrade. Patches and hotfixes are used to fix problems with an application or OS. Updates can include patches and hotfixes for the previous version. Upgrades are to improve the function of the application or the OS. Upgrades also add additional functionality and modifications all rolled into one change.

When software changes are needed, test the change on 10 percent or less of the computers and servers in the facility. Have users with more access test the functionality of the applications with the changes to make sure there are no glitches or problems before changing the rest of the computers and servers. When an application uses a thin client, the change needs to affect only the server. The users can see the change when they access the server through a web browser. When an application uses a thick client, the change may need to be made on the server and all the computers that use the application.

Whenever a change is made in the HIT environment, the change should be approved and documented. The change management documentation should include the following information:

- Device name, model number, and location
- Replacement parts
- Scheduled start and finish time of the change
- Actual start and finish time of the change
- Number of users who will be affected
- The notification of change sent to users affected
- Whether downtime is required
- Results from testing the change
- Rollback plan in case of failure
- Manager or supervisor approval

The change management documentation includes all this information, so if a problem is discovered down the road, documentation exists to pin down the point of the possible cause of the problem.

A workstation often works with peripheral devices to help manage and facilitate healthcare. The following section provides further information about these devices.

Peripheral Devices

Every facility has many peripheral devices, and HIT technicians need to know how to install them and offer basic support. These devices are becoming more mobile as medicine becomes more mobile as well. Also, more devices are introduced to the medical field as the move to include more technology in medical practice expands. When you install a new device, be sure to document information about the device. This documentation will be valuable for future reference.

The following imaging devices are widely used in facilities:

- A **barcode scanner** (see Figure 5-32) is mainly used for inventory of medicines and to confirm a patient's identity before administering medication. Barcode scanners can be used to track test specimens, surgical tool sterilization, or many other uses. Many barcode scanners use USB connections, so they are hot swappable and easily installed. Most barcode scanners come with proprietary software on a CD that must be installed for the device to function. The vendor provides specific directions for installing the software, or the vendor can install the device on site.

> **barcode scanner**—A device used to identify patients or medication, manage medication, track test specimens, and so on. The device reads a barcode and inputs the data into an IS.

Figure 5-32   A barcode scanner is used to inventory medicine and confirm a patient's identity.

Photo credit: Robert Kneschke

- A **document scanner** (see Figure 5-33) is mainly used to scan documents to be recorded into a patient's EHR/EMR. Document scanners are needed throughout the facility, so all documents that have anything written about a patient can be recorded permanently into the patient's EHR/EMR. Most document scanners use a USB connection, so they are hot swappable and easily installed. Some document scanners have an auto setup when first connected or may come with proprietary software on a CD that must be installed for the device to function. Often document scanners are used by an application and need to be compatible with all applications they need to interface with. Verify with the vendors of the applications that the document scanner is compatible before purchasing a new document scanner.

document scanner—A device used to scan paper documents into an electronic image or document.

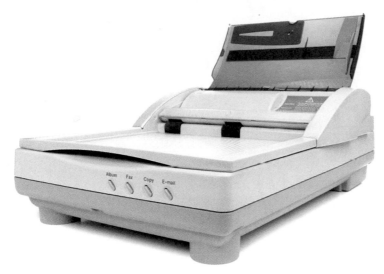

Figure 5-33 A facility uses document scanners to scan written information about a patient.

Photo credit: Roman Milert

- A **card or badge scanner** (see Figure 5-34) is used for security and convenience. A card or badge scanner works with applications, similar to a document scanner. A card scanner is frequently used to scan insurance cards to conveniently enter insurance data into a financial IS. Check with the vendor for installation instructions. Also verify that the card or badge scanner is compatible with the applications.

card or badge scanner—A device used for security and convenience that scans a card or badge to transfer data or detect identity.

Figure 5-34   A badge scanner is used for security and convenience.

Photo credit: Artur Golbert

- Printers and fax machines are installed the same way and sometimes are combined into the same machine. A printer or fax machine can be installed directly to a computer (called a local printer) or it can be connected directly to the network (called a network printer). If the printer or fax machine is installed locally, it likely uses a USB connection. When the device is connected to the computer, it tries to automatically install. If a driver is needed, it can be found on the manufacturer's website or on the CD that came with the printer or fax machine.

  When you first connect a network printer or fax machine to the network, use the control panel on the front of the device to assign it a static IP address. The printer driver must be installed on each computer that will use it. Install the printer using the IP address or shared name.

- Cameras are used in many areas of healthcare to visually document patient condition. For example, a Wound Care Center might document the progress of a wound being treated over a period of time. Cameras may use a USB connection or a memory card reader to copy image files from a memory card. The images are saved to the patient's EHR/EMR.

- **Signature pads** (see Figure 5-35) are used to transfer written signatures into an electronic image. Signature pads are usually USB and easily installed. Verify with the vendor about any applications a signature pad needs to interface with to make sure it is compatible.

signature pad—A device used to transfer written signatures into an electronic image.

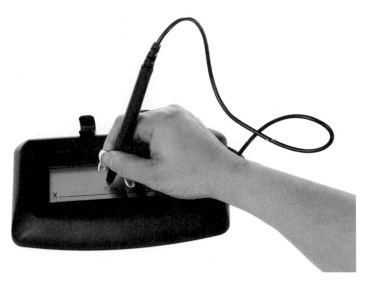

Figure 5-35   A signature pad creates an electronic image of a signature.

Photo credit: Glenda Powers

To make the installation process easier, gather the software and drivers necessary for installing or deploying equipment on a shared server for easy access from anywhere in the facility. Store documentation with step-by-step instructions on how to install any device and software on the shared server as well.

Mobile Storage

Mobile storage devices come in many different types and sizes. Security is a concern for mobile storage devices. Because mobile storage devices are small and easily transported, they are easy to misplace or steal. Each facility's security officer must evaluate and decide if using mobile storage devices will be allowed for storing e-PHI. If using mobile storage devices is approved, these devices must be encrypted and use password protection. The following sections cover devices used for storage.

Flash Drives and External Hard Drives

Flash drives are memory devices with a USB connection. Flash drives have no moving parts and do not require power to retain data. External hard drives also use a USB connection. Both flash drives and external hard drives are easy to connect and access from any computer with a USB port. External hard drives can be used as a media for performing backups because they are easy to store offsite in case of a catastrophic event that destroys the backups stored on site. The problem with using external hard drives as a backup is the reliance on human intervention. Human error might cause a backup to not write correctly; the media may be lost, stolen, or damaged; or the media might be accidentally left on site, which makes it vulnerable to data corruption and even destruction of all copies of the backup.

Many portable media players, such as an MP3 player, can store data or images. Portable media players should be viewed as a similar security risk as flash drives or external drives.

DVDs and CDs

DVDs and CDs are sometimes used to back up or move data, but human intervention is a risk to the backup. DVDs can hold more data than CDs. DVDs and CDs are better used for copying a medical image to a disk to take to an off campus facility that cannot share data over the network securely. For example, a patient's primary care physician (PCP) might send a patient to a hospital for an MRI. The MRI image can be copied to a DVD or CD that also contains the software needed to view the image on another computer. Any DVD or CD not required to be kept for a patient's EHR/EMR must be destroyed. Most shredders today have the capability to destroy a DVD or CD.

SD Cards

Secure digital (SD) cards are usually used to store images in a camera, although SD cards can hold data other than images. SD cards are generally not used for long term storage.

Tapes

Tapes are used as a media for backups. Tapes can hold large amounts of data for a long period of time. Tapes should be stored offsite in case of a catastrophic event at the facility. Tapes are quickly being replaced by storage area networks (SANs). A SAN is a dedicated network providing consolidated storage.

EXAM TIP   For the Healthcare IT exam, you need to be familiar with the different kinds of mobile storage devices and how to secure them.

Mobile Computing Devices

Mobile computing devices are the focus of making healthcare mobile. As healthcare providers have access to patient information and records on the move, they can move more quickly and efficiently. HIT technicians need to understand the uses and basic support of mobile devices because they are used more frequently in healthcare.

Tablet computers are smaller laptop computers but may not have a keyboard. Most tablet computers have a touchscreen that enables a signature on electronic documents without having to scan a paper-signed document. Tablet computers should be password protected and encrypted.

Smartphones are cellular phones that also function as a computer with limited capability. Operating systems on smartphones are Blackberry OS, Windows Mobile, Google Android, or Apple iOS. Smartphones enable healthcare providers to be contacted without having access to the network or computer. Some vendors allow healthcare providers to access an application using a mobile device. For example, some PACS vendors provide a smartphone app that enables viewing of medical images on the phone. Allowing access to e-PHI on smartphones is a security risk. Phones are easily misplaced, lost, or stolen, even more often than laptop computers. Any smartphone with access to e-PHI must be encrypted with password protection and time lockout. Also, software can be installed on a smartphone that can remotely wipe a device when prompted by the security administrator.

HIT in the Real World

While working on the clinical IS support team we received a support call from one of our facilities because the perioperative IS had become so sluggish as to almost make the IS useless. This made the support call a very high priority because this issue meant healthcare providers were unable to access patient records or document current information about the patient. The nurse who called it in told me the entire surgery department had gone to downtime procedures because it was so frustrating trying to use the sluggish perioperative IS. The perioperative IS had recently been installed at this facility, maybe three months earlier. We were able to see the response times of the messages in the interface to demonstrate that the system was in fact running slowly to the point that a simple request for a patient record would easily take a minute to retrieve.

We discovered that the server running the application and interfaces with other information systems was almost out of memory. This didn't seem right because it was a new server for a new IS. We learned when data messages are sent through the interface, a log of the message is created and stored on the server. The log is used for troubleshooting when there is an error with the interface.

We checked the logs and discovered the log files had grown so large that they had filled up most of the memory on the server. We had logs that were months old from all the way back to the time of the deployment. We got change management approval; then we deleted the old logs, and the system started working again.

A few months down the road we received another support call from another one of our facilities because the perioperative IS had become sluggish, making the IS nearly useless. The perioperative IS had recently been installed at this facility maybe two or three months earlier. Starting to sound familiar? I thought so, too. I searched through our records of support calls for the documentation of how we resolved the other facility's problem, and knew the steps needed to resolve the problem at this facility. We got change management approval; then we deleted the old logs, and the system start working again.

I thought I had seen the end of this problem because both perioperative information systems were working. I was wrong. It wasn't maybe a couple weeks later when we received another support call from the first facility saying the perioperative IS was acting sluggish again. Because this issue was recurring at the same facility, we placed a support call to the vendor. The vendor support team remoted into our server and discovered the logs had not been set to automatically delete after a set period of time had passed. They taught us how to set the logs to automatically delete when they become a week old. We then applied this same setting at all other facilities with this perioperative IS.

In order to prevent this from happening again, we added a point to the checklist of deployment milestones to verify this setting has been applied.

As HIT technicians we are responsible for learning from our own mistakes and taking actions to make sure the same mistakes don't happen again. When we discover a problem, it is crucial to fully document what was done to correct the issue and how it was done, too. With proper documentation, if a problem arises again, the finding a resolution is much faster, and healthcare providers don't need to be without critical patient information for very long.

Chapter Summary

How the Internet or an Intranet Works

- An Internet Service Provider (ISP) provides a facility access to the Internet, usually through a T-line. T-lines carry data over fiber-optic lines or copper wire.

- An intranet is the private network secured within a facility.

- HTTP, HTTPS, FTP, and RDP use a client-server architecture.

- Transmission Control Protocol (TCP) is responsible for guaranteeing the data is received after traversing the network.

- Internet Protocol (IP) is responsible for breaking down messages into packets small enough to travel through the network and for finding the best path over the network.

- The domain name service (DNS) resolves domain names into the IP address that the network understands to reach the correct computer on the intranet or Internet.

- Wireless connections to a local network use the Wireless Fidelity (Wi-Fi) technology.

- A wireless access point (WAP or AP) is a device that enables a wireless computer, printer, or other device to connect to a network.

- Programming languages used to support or build hospital intranet resources include SQL, HTML, XML, PHP, or ASP. Other tools are APIs and Adobe Flash.

How a Network Works

- An ad hoc network is a wireless, decentralized, temporary, and peer-to-peer connection.

- An infrastructure is a centralized network where devices connect through an access point.

- When setting up a wireless infrastructure, consider obstacles that might interfere with the wireless signal.

- Wi-Fi Protected Access 2 (WPA2) is the most current and secure encryption available for wireless networks.

- The SSID should be disabled on the network used by employees and information systems of a facility that shares e-PHI.

- A router is a network device that separates one network from another and enables traffic between the two networks. Besides providing connectivity between two networks, a router's second most important purpose is to stand as a firewall between the network it protects and another network or the Internet to make sure that unwanted traffic does not pass through.

- The dynamic host configuration protocol (DHCP) automatically assigns a dynamic IP address to a device when it joins a network unless that device has been assigned a static IP address.

- **Ipconfig**, **ping**, and **tracert** are commands used in the command prompt window to troubleshoot a network connection.

- Common network problems include duplicate IP addresses, broken cables and crosstalk, interference, poor AP placement, lost connectivity to the ISP, and power failure.

Managing Network Resources

- An application and computing device used to access the IS is provided as a thick client, a thin client, or as terminal services.

- Application service providers (ASPs) and cloud solutions are offered as software-as-a-service (SaaS).

- When configuring a server for an IS, consider security risks, high traffic and load balancing, hardware and software specifications required by vendors, and purging old logs.

- Three different types of backups should be performed regularly: daily, differential, and incremental.

Configuring a Workstation and Peripherals

- When deploying a computer, printer, or server, document important information for reference in case the device fails.

- Use a ghost image to efficiently deploy a large number of computers.

- All computers and servers should always have antivirus software with up-to-date virus definitions.

- Different types of communication standards that a computer or server might use include Universal Serial Bus (USB), IEEE 1394, small computer system interface (SCSI), or Bluetooth.

- When a problem presents with a mouse, monitor, printer, power, or software, try some simple troubleshooting steps before replacing the broken device.

- Common peripheral devices found in a hospital supported by HIT technicians include a barcode scanner, document scanner, card or badge scanner, or signature pads.

- Mobile storage devices create a security concern because of the size and portability. Common mobile storage devices include flash drives and external drives, DVDs and CDs, SD cards, and tapes.

- Mobile computing devices are the focus of making healthcare mobile. HIT technicians need to understand the uses and basic support of mobile devices as they are used more frequently in healthcare.

Key Terms

- active directory
- active server pages (ASP or ASP.NET)
- ad hoc
- Adobe Flash
- advanced encryption standard (AES)
- application program interface (API)
- application service provider (ASP)
- barcode scanner
- Bluetooth
- card or badge scanner
- client-server architecture
- cloud computing
- default gateway
- disk image
- document scanner
- domain controller
- domain name service (DNS)
- dynamic host configuration protocol (DHCP)
- dynamic IP address
- extensible markup language (XML)

- fiber optic
- file transfer protocol (FTP)
- hot swappable
- hypertext markup language (HTML)
- hypertext preprocessor (PHP)
- hypertext transfer protocol (HTTP)
- hypertext transfer protocol secure (HTTPS)
- IEEE 1394
- infrastructure
- Infrastructure as a Service (IaaS)
- Internet modem
- Internet Protocol (IP)
- Internet service provider (ISP)
- intranet
- IP address
- ipconfig
- local area network (LAN)
- mainframe
- network address translation (NAT)
- Open Systems Interconnection model (OSI model)
- parallel communication
- ping
- Platform as a Service (Paas)
- port
- port forwarding
- print server
- network address translation (NAT)
- remote authentication dial in user services (RADIUS)
- remote desktop protocol (RDP)
- router
- serial communication
- service set identifier (SSID)
- signature pad

- small computer system interface (SCSI)
- software-as-a-service (SaaS)
- static IP address
- structured query language (SQL)
- subnet mask
- switch
- T-line
- TCP/IP
- terminal services
- tracert
- transmission control protocol (TCP)
- universal serial bus (USB)
- virtualization
- virus definitions
- wide area network (WAN)
- Wi-Fi protected access (WPA)
- Wi-Fi protected access 2 (WPA2)
- wired equivalent privacy (WEP)
- wireless access point (WAP or AP)
- wireless fidelity (Wi-Fi)

Acronym Drill

Acronyms sometimes get confusing, especially when a single sentence can have four or five. As an HIT professional, you need to know the acronyms and what they stand for. Fill in the blank with the correct acronym for the sentence.

1. _____ is responsible for guaranteeing the data is received after traversing the network. _____ is responsible for reassembling those packets at the receiving end and for finding the path to use to get the packets across the network.

   Answer: _____

2. Pinging a domain name is a great tool for verifying if the _____ service is active.

   Answer: _____

3. An _____ is a segment of programming code that can be used by many programs.

   Answer: _____

4. _____ is the most current and secure encryption available for wireless networks.

   Answer: _____

5. When a wireless network contains sensitive data, the _____ broadcasting is disabled.

   Answer: _____

6. _____ automatically assigns a dynamic IP address to a device when it joins a network.

   Answer: _____

7. Both _____ and cloud solutions are offered as _____.

   Answer: _____

8. _____ and _____ are best used for copying a medical image to a disk to take to an off campus facility that cannot share data over the network securely.

   Answer: _____

Review Questions

1. What service does an ISP provide?

   Answer: _____

2. What are the seven layers of the OSI model?

   Answer: _____

   _____

3. Which protocol is used to provide a window to view the desktop of another computer?

   Answer: _____

4. What is the purpose of the DNS?

   Answer: _____

   _____

5. Why might a facility choose to use a cloud-based solution for HIS requirements?

Answer: _____

_____

_____

_____

6. What is the purpose for using Structured Query Language?

Answer: _____

7. Why would a web page use PHP?

Answer: _____

_____

_____

_____

8. What are some of the obstacles that must be considered when designing a wireless infrastructure?

Answer: _____

_____

_____

_____

_____

_____

9. Why did WPA2 replace WPA wireless encryption?

Answer: _____

_____

_____

_____

10. What is the purpose of NAT when used by a router?

Answer: _____

_____

11. What is the purpose of pinging another device on a network?

    Answer: _____

    _____

12. What is the difference between a thick client and a thin client?

    Answer: _____

    _____

    _____

13. What are some issues to consider when supporting servers so that servers perform well and are protected?

    Answer: _____

    _____

14. What is the difference between a differential backup and an incremental backup?

    Answer: _____

    _____

    _____

    _____

15. What information should be documented when deploying a new computer, printer, or server for reference in case the device fails?

    Answer: _____

    _____

    _____

    _____

    _____

16. Why is it important that virus definitions be updated regularly?

    Answer: _____

    _____

17. Why might a monitor need to use a DVI connection rather than a VGA connection?

Answer: _____

_____

_____

_____

18. When creating a change management documentation, what information should be included?

Answer: _____

_____

_____

_____

_____

_____

_____

_____

_____

_____

19. What are common peripheral devices found in a hospital supported by an HIT technician?

Answer: _____

_____

20. Why is it a security risk to allow access to e-PHI on smartphones?

Answer: _____

_____

_____

Practical Application

1. There are several ways to copy text from the command prompt window. In the chapter you learned two methods. Research on the Internet and find a third method for copying text from the command prompt window.

   Answer: _____

   _____

   _____

   _____

   _____

   _____

   _____

   _____

   _____

   _____

   _____

   _____

   _____

   _____

2. Sometimes it is easy to lose track of which IP addresses are used on a network. It's not a bad idea to occasionally run a network scanner to report all IP addresses currently in use on the network. On the internet, find freeware software on the for a network scanner to find IP addresses on the network you are connected to. What freeware software did you use? What IP addresses or how many IP address did you find in use on your network?

   Answer: _____

   _____

CHAPTER 6
Medical Business Operations

In this chapter you learn about:

- The clinical environment
- How to support clinical software
- How healthcare interfaces work

Knowing how IT operations work in any organization is not enough to work in the HIT environment. To work successfully in a hospital, you need to know about the business of a hospital. The purpose of the CompTIA Healthcare IT Technician certificate is to help IT trained professionals cross over to the healthcare IT field. Knowing common medical terms and the specifics of healthcare IT is necessary for this transition.

This chapter begins by defining some commonly used medical terms, devices, and departments.

Understanding the Clinical Environment

Objectives element:

4.1.   Identify commonly used medical terms and devices.

Devices: Portable x-ray machine, MRI, vitals cuff, EKG, EEG, Ultrasound, PET, CT, Vascular/Nuclear Stress Test, Glucose monitor

Basic clinical terms: Imaging, PCP, Stat, Acuity, Code blue/rapid response, Trauma levels, Controlled substance (levels), EI IR/EMR

Common medical departments:

Inpatient: OBGYN, ONC, PEDS, FBC/L&D/Stork/NICU, ICU/CCU, TCU/PCU, MED/SURG, Behavior Health, PACU, OR/UR, and ER

Outpatient: OBGYN, ONC, PEDS, Plastic Surgery, ENT, Respiratory, Physical therapy, Cardiovascular, Occupational therapy, Ambulatory/Day surgery, Radiology, Laboratory, Ophthalmology, Dermatology, Nuclear

4.2.   Explain aspects of a typical clinical environment.

Basic workflow: Registration, Consultation, Examination

Clinical processes: Computerized physician order entry, transcription, dictation, referrals/consults, digital signatures

Knowing common medical terms and devices helps HIT technicians relate and communicate better with their medical co-workers. You can better assist the employees of the hospital when you understand more about the equipment and terms they use daily. Another reason to know about medical devices is that it wouldn't be unexpected for the HIT department at a hospital to receive a support call concerning a broken device that is not supported by the HIT department. You need to be familiar enough with the device to point the caller in the right direction for help or know the vendor contact information to request support.

Some of these terms and devices have already been mentioned in earlier chapters. The sections that follow review the terms you're already familiar with and as well as those that haven't yet been covered.

Medical Terms, Imaging, and Tests

Part of being an HIT technician is translating between medical and technological terminology. As you work in a facility, you might hear several terms with which you might not already be familiar. The section that follows outlines some of the terms you will hear in a hospital, so you can follow a conversation with medical personnel.

Medical Terms

The electronic health record (EHR) or electronic medical record (EMR) is the record of the patient's medical condition and history that healthcare providers refer to in order to make decisions on a patient's care. Remember from Chapter 1, "Introducing Healthcare IT," that the EHR and the EMR are not exactly the same thing. The EMR is the collection of patient information from all visits at *one* hospital. The EHR is the collection of patient information from *all* hospitals the patient has visited.

A **primary care physician (PCP)** is a doctor who has an ongoing relationship with a patient and provides primary care for that patient. The PCP is usually the first physician a patient sees when he experiences a new illness or medical condition and for regular checkups. The PCP offers referrals to specialists when needed and provides ongoing healthcare management.

> **primary care physician (PCP)**—A doctor who has an ongoing relationship with a patient and provides primary care for that patient.

The Drug Enforcement Administration (DEA) is a U.S. Department of Justice agency responsible for enforcing the controlled substance laws and regulations. A **controlled substance** is a drug or substance regulated by the government. This regulation includes the manufacture, possession, or use of the controlled substance. Controlled substances are divided into five classifications called schedules, which are listed in Table 6-1.

> **controlled substance**—A drug or substance regulated by the government.

Table 6-1 Controlled Substance Schedules or Classifications as Determined by the DEA

Classification	Description	Examples
Schedule I	High potential for abuse. No accepted medical use in treatment. No accepted safety standards for use under medical treatment.	Heroin, LSD, marijuana, and ecstasy
Schedule II	High potential for abuse. May lead to severe psychological or physical dependence.	Morphine, opium, oxycodone, fentanyl, methamphetamine, cocaine, and pentobarbital
Schedule III	Potential for abuse is less than substances in schedules I and II. May lead to moderate or low physical dependence. May lead to high psychological dependence.	Less than 90 milligrams of codeine per dosage, buprenorphine products, and anabolic steroids
Schedule IV	Low potential for abuse relative to substances in schedule III	Propoxyphene and diazepam
Schedule V	Low potential for abuse relative to substances in schedule IV. Primarily small amounts of narcotics used for antitussive, antidiarrheal, and analgesic purposes.	Cough preparations containing less than 200 milligrams of codeine per 100 milliliters or grams

EXAM TIP   For the Healthcare IT exam, you need to be familiar with the controlled substance schedule. Learn the five levels and how they differ.

Patient acuity describes the level of care that a patient requires. Measuring patient acuity is necessary to determine staffing levels needed to care for all the patients in the hospital. The guidelines for measuring acuity vary from hospital to hospital and even unit to unit within a hospital. Generally, a patient with low acuity is an easy patient to care for, relatively healthy, and does not require much of a healthcare provider's time and effort. A patient with high acuity is a very sick patient whose healthcare needs require a lot of a healthcare provider's time and effort.

Hospitals have a hospital incident command system (HICS) to establish procedures for emergency situations. The codes usually are a color or number that has been assigned a meaning. Codes are either called out over the intercom or sent to employee pagers. The code assignments change from hospital to hospital. Hospitals display their coding scheme on placards on the walls of nursing stations or on the back of ID badges of employees, as shown in Figure 6-1. Usually, a **code blue** means immediate care is needed for a patient who is in critical condition. A code blue team quickly arrives to care for the patient. When a patient is almost to the point of a code blue, a nurse or other medical personnel can issue a **rapid response**. During a rapid response, only part of the code blue team arrives to try to prevent a code blue. "Stat" is another term used in healthcare to express urgency. "Stat" comes from the Latin word *statim*, meaning immediately.

> **EXAM TIP**   For the Healthcare IT exam, you need to be familiar with what hospital codes are, especially code blue and rapid response.

Figure 6-1   Hospitals sometimes display their coding scheme on the back of ID badges of employees.

> **code blue**—A code usually used to indicate a patient is in critical condition and requires immediate intervention.
>
> **rapid response**—A code used when a patient is about to go into a code blue.

Not all hospitals are equipped to care for a patient with a severe trauma. Hospitals are assigned a trauma center designation level to indicate the capability to care for trauma patients. This designation has much more relevance than just the readiness of the ED. Many qualifications are considered such as readiness of all the departments, availability of staff and equipment, and involvement in ongoing preparation. The guidelines for trauma center level standards vary from state to state. States use a three-, four-, or five-level classification. A Level I trauma center is the most equipped facility to care for a trauma patient because that facility has a full range of specialists and equipment available at all times. Table 6-2 gives a general overview of qualifications in a five-level trauma classification.

Table 6-2 Trauma Center Designation and Qualifications

Trauma Level	Qualifications
I	The trauma center is ready for the highest level of surgical care to trauma patients by providing equipment and a full range of specialists, including a certain number of surgeons, emergency physicians, and anesthesiologists at all times inside the hospital and not just on call from home. The hospital is also required to have a residency program for training physicians.
II	The trauma center provides comprehensive trauma care and collaborates with a Level I center.
III	The trauma center provides emergency resuscitation, surgery, and intensive care to most trauma patients. Other patients are transferred to a Level I or Level II trauma center.
IV	The trauma center provides initial evaluation, stabilization, and diagnostic services. Patients are transferred to a higher level of care facility when needed.
V	The trauma center provides initial evaluation, stabilization, and diagnostic services. Patients are transferred to a higher level of care facility when needed. If not open all hours, the trauma center must have an after-hours response protocol.

A **blood pressure cuff** is a device used to measure blood pressure. A blood pressure cuff has many names: BP cuff, **vitals cuff**, or sphygmomanometer. Usually healthcare providers just say blood pressure cuff. A blood pressure cuff can either be manual or automatic (see Figure 6-2). A manual blood pressure cuff is used with a stethoscope.

> **blood pressure cuff**—A device used to measure blood pressure. Also called BP cuff, vitals cuff, or sphygmomanometer.
>
> **vitals cuff**—See blood pressure cuff.

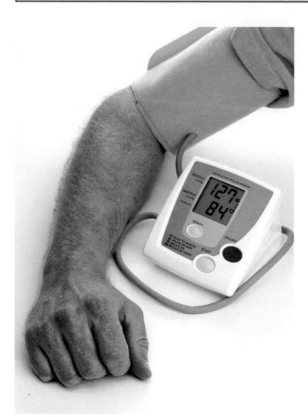

Figure 6-2   An automatic blood pressure cuff measures the blood pressure in a patient.

Photo credit: Serenethos

Medical Imaging

Imaging is the process to create images of the body for clinical purposes. Several different departments in a hospital have the capability to create medical images, such as radiology, nuclear medicine, or endoscopy. The following list describes some of the equipment used for imaging:

- The **portable X-ray machine**, as shown in Figure 6-3, is a mobile X-ray machine that is small enough to be rolled to a patient's room. Some portable X-ray machines are designed to be taken to a patient's house. After the image is taken, the machine is connected to the network to transfer the image to the PACS IS.

portable X-ray machine—A mobile X-ray machine that is small enough to be rolled to a patient's room or taken to a patient's house.

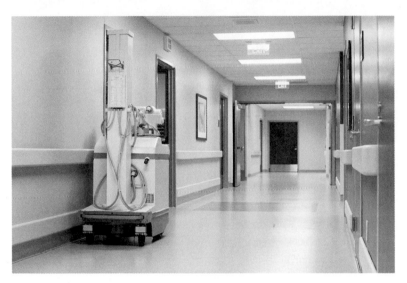

Figure 6-3   A portable X-ray machine can be rolled to a patient's room.

- An **ultrasound** is an image taken of soft tissue using high-frequency sound waves and echoes. Ultrasounds are often chosen because there are no known bad effects from ultrasounds. An ultrasound machine, as shown in Figure 6-4, is usually on a rolling cart but can be as small and portable as a handheld device. Ultrasounds are commonly used for viewing images of a fetus to determine gender, position, or condition but also might be used to look for blood clots or to measure bladder size.

ultrasound—An imaging process that uses sound waves to create a picture of soft tissues inside the body.

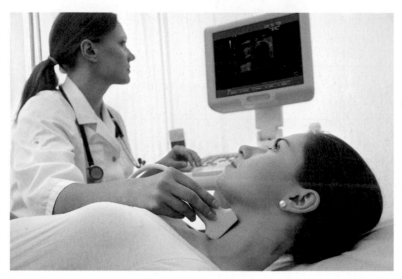

Figure 6-4   An ultrasound machine can be as small as a handheld device.

Photo credit: Alexander Raths

> - A computed tomography (CT) is imaging that uses x-rays along with computing algorithms. A patient lies down in a CT machine while the CT machine rotates around the patient, as shown in Figure 6-5. The CT produces cross-sectional images (tomography) of the patient's body. A CT machine produces an image with 100 times more clarity than normal X-ray imaging.

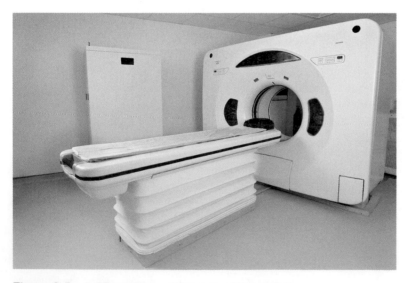

Figure 6-5   A CT machine rotates around the patient.

Photo credit: Hakan Kızıltan

- Magnetic resonance imaging (MRI) is imaging that uses strong magnetic fields and radio signals to create an image of a patient's body. A patient lies down in an MRI machine, as shown in Figure 6-6, and must remain still for extended periods of time in a noisy, cramped space. An MRI machine can see tendons and ligaments when X-rays cannot. Because of the strong magnetic field, all personnel, including HIT technicians, must take extra precaution when entering a room with an MRI machine. Absolutely no metal must enter the room because it can cause a dangerous situation as the magnetic field pulls the object to the machine. Metal objects include keys, jewelry, IV poles, oxygen tanks, pacemakers, or metal pins in the body.

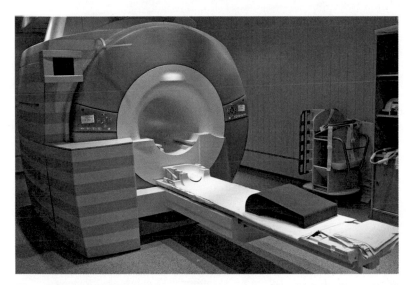

Figure 6-6   An MRI machine uses strong magnets, which is dangerous if you have any metal on your person.

Photo credit: smart.art

- A positron emission tomography (PET) is imaging that creates an image of the body or function of an organ. A radioactive tracer is introduced to the patient's body, usually injected into the patient's bloodstream. A PET scanner, as shown in Figure 6-7, records the location of the tracer as it is absorbed into the body. When a PET scan is used with a CT scan, a three-dimensional image can be created.

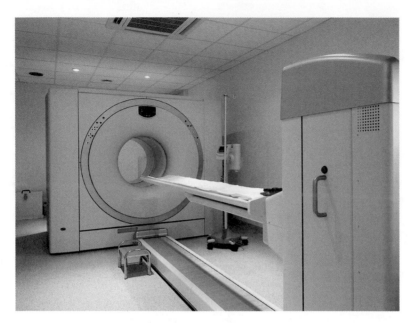

Figure 6-7   A PET scanner uses a radioactive tracer and creates an image as the tracer is absorbed into the body.

Photo credit: grieze

Medical Tests

> **EXAM TIP**   Although medical tests are not on the Healthcare IT exam, the devices used to perform the tests are. Pay attention to the devices used to perform medical tests and why they might be used.

Some medical conditions, such as diabetes mellitus, require a patient to monitor the glucose concentration levels in her blood. Glucose is a kind of sugar the body uses as a source of energy. A patient uses a **glucose monitor** to measure blood glucose levels (see Figure 6-8). Usually the device is small and portable, and the test needs only a small drop of blood usually from a finger prick. Another option for some patients is a continuous glucose monitor. This device is worn like a pager and has a disposable sensor placed just under the skin.

> **glucose monitor**—A device used to measure the amount of glucose in a blood sample.

Figure 6-8 A glucose monitor is small and portable.

Photo credit: evgenyb

Natural electrical waves of electricity occur in a brain. An **electroencephalogram (EEG)** measures the frequency of brain waves. During an EEG test, sensors are attached to a patient's head to measure the electrical activity. Usually the sensors are attached to a cap placed on the patient's head, as shown in Figure 6-9. The EEG machine translates the electrical activity into waves on a monitor display. EEG results are used to diagnose brain disorders or dysfunction; for example, epilepsy. Usually the symptom needs to be presenting, such as a seizure, for an accurate and beneficial recording.

> **electroencephalogram (EEG)**—A test that measures the frequency of brain waves.

Natural electrical pulses cause the heart muscle to contract and pump blood through the heart's chambers. An **electrocardiogram (EKG or ECG)** tests for problems with the electrical activity of the heart. During the test, electrodes or sensors are placed on the chest area to measure the electrical activity. The EKG machine translates the electrical activity into line tracings on paper or a monitor display, as shown in Figure 6-10. EKG results are used to determine the cause of symptoms of heart diseases or conditions or to measure progress of treatment of a heart disease or condition.

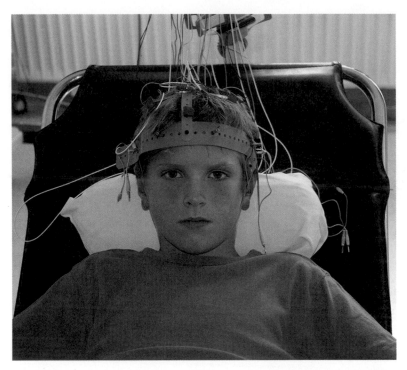

Figure 6-9 Sensors used for an EEG usually are attached to a cap that the patient wears.

Photo credit: Marcus Scholz

> **electrocardiogram (EKG or ECG)**—A test that indicates problems with the electrical activity of the heart.

Sometimes doctors order a **vascular stress test** to determine the capability of veins to return blood from the lower limbs to the heart. The patient usually starts out walking on a treadmill or pedaling a stationary bike to get the blood flowing, as shown in Figure 6-11. Electrodes or sensors placed on the patient's chest record the EKG results.

> **vascular stress test**—A physical test using an EKG that determines the capability of veins to return blood from the lower limbs to the heart.

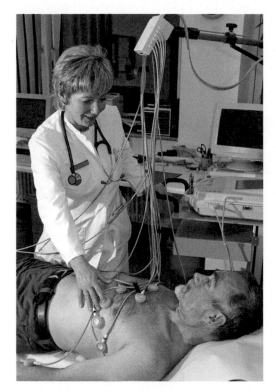

Figure 6-10   EKG results are displayed on a monitor by the patient's bed.

Photo credit: Alexander Raths

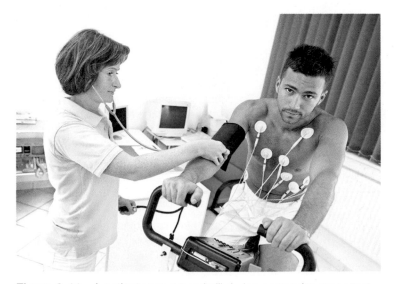

Figure 6-11   A patient uses a treadmill during a vascular stress test.

Photo credit: nyul

A **nuclear stress test** is used to diagnose and treat some heart disorders. The test involves a vascular stress test combined with a PET scan. A patient starts with a PET scan to record the patient's blood flow at a resting heart rate. Then the patient takes the vascular stress test to reach a target heart rate. A patient PET scan is taken to record any blockage of blood flow or how well the blood flows through the heart.

> **nuclear stress test**—A test using both two PET scans and a vascular stress test to test how well the blood flows through the heart of a patient.

Medical Departments

HIT technicians need to be familiar with the medical departments in the hospital. Table 6-3 describes the departments for inpatient procedures, and Table 6-4 describes the departments for outpatient procedures.

Table 6-3   Inpatient Departments

Department	Typical Abbreviations	Specialization
Obstetrics and Gynecology	OB/GYN, OBG, O&G	Deals with female reproductive organs. Obstetricians care for women who are pregnant, and gynecologists care for women at any other time.
Labor and Delivery	L&D, Stork, Family Birthing Center (FBC)	Cares for new mothers and babies during delivery.
Postpartum	Mother/Baby	Cares for new mothers and babies after delivery.
Neonatal Intensive Care Unit	NICU	Cares for babies in critical condition. When a patient leaves the NICU and needs to be readmitted to the hospital, this returning patient must go to the pediatric department.
Pediatrics	PEDS	Cares for patients who are infants, children, or adolescents.
Oncology	ONC	Cares for patients who have cancer.
Intensive Care Unit	ICU, critical care unit (CCU)	Cares for patients in critical life-threatening condition. Usually has a lower nurse-to-patient ratio.

Department	Typical Abbreviations	Specialization
Transitional Care Unit	TCU, progressive care unit (PCU), step-down floor	Cares for patients not quite needing ICU care but who need more than general nursing.
Medical/Surgical Nursing Unit	MED/SURG, floor	Provides general care for adult patients in a hospital.
Behavior Health	Psych	Cares for patients with mental health conditions or rehabilitation.
Operating Room	OR	Offers surgical procedures.
Post Anesthesia Care Unit	PACU	Cares for patients leaving the OR as the anesthesia wears off.
Emergency Department	ED, emergency room (ER), emergency center (EC)	Cares for patients with new and acute medical conditions.

Table 6-4 Outpatient Departments

Department	Typical Abbreviations	Specialization
Obstetrics and Gynecology	OB/GYN, OBG, O&G	Deals with female reproductive organs. Obstetricians care for women who are pregnant, and gynecologists care for women at any other time.
Pediatrics	PEDS	Cares for patients who are infants, children, or adolescents.
Oncology	ONC	Cares for patients who have cancer.
Plastic Surgery		Offers surgical procedures to reconstruct or restore form or function of the body.
Ear, Nose, Throat	ENT	Cares for patients with a condition involving the ears, nose, or throat.
Respiratory		Cares for patients with respiratory conditions, such as asthma.
Physical Therapy	PT	Offers physical rehabilitation to restore physical function to an injured patient as he recovers.

Table 6-4 Continued

Department	Typical Abbreviations	Specialization
Occupational Therapy	OT	Offers rehabilitation to disabled patients to restore meaningful and purposeful activities of daily living.
Cardiovascular		Cares for patients with conditions of the heart or blood vessels.
Ambulatory/Day Surgery		Offers surgical procedures that do not require an overnight stay at the hospital.
Radiology		Creates medical images.
Laboratory	Lab	Performs testing and research for medical practice.
Ophthalmology	Op, OP	Cares for patients with disorders or diseases of the eye.
Dermatology	DERM	Cares for patients with conditions of the skin.
Nuclear	NUC	Deals with the use of radioactive substances for diagnosis, treatment, and research of medical conditions.

Clinical Environment

Recall that when a patient arrives at a hospital, he goes through a registration process. While speaking with registration staff, the patient is asked questions to fill out his patient information. This information is entered into the HIS and becomes part of the patient's registration record. During the registration process, the patient is assigned a medical record number (MRN), if he doesn't already have one. The MRN is a unique identifier for the patient. The patient might be asked for the following information.

- Full name
- Address
- Employer
- Next of kin
- Billing and insurance information
- Referring and family physician information

A doctor or nurse conducts an **examination**, or exam, to determine the cause of symptoms a patient is experiencing. During the exam, the doctor might order blood work or other lab tests, which means a specimen will be collected from the patient. Sometimes the first doctor a patient sees (the PCP or emergency physician) cannot diagnose or treat a condition and might need to consult another doctor. A **consultation** is when a doctor seeks the expertise of another doctor in a specialized field. A **referral** is when a doctor refers a patient to go see a specialist.

> **examination**—When a healthcare provider evaluates a patient and his medical conditions. This might include tests for a complete understanding of the cause of the symptoms. Also called an exam.
>
> **consultation**—When a doctor seeks the expertise of another doctor in a specialized field.
>
> **referral**—When a doctor refers a patient to go see a specialist.

A doctor uses a computerized physician order entry (CPOE) IS to enter orders for a patient. Using the CPOE reduces the time it takes to send orders to other departments through the HIS when the doctor enters the order himself rather than asking a nurse or other healthcare provider to enter the order. The CPOE is usually different from the order entry IS that the nurses use. The CPOE is customized to the doctor's needs because it has the capability for prescriptions to be entered.

A doctor dictates notes about the patient to a dictation application. Dictation applications usually use a microphone hooked up to a computer or a telephone that dials into the application. Dictation is becoming more mobile as physicians are starting to use mobile phones for dictating, as demonstrated in Figure 6-12.

In the past, transcription personnel would transcribe the recorded voice to text. Today, voice recognition software, also called transcription software, is used to transcribe the dictation into text. Transcription personnel are still used to ensure that the transcription software translated correctly what the physician dictated. This text, called notes, is entered into the patient's EMR. After the doctor finishes all his notes and orders on a patient, he must digitally sign the chart to indicate that he agrees with what has been entered into the patient's EMR. A chart is usually signed digitally while the doctor is logged in to view the chart and clicks a button that signs the chart. Figure 6-13 shows a confirmation message before finalizing the digital signature on a patient's chart in an EHR IS. The digital signature includes a date, timestamp, and text that says something like "electronically signed by," and then the doctor's name.

Figure 6-12 Using mobile phones or tablets to enter dictation about a patient is becoming more popular among physicians.

Photo credit: 夢見る詩人

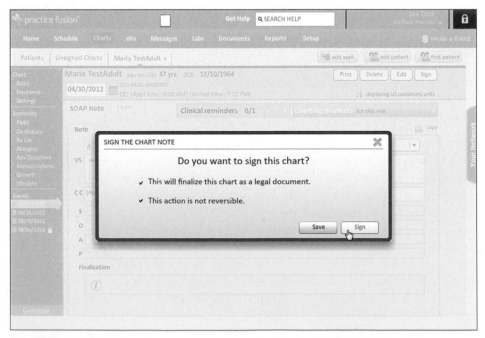

Figure 6-13 A confirmation message appears before finalizing the digital signature on a patient's chart in an EHR IS.

http://www.practicefusion.com

Supporting Software Used in Healthcare Facilities

Objectives element:

4.1   Identify commonly used medical terms and devices.

Interfaces: e-prescribing, ICD10, CPT, SNOMED, NDCID, PACS, E/M codes

Clinical software and modules: Patient tracking, Scheduling, Order entry, Practice management, Billing/coding, Tracking/auditing

4.5   Explain the basics of document imaging.

File types: TIFF, PDF, JPG, GIF

Characteristics: Quality, Size, Resolution, Compression

Scanning and indexing: Metadata, Storage, and Retrieval

OCR and structured data

4.6   Given a scenario, determine common clinical software problems.

Locate the affected modules or fields.

Determine file/data types.

Escalation procedures to proper support tier: vendor or local application support.

4.7   Describe change control best practices and their system-wide effects.

Procedural systematic customization, Governance board, System patching/updates, Appropriate scheduling

Change control environments: Development, QA/Test, User test, Production/live

When an HIT technician arrives on the job the first day, most likely she will know only a little about what is needed to do her job because information systems at a hospital are likely to be specific for this hospital. Vendors have their own ways to present the same solutions, and it's unreasonable to thoroughly know them all. The HIT technician needs to know the basics of clinical software, what problem the software solves, and about the technology used behind the software. With this knowledge, she can quickly learn the information systems used at her new job.

Clinical Software and Modules

The clinical software used in healthcare facilities can all be provided by one vendor or can be provided by several different vendors. Usually, smaller hospitals find it cost-effective to have one vendor provide all the software needed in modules and these modules make up one big clinical system. Larger hospitals are more likely to afford the interfacing equipment, software, and support needed to use multiple vendors. The benefit of using multiple vendors is the facility can pick and choose the best of each software area.

Several areas of hospital operations use software to facilitate healthcare. Earlier chapters have already mentioned these, but the following sections discuss these further.

Scheduling Software

Scheduling software, as shown in Figure 6-14, is used in several different departments of a hospital to schedule services offered. Any department or physician's office that can predict when patients need services use scheduling software. For example, departments that offer surgery, therapy, imaging, lab tests, or follow-up visits use scheduling software. Scheduling software helps departments know how many staff members need to be scheduled to work. It also keeps patient flow in an organized and orderly way. Scheduling software specifically designed for healthcare offer conveniences, such as reserving rooms, procedures, and personnel based on the type of procedure or service. Most information systems designed for a specific department that is responsible for organizing schedules for services include a module in the IS used for scheduling. For example, many perioperative information systems include a scheduling module used to schedule inpatient and outpatient surgeries.

> **scheduling software**—Software used to schedule services offered that might include features that can reserve rooms, procedures, and personnel based on the type of procedure or service.

Figure 6-14   Scheduling software helps keep departments and practices organized and running smoothly.

http://www.practicefusion.com

Patient Tracking Software

Patient tracking software is used to follow and record patient flow through a patient's changing medical status, lab studies, imaging, or other diagnostic and treatment services. Keeping track of patient flow helps the hospital administration justify if additional staff or equipment is needed or if the facility needs to be expanded to accommodate an unbalanced patient population. The patient flow data is also collected to see how long each service during a patient's stay takes, for example, how long a patient spends in radiology for an MRI. Patient tracking software can also focus on a specific patient population, such as all patients who have visited the ED.

Another type of patient tracking software tracks the physical location of a patient in a hospital using **radio frequency identification (RFID)** technology. This patient tracking software and devices are commonly used in the nursery to prevent kidnapping. Devices are attached on the ankle of a newborn baby until the baby is discharged. The system initiates an alarm that alerts personnel when a baby's anklet is cut or the baby leaves the unit. Also, adult patients wear wristbands with RFID technology to track their locations, as shown in Figure 6-15.

> **radio frequency identification (RFID)**—A technology that uses radio frequency to track or locate a transponder, or tag.

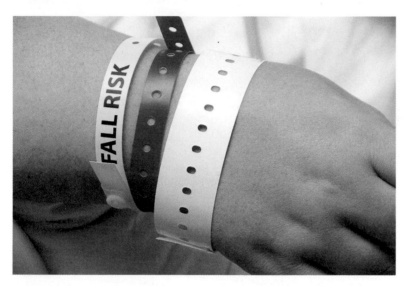

Figure 6-15   RFID wristbands are worn by patients to track their locations.

Photo credit: Rob Byron

Order Entry Software

Order entry (OE) software facilitates the creation, duplication, and safety of orders given by healthcare providers. A single facility produces thousands of orders daily for lab tests, procedures, medication, and nutrition services. Using an order entry system eliminates the cumbersome paper system and provides faster, safer, and higher quality healthcare. Most OE information systems alert users of conflicts while entering orders. For example, the user will be alerted if the order being entered is a duplicate or if a patient is allergic to a medication, and the user will be reminded when an order needs to be completed. OE information systems also provide a historical summary of the orders a patient has received to better provide information to healthcare providers for proper treatment of a patient's condition.

A physician can use **e-prescribing software** to electronically write a prescription for a patient. The prescriptions can go to the hospital's pharmacy or to a pharmacy outside the hospital. An e-prescribing IS uses the **national drug code identifier (NDCID)** to identify the drug being prescribed.

> **e-prescribing software**—Software used by physicians to electronically write prescriptions for patients.
>
> **national drug code identifier (NDCID)**—A code assigned to each drug used by the FDA to maintain a list of drugs being produced.

An e-prescribing IS offers these benefits:

- Eliminates paper and decreases chances for error. An e-prescribing IS immediately sends the prescription to the pharmacy of the patient's choice, which ensures no errors due to interpretation of handwriting.

- Verifies that the patient is not allergic to the medication by checking against the patient's allergies indicated in the patient's EHR/EMR.

- Verifies that the medication does not have an adverse drug interaction with a medication the patient is currently taking as indicated in the patient's EHR/EMR.

- When a patient's registration changes, the medication reconciliation checks on the medications a patient is prescribed to make sure the patient does not have duplicate prescriptions or a prescription with an allergy or adverse interaction with another prescription.

As explained in Chapter 2, "Introducing Data Flow in HIT," bedside medication verification ensures that the correct patient is receiving the correct medicine.

Practice Management Software

Practice management software is an all-encompassing software solution to manage both clinical and business needs in a small- to medium-sized medical office, such as a physician's practice or an outpatient medical office. The software handles day-to-day activities, anywhere from charting on patients, scheduling, or billing. Often, practice management software is interfaced with the EHR/EMR solution or connected to a hospital's network to share patient data.

> **practice management software**—Software used in small- to medium-sized medical offices for both clinical and business needs.

Billing and Coding Software

Billing and coding software is commonly included with practice management software or comes as independent software used in larger facilities. A healthcare provider fills out a **superbill**, paper or electronic, indicating the services rendered to a patient for billing, as shown in Figure 6-16. The coding module receives information from the HIS about procedures, patient care, and other billable items from a patient's EHR or EMR. The coding module translates the billable items into standardized numeric codes. Two coding systems are used. The first coding system is an international classification of diseases, version 10 (ICD-10). ICD-10 codes describe diagnosis or classification of diseases or illnesses. The second coding system is **current procedural terminology (CPT)**. CPT describes the procedure or treatments offered by healthcare providers. Hospitals need to bill for more than just the supplies and procedures, but also bill for the time and effort of healthcare providers' work. **Evaluation and management (E/M) codes** are a subcategory of CPT codes that describe the level of care provided to a patient. In simple terms, ICD-10 codes justify billing the CPT codes. Figure 6-17 shows the diagnosis and CPT codes being entered for a patient who has received an H1N1 vaccine.

> **billing and coding software**—Software that receives data from a patient's EHR/EMR, converts the data into billable items, and submits the bill to the insurance company for reimbursement.
>
> **superbill**—An itemized form used by healthcare providers to indicate services rendered. The superbill is the primary source for creating a claim to be submitted to the payer.
>
> **current procedural terminology (CPT)**—Coding system maintained by the American Medical Association (AMA) to represent procedures or treatments offered by healthcare providers.
>
> **evaluation and management (E/M) codes**—Subcategory of CPT codes that are used to describe the level of care provided to a patient.

Figure 6-16   A healthcare provider fills out a superbill to indicate the services rendered to a patient for billing.

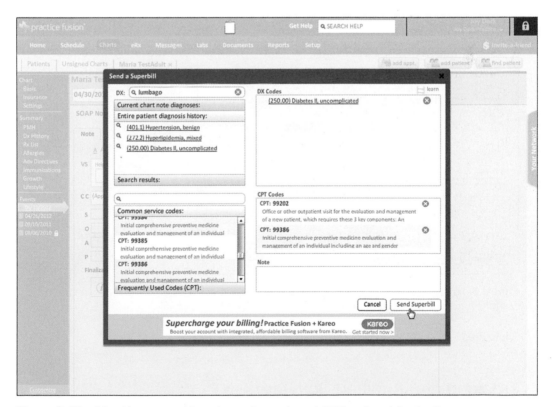

Figure 6-17   A healthcare provider selects diagnosis and CPT codes while charting on a patient who received an H1N1 vaccine.

http://www.practicefusion.com

The billing module collects the CPT codes and gives the codes a monetary value. The claim is sent to insurance companies, government agencies, or patients for reimbursement (see Figure 6-18). Although coding and billing software are advanced and capable, human verification is still needed. Considering how picky insurance companies are about having the right codes, coding and billing require personnel to verify codes and claims before submitting the bills to the insurance companies. This process can be outsourced to a healthcare clearinghouse.

Figure 6-18 This bill has the CPT codes used to request reimbursement from an insurance company, government agency, or patient.

Photo credit: qingwa

Tracking and Auditing Software

Every patient has the right by law to request to see who has accessed their health records. All software that contains e-PHI must have a tracking or auditing system (see Figure 6-19) to report who has viewed a patient's information.

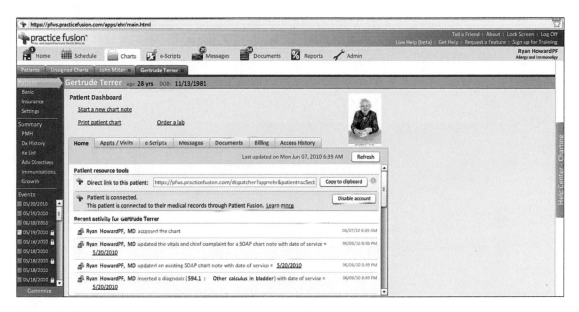

Figure 6-19   Healthcare information systems must audit who has accessed a patient's record.

http://www.practicefusion.com

Document Imaging

Digital images are used in healthcare for two primary purposes:

- For medical images of the human body
- To create a fully digital EHR/EMR from paper patient records

Medical Images of the Human Body

The medical images of the human body can be saved in a digital format (see Figure 6-20). Usually these images are stored as either **digital imaging and communication in medicine (DICOM)** or, when animated, **graphics interchange format (GIF)**. DICOM is the standard in the medical field for saving digital images. DICOM was designed specifically for medical imaging. An example of this specific design for the medical field is the files that contain markers that relate the image to the patient so that the image cannot be separated from the patient. The types of imaging supported include CT, MRI, ultrasound, PET, and X-rays. Software used to create DICOM files usually comes with the imaging machine. Sometimes it is easier to get a visual on an image when the slices of an image are merged into animation, such as combining the images of a CT scan into a small movie. These types of files are saved in GIF.

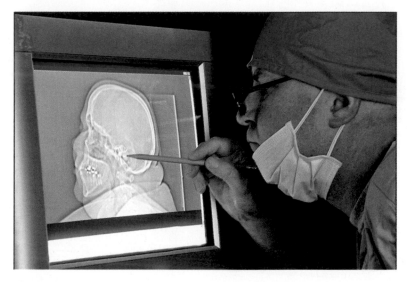

Figure 6-20   A medical image can be saved as a digital image.

Photo credit: Konstantin Sutyagin

> **digital imaging and communication in medicine (DICOM)**—The healthcare industry standard for medical digital imaging. DICOM is designed specifically for image handling, storing, printing, or transmitting. The file extension for this format is .dcm.
>
> **graphics interchange format (GIF)**—An image file format that supports data compression and animation. GIF supports only 256 colors, so some quality is lost on colored images. The file extension for this format is .gif.

After a medical image has been created, it is sent to the **picture archiving and communication system (PACS)**. PACS centralizes all the different types of medical images into one IS. PACS is designed to store and retrieve medical images, as well as communicate medical images with other information systems, such as the EHR/EMR IS. Having all the different types of medical images in a central IS means that radiologists can read digital studies on one computer that has PACS installed, by simply searching for the patient and not each image.

> **picture archiving and communication system (PACS)**—An information system designed to store and retrieve different formats of medical imaging in one location, as well as communicate PACS images to other information systems.

Digital Images of Patient Records

Digital images are used in healthcare to create a fully digital EHR/EMR from paper patient records. Usually, these documents are stored as either **tagged image file format (TIFF) or portable document format (PDF)**. TIFF and PDF are desired formats because they support storing multiple pages in a single file. Other image formats are permissible, such as **joint photographic experts group (JPEG)** but are not as widely used because these are compressed and lose quality.

> **tagged image file format (TIFF)**—A widely supported image file format. TIFF images can be any resolution, color, or grayscale. The file extension for this format is .tif or .tiff.
>
> **portable document format (PDF)**—A widely used file format developed by Adobe Systems used to present digital documents in a printable view on a monitor. PDF files can be viewed using Adobe Acrobat software or many other PDF viewers or editors made by many software companies. The file extension for this format is .pdf.
>
> **joint photographic experts group (JPEG)**—An image file format that supports data compression. JPEG supports up to 16 million colors, but when compressed, the image loses clarity and sharpness. JPEG is generally used on the Internet. The file extension for this format is .jpg.

> **EXAM TIP** For the Healthcare IT exam, you need to be familiar with different file types and when they each might be used.

EHR/EMR vendors have their own specifications for images. These requirements are in place to make sure the images are legible. For example, one major imaging company requires images to be in either TIFF or PDF format, preferably TIFF. This company also requires the resolution to be at least 300 dpi in black and white, unless at a lesser resolution the document is still legible. The company also has file-naming conventions to ensure the file is stored with the correct patient record.

When a document needs to be digitized, personnel use a scanner to create a digital image of the document in a digital file format, such as TIFF or PDF. The image is read by an application, called an **optical character recognition (OCR)** program, which scans the image and translates the text from the image into pure text that is searchable. When the words are in pure text, **systemized nomenclature of medicine – clinical terms (SNOMED-CT)** interprets the medical descriptions into standardized medical terminology. When the digital image is created, metadata is added to the file. The **metadata** acts like tags containing keywords, such as a patient's MRN, to make searching for a specific file faster and easier. The data captured from the document is indexed for searching and retrieving the document or its contents at a later time. Key words and phrases are targeted for indexing to make searching for a specific record easy, such as the patient name, SSN, or MRN.

---

optical character recognition (OCR)—A technology that translates printed lettering into pure text that can be searched and manipulated on a computer.

systemized nomenclature of medicine—clinical terms (SNOMED-CT)—A medical terminology standard used internationally to create consistency in keywords in medical documentation. SNOMED-CT technology translates several ways to describe the same medical term into a single code.

metadata—Data about data. In imaging, metadata tags files with keywords to easily search for the file.

Types of documents to be scanned are classified into three categories:

- *Structured documentation* is a form that has fields for specific information in the same location on every document scanned, such as an insurance information form.

- *Semi-structured documentation* has some portions of the form constant, but other items can vary, such as a list of billable items on an invoice to an insurance company.

- *Unstructured documentation* has no constant fields, and appearance is flexible.

Change Control

While supporting software of any kind, the **change management** process plays a key role when an IS requires a systemwide change. The change management process is designed to prevent as many failures as possible during and after a change. To start a change, an HIT technician documents a plan for implementing the change. The contents of the change management documentation are discussed in Chapter 5, "IT Operations." When deciding to suggest what day and time a change should happen, consider all users that will be affected. If the change requires a computer or system to be down or offline, called downtime, choosing off hours might be best to decrease the number of healthcare providers who will be affected. Also consider if support needs to be available in case of a failure during the change. If it is a major change and needs to happen after hours, it might be necessary for support personnel to work during the change to monitor the progress and check for failures.

> **change management**—A process to define a change needed, the steps to take to complete it, the results of the change, and the time frame for completion. Also called change control.

The change management documentation is submitted to a **change advisory board (CAB)**, also called a **governance board**, for approval. After the CAB approves the change, the hard work begins. Four environments or versions of each IS are used to assist with the change:

- **Development**: The environment using test or fake data used by engineers to create the change

- **QA/Test**: The environment used by HIT technicians and analysts using test or fake data to verify the developed change is functioning and meets the needs of the change request. (QA stands for quality assurance.)

- **User Test**: The environment used by healthcare providers using real data, usually approximately 10% of the live environment to double-check for failures in the change.

- **Production/Live**: The environment used by healthcare providers daily using real data.

> **change advisory board (CAB)**—The board within an IT company that decides if a change management request is a benefit to the company or a liability. Also called a governance board.
>
> **governance board**—See change advisory board (CAB).

> **EXAM TIP**   For the Healthcare IT exam, you need to be familiar with the change control process and the four environments involved.

The first three environments separate the change process from the live systems and are necessary to make sure that while a change is developed and tested, the live IS environments are not affected. The change moves from the first environment all the way through to the last, where the users finally experience the change. After the change is implemented in the live environment, and any issues are resolved, the change is documented fully for every step in the change control management system.

Support Requests

Each facility will have different protocols for support escalation. The best idea is to start low and escalate higher or broader as necessary. For example, if an HIT technician receives a support call saying the medical record images are corrupted, he starts trying to determine the cause of the issue. He checks for issues he can resolve on his own, such as a bad cable. If the HIT technician cannot resolve the issue but knows the issue is a problem with the interface corrupting the image, the support call should be assigned to an interface analyst.

However, sometimes the service-level agreement (SLA) established with a vendor states that all support will go directly to the vendor. Some vendors support only the software; others support both software and hardware. HIT technicians need to be familiar with the SLAs with each of the vendors to ensure that support calls are escalated to the correct team and as quickly as possible.

To understand where the failure is that is causing the problem the user is experiencing, you must listen for clues from the user and ask the user questions that can lead to the root of the problem. For example, a user might call saying he cannot see the final results from lab tests on a patient. This is a vague description of the problem, and you should ask the user more questions to pinpoint what exactly the problem is. The user might actually mean that there is simply no reference range with the result to indicate what a normal range for a result is. Figure 6-21 shows what an example of a lab result might look like.

Figure 6-21   An example of lab results for a patient in an EHR IS.

http://www.practicefusion.com

The main concept to offering support is to own the issue. Take ownership of an issue no matter what the issue is, how it was caused, or who is responsible for fixing it. When an HIT technician is aware of an issue, it is his responsibility to follow it through to resolution. Remember that when a healthcare provider experiences an issue with an IS, patient care is affected. It is your responsibility as HIT personnel to make sure that all issues are resolved in a timely manner.

How a Healthcare Interface Works

Objectives element:

4.1   Identify commonly used medical terms and devices.

Interfaces: HL7, CCD, CCR

4.3   Identify and label different components of medical interfaces.

HL7: Standard contents, Provider types, AL1, BLG, IN1, MSH, OBR, PID, SCH

e-prescribing: Medication reconciliation, Bedside medication verification, Allergy interactions, Formulary checking

Billing: EMR/EHR outbound communication, Types of codes, Clearinghouse

4.4   Determine common interface problems and escalate when necessary.

HL7: Threads/nodes deactivated, Improperly formatted patient demographics, Communication link (fax, network, Internet)

e-prescribing: Improperly formatted patient demographics, Improperly formatted script, Deactivated medication, Controlled substance, Communication link (fax, network, Internet)

Medical devices: Power, Network, I/O, Configuration settings

Billing: Improperly formatted patient demographics, Improperly formatted superbill, Communication link (fax, network, Internet), I/O, Software configuration settings

Recall from Chapter 2 that interfaces are used for communication between information systems. Healthcare interfaces must have a common form of communication for all possible vendors, information systems, or applications to share data accurately and efficiently. If there weren't a standard and common form of communication between two different information systems, data could become corrupted and information could be misrepresented about a patient. Health Level Seven International (HL7) is the communication standard accepted and used by healthcare entities today.

A **continuity of care document (CCD)** can be created by an HIS using HL7 formatting to provide an easily transferred snapshot of a patient's record. This information can be easily read by a person or by an IS. A CCD is commonly used to send relevant information about a patient from one healthcare provider to another, for example when a patient is referred to a specialist. A **continuity of care record (CCR)** is a collection of CCDs, spanning multiple patient visits, sometimes called patient encounters. Many CCDs can make up a CCR.

> **continuity of care document (CCD)**—A version of a patient's record for transferring relevant data. A CCD is easily read by both a person or an IS.
>
> **continuity of care record (CCR)**—A collection of CCDs.

HL7 Message

An interface moves information through the network in messages. The medical community uses HL7 formatted messages to ensure that all medical devices and platforms can communicate without corrupting data. HL7 messages might communicate patient demographics, insurance information, orders, results, or changes in registration status between information systems.

Every message contains segments that contain fields. HL7 is highly customizable. The interface engine can receive a message from a sending IS and manipulate the data and the field assignments to accommodate what the destination IS expects to receive in each field. Some information systems have the capability to customize the HL7 content. However, because not all information systems on a network have this capability, usually the manipulation of the message is left to the interface engine.

Remember from Chapter 2 that the interface engine can monitor the incoming and outgoing **thread** connection status on the interface engine with the display on the dashboard. The interface engine touches only the interface on one side of the connection; therefore, it cannot monitor the thread connection status on the application side of the interface (see Figure 6-22).

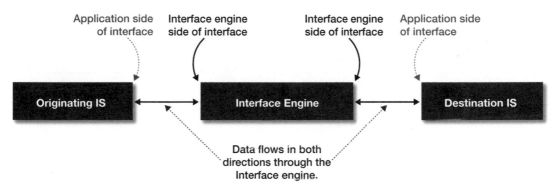

thread—The interface pipeline that connects two information systems.

Application side of interface

Interface engine side of interface

Interface engine side of interface

Application side of interface

Originating IS

Interface Engine

Destination IS

Data flows in both directions through the Interface engine.

Figure 6-22   The interface thread connection status is monitored on the interface engine side and not on the application side.

An HL7 segment begins with an abbreviation indicating the type of information contained in the segment. For example, MSH stands for the message header, which contains information about the message type and date/time stamp. The message shown in Figure 6-23 has been parsed so that the segments are more easily identified. Each of the segment abbreviations are in red. The vertical bar | separates each field. Two vertical bars together indicate the field is present but contains no data. The caret symbol ^ indicates a subfield.

```
MSH|^~\&|PATACCT|999|MCKESSON|999|20120320115714||ADT^A03|3163|P|2.3|3
163||||US|
EVN|A03|20120320115400|||GDC|
PID|1||2||MOUSE^MICKEY|||17620824|M||W|2525 OAK STREET^^DES
MOINES^IA^50302|153||||D|C|2000008|||||CO|||||
PD1||||||||Y||||N|N^N|
PV1|1|O|RAD|3|||107^DUCK^DAFFY^L|||RAD||||1||N|107^DUCK^DAFFY^L|E||H||
||||||||||||||01^DC TO HOME OR SELF CARE (RO
DISCHA)|||||||||20120320115400|20120320115400||||||
DG1|1|I9||HEADACHES|||||||||||||||
GT1|1|2|JAMES^TEST|||324 6TH AVE^^CEDAR
RAPIDS^IA^52402|||||M||||||1||||||||||||||||||||||||||||||||||||||||||||||||
IN1|1|2|411|AETNA|REG TO ENTER^^REG TO
ENTER^OK^00000||||||||||C|JAMES|G8^OTHER
RELATIONSHIP|||Y|CO|1|||||Y||||||||||||||||1|M|SAME^^^^|Y||3|||
```

Figure 6-23   This HL7 message is parsed to easily view segments and fields.

Table 6-5 lists some common segments abbreviations given with a description.

Table 6-5   Some HL7 Segments and Their Abbreviations

Segment	Description
AL1	Allergy information
BLG	Billing information
DG1	Diagnosis information
EVN	Event type
IN1	Insurance information
MSH	Message header, contains the type of HL7 message
OBR	Order information, contains observation request
OBX	Order information, contains observation result
PID	Patient identification
SCH	Schedule activity or appointments

In some of the segments, healthcare providers might be referenced, including the type of provider. Healthcare providers specified in an HL7 message might include the following types of providers:

- Referring physician
- Attending physician
- Admitting physician
- Consulting physician
- Primary care provider

Typical Interface Issues

Interfaces are detailed and are occasionally manipulated in the interface engine. It is not uncommon to have a mistake because of all the intervention in the interface. The following list describes a few common errors that are quickly and easily resolved:

- The interface might have a thread deactivated on either the application side or the interface engine side of the connection. Deactivated threads do not allow data to pass. The interface engine dashboard displays the monitoring of the threads that have lost connection to be proactive about this issue.

- A **node** has not been activated with the IS to which it is trying to connect. For example, the IS might require a node for a workstation to be activated or registered with the IS as an authorized access point to send or receive information from the IS.

> **node**—A connection point to an IS.

- If patient demographics are not properly formatted, the message might fail; for example, if letters are entered into the field (that accepts only numbers) for a phone number, or if a number is entered into the first name field that accepts only letters. Another example is if the message uses the wrong symbol to separate fields, such as using a colon instead of a vertical bar.

- If the network fails, so will the interface connection. The most common mistake with a fax connection is dialing the wrong number or the queue that receives faxes runs out of memory.

- In e-prescribing, if a prescription is improperly formatted or does not contain all necessary information entered by the physician, such as number of refills or quantity, an error occurs.

- In e-prescribing, if a medication is no longer available an error occurs. A medication will no longer be available if the FDA removes approval of a drug or if the drug lot in the inventory expires.

- In e-prescribing, when prescribing a controlled substance, the proper authorization for the prescription must be included.

- If a device or machine connected to the interface loses power, the interface will fail. For example, if a lab analyzer goes offline, the HIS will not receive the results from the lab tests performed by that analyzer. When a device or machine is offline, the end of the thread on the interface engine might appear to still be connected. For threads that are not frequently used, the interface engine will wait for extended periods of time for the device to send data, expecting the application side of the interface to open at any moment.

- In billing, if the superbill has improperly formatted data entered by the healthcare provider, an error will occur.

> **EXAM TIP**   For the Healthcare IT exam, you need to identify which segment might contain a problem in an example HL7 message.

When these errors occur, deciding where the breakdown is happening can be difficult. You must view the HL7 message that leaves the originating application, the arriving message at the interface engine, the leaving message from the interface engine, and the message arriving at the destination application. Figure 6-24 illustrates that the interface can break down at any point of connection to an application or the interface engine. Check the messages sent or received at each of these connection points to make sure the message has not been corrupted. When you view all those messages, compare them to each other to find out where the message changes. When comparing the messages, remember that the interface engine can manipulate the data so that not all segments in the outgoing message look exactly the same as the incoming message because some information might be dropped or moved. The HIT technician must know the requirements of each IS that sends and receives HL7 messages to make sure the messages conform to the requirements of the sending IS and receiving IS to prevent corrupting data. The application analyst can make changes to the outgoing HL7 message content.

Figure 6-24   There are several points where a message can be checked on an interface to find out where the interface is broken.

HIT in the Real World

The following incident is a story from one of my former co-workers. She was one of the interface analysts for the clinical information systems at all the hospitals we supported.

While working at a healthcare company in Tennessee, there was a change made to the live environment for one of our facilities in Alabama that was not recorded through the change control process. A change was made to an application script that converted a lab report. The change stripped out a large portion of the lab report to condense the file size and submit only a certain portion of the lab result. The change made to the script accidentally caused the size of the file to grow to such a large size that the application crashed.

When this issue was reported, the normal troubleshooting process was followed without any success. After five hours of troubleshooting the issue, she began to review the file that runs application scripts and could only reason that the problem was with one of the scripts. Because the master file called more than 200 scripts, she was forced to rewrite the master file adding back one script at a time and adding only the scripts that were essential for operation. At the end of the day, it took 10 hours to build a new master file and test 20 scripts of the 200-plus scripts, and there were still more scripts to test. The next two weeks were spent verifying the additional scripts and the purpose of each one. At the end of the two weeks, she discovered the change that caused the issue and tracked down the person who changed the original script for the lab report.

This issue could have been solved within one hour if the proper process had been followed. One of the first steps to troubleshooting is checking for any changes made recently to the affected system. If the employee who made the change would have entered a change control record for the script alteration, my former co-worker would have started her troubleshooting efforts there and quickly have seen that the script had changed the way it processed lab reports. Instead, several resources spent two weeks rewriting a master file and testing more than 200 scripts while searching for a root cause of the issue.

Chapter Summary

Understanding the Clinical Environment

- The EMR is the collection of patient information from all visits at one hospital. The EHR is the collection of patient information from all hospitals the patient has visited.

- A primary care physician (PCP) is a doctor who has an ongoing relationship with a patient and provides primary care for that patient.

- A controlled substance is a drug or substance that is regulated by the government.

- Patient acuity describes the level of care that a patient requires.

- Hospitals have a hospital incident command system (HICS) to establish procedures for emergency situations. Usually a code blue means immediate care is needed for a patient that is in critical condition. When a patient is almost to the point of a code blue, a nurse or other medical personnel can issue a rapid response to call only a part of the code blue team.

- A blood pressure cuff, or vitals cuff, is a device used to measure blood pressure.

- A portable X-ray machine is a mobile X-ray machine that is small enough to be rolled to a patient's room.

- An ultrasound is an image taken of soft tissue using high-frequency sound waves and echoes.

- A computed tomography (CT) is imaging that uses X-rays along with computing algorithms.

- Magnetic resonance imaging (MRI) is imaging that uses strong magnetic fields and radio signals to create an image of a patient's body.

- A positron emission tomography (PET) is imaging that creates an image of the body or function of an organ using a CT scan with a radioactive tracer.

- A glucose monitor measures blood glucose levels.

- An electroencephalogram (EEG) measures the frequency of brain waves.

- An electrocardiogram (EKG or ECG) tests for problems with the electrical activity of the heart.

- A vascular stress test determines the capability of veins to return blood from the lower limbs to the heart.

- A nuclear stress test is used to diagnose and treat some heart disorders. The test combines two PET scans before and after a vascular stress test.

- Common inpatient departments include OB/GYN, oncology, pediatrics, labor and delivery/NICU, ICU, transitional care unit, medical/surgical nursing unit, behavior health, post anesthesia care unit, operating room, and the Emergency Department.

- Common outpatient departments include OB/GYN, Oncology, Pediatrics, Plastic Surgery, Ear/Nose/Throat, Respiratory, Physical Therapy, Cardiovascular, Occupational Therapy, Day Surgery, Radiology, Laboratory, Ophthalmology, Dermatology, and Nuclear.

- A doctor or nurse examines a patient to determine the cause of symptoms the patient is experiencing. The doctor may consult another doctor for a second opinion or refer the patient to a specialist.

- A doctor uses a computerized physician order entry (CPOE) to enter orders for a patient. When a doctor is ready to enter notes about a patient into the patient's record, she may dictate the notes, which are transcribed into text. The doctor then digitally signs the patient's record confirming the notes are accurate.

Supporting Software Used in Healthcare Facilities

- Scheduling software is used in several different departments of a hospital to schedule services offered.

- Patient tracking software is used to follow and record patient flow through a patient's changing medical status, lab studies, imaging, or other diagnostic and treatment services. Or patient tracking software tracks the physical location of a patient in a hospital using radio frequency identification (RFID) technology.

- Order entry (OE) software facilitates the creation, duplication, and safety of orders given by healthcare providers.

- A physician can use e-prescribing software to electronically write a prescription for a patient.

- Practice management software is an all-encompassing software solution to manage both clinical and business needs in a small- to medium-sized medical office, such as a physician's practice or an outpatient medical office.

- Billing and coding software receives data from a patient's EHR or EMR, converts the data into billable items, and submits the bill to the insurance company for reimbursement.

- ICD-10 codes describe diagnosis or classification of diseases or illnesses. Current procedural terminology (CPT) describes the procedure or treatments offered by healthcare providers. Evaluation and management (E/M) codes are a subcategory of CPT codes, which describe the level of care provided to a patient. ICD-10 codes justify billing the CPT codes.

- All software that contains e-PHI must have a tracking or auditing system to report who has viewed a patient's information.

- Digital imaging and communication in medicine (DICOM) is the standard in the medical field for saving digital images.

- Sometimes it is easier to save an image as a GIF to get a visual on an image when the slices of an image are merged into animation, such as combining the images of a CT scan into a small movie.

- Picture archiving and communication system (PACS) centralizes all the different types of medical images into one information system, stores and retrieves medical images, and communicates medical images with other information systems.

- Tagged image file format (TIFF) and portable document format (PDF) are used in healthcare to create a fully digital EHR/EMR from paper patient records.

- An optical character recognition (OCR) program scans an image and translates the text from the image into pure text that is searchable.

- Systemized nomenclature of medicine—clinical terms (SNOMED-CT) interprets the medical descriptions into standardized medical terminology.

- The metadata is data about the data that acts like tags containing keywords, such as a patient's MRN, to make searching for a specific file faster and easier.

- Scanned documents are classified as structured, semi-structured, or unstructured documents based on how consistent the scanned images are.

- Change management, also called change control, is a process to define a change needed, the steps to take to complete it, the results of the change, and the timeframe for completion. The change advisory board (CAB), or governance board, is responsible for approving pending change management requests.

- Four IS environments used during the change management process are development, QA/test, user test, and production/live.

- When a support call needs to be escalated, the best idea is to start low and escalate higher or broader as necessary. However, sometimes the SLA established with a vendor states that all support will go directly to the vendor.

- To understand where the failure is that is causing the problem the user is experiencing, you need to listen for clues from the user and ask the user questions that will lead to the root of the problem.

- The main concept to offering support is to own the issue by taking ownership of an issue no matter what the issue is, how it was caused, or who is responsible for fixing it, and to follow it through to resolution.

How a Healthcare Interface Works

- A continuity of care document (CCD) provides an easily transferred snapshot of a patient's record, which can be easily read by a person or by an IS. A continuity of care record (CCR) is a collection of CCDs, spanning multiple patient visits, sometimes called patient encounters.

- The medical community uses HL7 formatted messages that might communicate patient demographics, insurance information, orders, results, or changes in registration status between information systems through an interface.

- An HL7 segment begins with an abbreviation indicating the type of information contained in the segment. Common segments include the following:
    - AL1—allergy information
    - BLG—billing information
    - DG1—diagnosis information
    - EVN—event type
    - IN1—insurance information
    - MSH—message header
    - OBR—order information/requests
    - OBX—order information/results
    - PID—patient information
    - SCH—schedule activity or appointments

- Provider types include referring physician, attending physician, admitting physician, consulting physician, or primary care provider.

- A thread is the interface pipeline that connects two information systems. A node is a connection point to an IS.

Key Terms

- billing and coding software
- blood pressure cuff
- change advisory board (CAB)
- change management
- code blue
- consultation
- continuity of care document (CCD)
- continuity of care record (CCR)
- controlled substance
- current procedural terminology (CPT)
- digital imaging and communication in medicine (DICOM)
- electrocardiogram (EKG or ECG)
- electroencephalogram (EEG)
- evaluation and management (E/M) codes
- examination
- glucose monitor
- governance board
- graphics interchange format (GIF)
- e-prescribing software
- joint photographic experts group (JPEG)
- metadata
- national drug code identifier (NDCID)
- node
- nuclear stress test
- optical character recognition (OCR)
- picture archiving and communication system (PACS)
- portable document format (PDF)
- portable X-ray machine
- practice management software
- primary care physician (PCP)
- radio frequency identification (RFID)

- rapid response
- referral
- scheduling software
- superbill
- systemized nomenclature of medicine—clinical terms (SNOMED-CT)
- tagged image file format (TIFF)
- thread
- ultrasound
- vascular stress test
- vitals cuff

Acronym Drill

Acronyms sometimes get confusing, especially when a single sentence can have four or five. As an HIT professional, you need to know the acronyms and what they stand for. Fill in the blank with the correct acronym for the sentence.

1. The _____ is usually the first physician a patient sees when he experiences a new illness or medical condition and for regular checkups.

   Answer: _____

2. A _____ is imaging that creates an image of the body or function of an organ using a _____ scan with a radioactive tracer.

   Answer: _____

3. An _____ or _____ tests for problems with the electrical activity of the heart.

   Answer: _____

4. The _____ cares for preterm babies.

   Answer: _____

5. The _____ provides general care for adult patients in a hospital.

   Answer: _____

6. The _____ cares for patients leaving the OR as the anesthesia wears off.

   Answer: _____

7. The _____ is a code assigned to each drug used by the FDA to maintain a list of drugs being produced.

   Answer: _____

8. _____ codes justify billing the _____ codes.

   Answer: _____

9. _____ technology translates several ways to describe the same medical term into a single code.

   Answer: _____

10. Every _____ message contains an _____ segment that contains information about the message type and date/time stamp.

    Answer: _____

Review Questions

1. What is the difference between an EMR and an EHR?

   Answer: _____

   _____

2. What does a healthcare provider mean when he orders a medication to be given "stat?"

   Answer: _____

3. Which level trauma center is most equipped to care for a trauma patient because the facility has a full range of specialists and equipment available at all times?

   Answer: _____

4. Why might a physician order a CT scan over an X-ray for a patient?

   Answer: _____

   _____

5. Why must all employees, including HIT personnel, be careful when entering a room with an MRI machine present?

   Answer: _____

   _____

   _____

   _____

   _____

6. What is the difference between obstetrics and gynecology (OB/GYN)?

   Answer: _____

7. Which inpatient department cares for adolescents?

   Answer: _____

8. What service does occupational therapy (OT) offer?

   Answer: _____

9. What is the purpose of nuclear medicine?

   Answer: _____

10. What type of information might a patient give during registration?

    Answer: _____

    _____

    _____

11. How might computerized physician order entry (CPOE) be different from the order entry IS that nurses use?

    Answer: _____

12. How is scheduling software specifically designed for healthcare use?

    Answer: _____

    _____

13. What are two types of patient tracking software?

Answer: _____

_____

_____

_____

_____

14. Explain the difference between ICD-10 codes and CPT codes.

Answer: _____

_____

_____

_____

_____

15. What services does a healthcare clearinghouse offer?

Answer: _____

_____

_____

16. What is the standard file format in the medical field for saving digital medical images?

Answer: _____

17. What is the technology that translates printed lettering from a scanned image into pure text that can be searched and manipulated on a computer?

Answer: _____

18. Why is it important to consider the time of day to implement a change when creating change management documentation to be submitted to a CAB for approval?

Answer: _____

_____

_____

_____

_____

_____

19. What is the difference between a continuity of care document and a continuity of care record?

    Answer: _____

    _____

    _____

20. What symbol in an HL7 segment separates fields? What does it mean when two symbols are side by side with nothing in between them?

    Answer: _____

    _____

Practical Application

1. Place the change management process steps in the correct order.

    ___ The completed change is documented.

    ___ The change is developed in the development environment.

    ___ Change management documentation is submitted to a CAB.

    ___ Change management documentation is created.

    ___ The CAB approves the change request.

    ___ Users test the change.

    ___ A change is requested for an IS.

    ___ The change is implemented in the live environment.

    ___ The change is tested for quality assurance in the QA/Test environment.

2. Identify these five machines and give a brief description of their purposes.

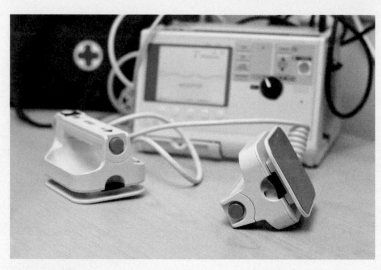

Figure 6-25a
Photo credit: Renewer

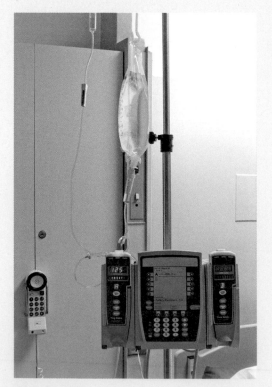

Figure 6-25b
Photo credit: Rob Byron

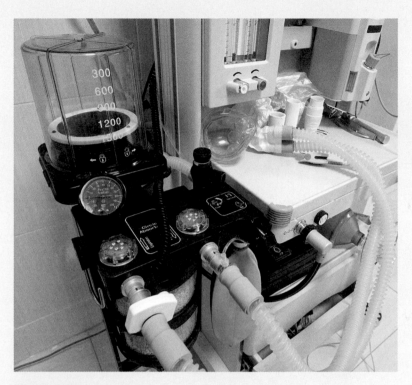

Figure 6-25c

Photo credit: Paul Vinten

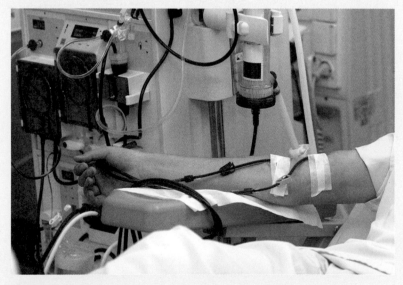

Figure 6-25d

Photo credit: picsfive

Figure 6-25e

Photo credit: lculig

a. _____

_____

b. _____

_____

c. _____

_____

d. _____

_____

e. _____

_____

3. Practice Fusion is a free EHR IS available through cloud computing. Students are able to create free accounts and explore using an EHR IS with test patients already set up. Go to http://www.practicefusion.com. Then go to the Sign Up webpage and create an account using "x Academic (I am a student)" as your Specialty. Find the Practice Fusions Features webpage and watch training videos about how to use the EHR IS. Practice doing what the training videos demonstrate when possible. Write down your Practice ID, username, and password.

Answer: _____

CHAPTER 7
Security

In this chapter you learn about:

- **What we are up against**
- **Permission levels**
- **Physical security**
- **Best practices for handling passwords**
- **Different encryption types**
- **How to secure a wireless network**
- **How to remotely access a secured network**
- **Securing backups**
- **How to dispose of protected health information (PHI)**

Security is a natural aspect of working in an industry surrounded by sensitive information. This is probably why security has been mentioned so many times in earlier chapters. As you learned in Chapter 3, "Regulatory Requirements," the law requires all covered entities to ensure security is maintained in all environments in which patient health information (PHI) or other sensitive information is used or stored. Compromised PHI might be used for identity theft, theft of narcotics, or plain ol' gossip. No matter if PHI is stolen or lost, it is a Health Insurance Portability and Accountability Act (HIPAA) violation with repercussions. It is our job as HIT technicians to not only establish and maintain technical safeguards, but to also educate users about social avenues of attack and how to protect PHI against these attacks.

This chapter begins with coverage of how secured data might be breached.

What Are We Up Against?

HI001 Objectives:

5.9 Identify common security risks and their prevention methods.

Social engineering—User training

Phishing—User training

Spamming—Filters

Malware—Access control

Spyware—Antispyware

People with malicious intentions have many avenues for attacking networks containing sensitive information. Software blocks many attacks, but sometimes user training is required to prevent a breach of confidentiality. The following sections review five common security risks and how to prevent them.

Social Engineering

Social engineering is a malicious attack directed at a person who has access to sensitive data, such as PHI. The attacker uses social skills to trick or manipulate a person who is authorized to access sensitive data. The attacker pretends to be an authorized identity. For example, the attacker might present himself as a new employee or repairman. Not all attacks come from outside the organization, though. Employees must also beware of other employees trying to access information for which they are not authorized.

> **social engineering**—A malicious attack using social skills directed at a person who has access to sensitive data.

> **EXAM TIP** For the Healthcare IT exam, you need to be familiar with different kinds of security threats and how they might enter a facility's network.

Phishing (pronounced "fishing") is a form of social engineering. The user is tricked or manipulated to give out sensitive data or into allowing unauthorized programs onto the computer or network. Phishing attacks come in many forms. A phishing attack might be an e-mail that appears to be official and is asking for information that can be used to hack into the network. Other phishing attacks might lure a user to open an attachment in an e-mail with malicious software or to download a cute screensaver that has malicious software attached.

> **phishing**—A form of social engineering in which an attacker tricks or manipulates a user to give out sensitive data or into allowing unauthorized programs onto the computer or network.

The only method to prevent social engineering is to educate employees about how attacks might present themselves and how to avoid them. Employees need to know what information is secured and should not be shared without verifying proper authorization. Employees should also understand the necessity to not freely surf the web while using a computer connected to the facility's network and visit only familiar websites necessary for work purposes. Using the firewall to block users from accessing unapproved websites while on the network is a good method to avoid unauthorized Internet use, as well as wasted time during work hours.

Electronic Attacks

Spam is unsolicited contact from an attacker. Spamming causes unnecessary network or Internet traffic, which can slow down the network for legitimate uses. Spam is usually an e-mail, but it can also come in other forms. For example, spam can come through a fax or text message. Spam is a waste of resources and just gets in the way.

> **spam**—Unsolicited contact that you did not ask for and don't want and might come from an attacker.

You can use a few methods to prevent spam mail from swamping a user's email inbox, including the following:

- Apply filters that either block or allow e-mail to pass through the e-mail server based on set criteria.
- Educate users to not freely give out their e-mail addresses.

- Educate users to not click links in spam e-mail.

- Educate users to not send spam e-mail, such as a forwarded e-mail of a funny picture or joke.

Malicious software, also called **malware**, is any program transmitted to a computer or network designed to cause damage without the knowledge of the user. Malware attacks are deployed through social engineering or spamming. To limit accidental installation of malware, most users are not allowed administrator privileges, which are required to install new software. **Spyware** is a type of malware that runs in the background on a computer and is designed to secretly collect information on a computer or network. **Antispyware** is a program designed to prevent spyware from being installed on a computer; however, the best method to prevent spyware is to be careful about clicking unknown links or downloading unknown software.

---

malicious software—Any program unknowingly transmitted to a computer or network designed to cause damage. Also called malware.

malware—See malicious software.

spyware—A type of malware designed to secretly collect information on a computer or network.

antispyware—A program designed to prevent spyware from being installed on a computer.

Understanding Permission Levels

HI001 Objectives:

5.4   Classify permission levels based on roles.

Read, Write, Modify, Full Access

One of the lines of defense is to assign permission levels to each user account on the domain. Before getting into the details of how this works, look at the overarching strategy to control access to computer resources. You can use two fundamental methods:

- **Authentication**: Authentication proves an individual is who he says he is and is accomplished by a variety of techniques including a username, password, badge with card reader, key fob, or biometric data such as a fingerprint. The best security is when at least two methods of authentication are used: A person proves he possesses an identity (such as a card reader badge) and also proves he knows secured knowledge (such as a password). After the person is authenticated, he is allowed access.

- **Authorization**: Authorization methods are used to define what resources a person can access after he is authenticated and what he can do with these resources (such as edit a record or only view it). Most often authorizing the type of access a person has to computer resources is accomplished by assigning permissions to a user account or user group.

As you learned in Chapter 5, "IT Operations," user permissions are controlled by grouping users in active directory (AD) and assigning permissions to each group. Each employee is assigned a user account in AD. This account can be put into one or more user groups. Each user group can be a job title or security-level group. Permission levels indicate the access a user group has to data on a computer or in an IS. The access assigned to standard users should be the bare minimum required to perform their job duties. Assigning access to users based on their job role is called role-based access control (RBAC).

Access is assigned to a specific folder or file. Following are four different types of access:

- **Read**: Can view data, but cannot alter data
- **Write**: Can view and create data, but cannot alter data already existing
- **Modify**: Can view, create, and alter data
- **Full Access**: Can view, create, alter, and delete data

> **EXAM TIP** For the Healthcare IT exam, you need to be familiar with the four different types of access to data.

When a person is hired, a new username is created for her to log in to the computers, network, and information systems. The security administrator in the HIT department places her username in AD groups to give her the access predetermined based on her job description or role. For example, for an employee who has in her job description the requirement to travel, her username is placed in the AD group that enables users to access the internal network using a VPN connection. Two other examples when an HIT employee needs to be in the AD group that gives his username the right to join a computer to the domain group; or in the AD that gives his username the authority to reset passwords.

If an employee requires more permissions than the standard permissions assigned for the job role, the manager or supervisor must submit a written request asking for an exception to the access normally granted for the job role. The manager should also know if a backup person with the same access is needed in case the employee is absent.

An administrator account has full access to the data on a system and can make security changes to other user accounts. Administrator accounts may be required to provide their password when making a change to the system. Only HIT technicians should be allowed administrative access to the computer. Anyone with an administrator account should have separate accounts, one with administrative access to use when needed and another without administrative privileges for daily use.

In addition to using AD groups to assign permissions to user accounts, AD groups can also affect permissions of computers, printers, and any other device that joins the domain. For example, computers have unique names and are joined to the domain on the network. The computer name is placed in an AD group that controls the screensaver behavior. One AD group is set so that the screensaver activates after five minutes of inactivity, is password protected, and uses the standard Windows 7 display. A separate AD group is set so that the screensaver activates after 15 minutes of inactivity, is password protected, and uses the standard Windows 7 display.

The reason two separate groups are created for screensavers is because any computer in a vulnerable position, such as in a patient's room, should have extra protection to have the screensaver activated quickly to prevent unauthorized use of the computer. In the administrative offices of a hospital, however, the computers are in locked offices, and it is rare for patients, visitors, or unauthorized personnel to be in proximity of those computers, so the screensaver is set to activate after 15 minutes to cut down on frustration of the user having to frequently unlock her computer.

Understanding Physical Security

HI001 Objectives:

5.1   Explain physical security controls.

Locations for servers, network hardware, printers, scanners, copiers

Access: servers, office, data closet, IDF/MDF, backups, key fobs, badges, biometrics

Environmental: HVAC, security lighting, surveillance, fire suppression, personnel, generator

Office hardware: locks, door locks, biometrics, privacy screens, UPS

Physical security is the first line of defense against malicious attacks on information systems. From where a printer is placed to the lock on the office door, all play a part in securing the sensitive data on the information systems. One goal of physical security is to ensure that only authorized personnel enter areas that have sensitive data. Any other person should be escorted by an authorized person. However, more threats exist against an IS other than hackers. Information systems need to be protected against destruction caused by other influences as well, such as a power surge or water pipe burst.

Following the guidelines set by the security officer at a facility aids in preventing theft or destruction of PHI and other sensitive information.

The next section starts with coverage of how the physical location of devices should help protect sensitive data.

Location and Access

Location is crucial to protecting hardware. Hardware should be in a controlled environment with limited access whenever possible. Hardware should never be allowed to leave the premises without permission or properly destroying or cleaning the data storage on the device.

The next few sections cover the physical safeguards.

Servers

Every facility has a data center containing servers, routers, and other shared hardware resources. Most servers, if not all, are located in the data center. The data center is usually near or in the IT department space in the facility for easy access, which is usually in the basement or first floor of a hospital. The data center contains rows of racks or cabinets with locks on each cabinet door, as shown in Figure 7-1. Inside the cabinets are the servers, routers, and other hardware devices. The door into the server room also has a secure lock. Some cabinets should still be empty to allow for future growth. The data center should have emergency power, preferably redundant emergency power.

Only authorized HIT employees should have login or physical access to the data center or data closet and devices contained in the data center. Not even all HIT personnel should have access. Server login should be accessible using only an administrator account for direct login to the server's operating system. This restriction does not affect access to the data on the server as viewed through using an IS.

Figure 7-1   The data center has rows of locked cabinets containing servers, routers, and other shared hardware.

Photo credits: Amy Walter

Backups are created in the data center. The backup media must be secured because it contains e-PHI. Only HIT personnel should handle backup devices, and these devices should always be kept in restricted areas or under lock and key when transported to offsite locations.

Backup media should be stored offsite or in a fireproof safe so that it is protected if a disaster (for example, fire, flood, or thief) happens in the data center.

Network Hardware

In Chapter 5 you learned about where to place wireless network devices. The cabling that reaches some of those devices originates in the **main distribution frame (MDF)**, which is usually in the data center, as shown in Figure 7-2. The MDF is the demarcation point, or demarc, between public and private wiring. Because cables have limitations for how far they can reach, **intermediate distribution frames (IDFs)** are usually located on each floor to reach each workstation or device on the floor that requires a wired connection.

main distribution frame (MDF)—A cable rack that connects and manages wiring used for telecommunication between a service provider and intermediate distribution frames (IDFs). The MDF connects private or public lines coming into a facility with the networking devices in the facility.

intermediate distribution frame (IDF)—A cable rack that connects and manages wiring used for telecommunication between the MDF and devices such as computers or network printers. IDFs are usually found on each floor of a building in a data closet.

Figure 7-2   The main distribution frame (MDF) is contained in cabinets in the data center.

Photo credit: Hartmut Menz

When designing a network, consider the following:

- Don't place an MDF or IDF near electrical equipment because it can cause interference and weaken the signal in the network.
- Static-free flooring should be installed.

- No ceiling tiles should be installed in a data closet where an IDF is located.
- A data closet where an IDF is located should have at least three feet of clearance between the IDF backboard and the door when closed to allow for proper ventilation.
- A data closet where an IDF is located must have a locked door.
- Network cables coming out of a cabinet should be neat and orderly, not tangled, as shown in Figure 7-3.

 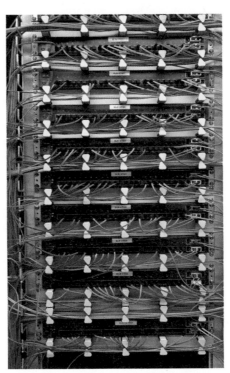

Figure 7-3 Tangled cables create problems with maintenance and ventilation. The cables in a data center should be orderly to ensure the equipment is accessible and air can circulate.

Photo credit: Fotoschuh

Printers, Scanners, and Copiers

Consider the following guidelines when deciding where to place a printer, scanner, or copier. Also educate users who use the device how to maintain privacy of sensitive information.

- Any device used for sensitive information should be out of view from unauthorized personnel, patients, or visitors. Place the device, such as a printer, behind the desk at a nursing station, but it would be better to have the device in an office with a door.

- Devices should be configured to use security features when available; for example, some network printers can be set to require a password to be used.

- Avoid storing sensitive information in electronic address books, such as an address book installed in memory on a fax machine, printer, or copier.

- Change any device passwords from the default setting to secure passwords.

- Work with vendors to ensure a device meets industry security standards and certifications.

Accessing Secured Resources

Before a user's permission to access a computer, file, folder, or network is allowed, the user must authenticate that he is the person sitting in front of the computer doing the work on the computer. Authentication proves that a user is who he says he is. In addition to knowing the correct username and password, you can use some physical controls to prevent a fraudulent person from trying to use the permissions of another user.

> **EXAM TIP** For the Healthcare IT exam, you need to be familiar with physical security measures to protect PHI.

All offices or facilities should be locked when not used by an employee with authority to any sensitive information in the room or facility. Methods for unlocking secured locks include the following:

- A log of who has which door keys should be maintained and reviewed annually. Keys should never be duplicated outside of the facility's management. Door locks should be changed whenever there is a personnel change for every door that person had access to. All keys possessed by an employee should be surrendered upon termination of that employee.

- A **key fob** is an electronic device designed to fit onto a key ring (see Figure 7-4). Key fobs display a number or code synched with the network authentication service. This code typically changes every 60 seconds. The code is entered when logging into the network. This method is one more layer of security to prove a person is authorized to access the network. The process proves the person is in possession of the key fob when he logs on.

> **key fob**—A device synched with a network authentication service that provides a code used to log in to a network or other system.

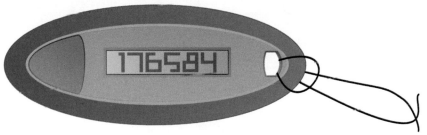

Figure 7-4 A key fob displays a code synched with the network authentication service.

Photo credit: Pix by Marti

- A **badge** is a smartcard that looks similar to a credit card with a strip or chip that identifies the person assigned to the card, as shown in Figure 7-5. Badges are usually used to unlock doors. RFID chips are mainly used today, which is the same technology used for patient tracking devices, as you learned in Chapter 6, "Medical Business Operations."

> **badge**—A card with a magnetic strip or chip that identifies the person assigned to the card.

- A **biometric scanner** is used to prove the identity of a person accessing a room or device. Biometric scanning devices can verify a number of unique identifiers of people, such as a handprint scan, retinal scan, or fingerprint scan. Figure 7-6 shows an example of a fingerprint scanner on a keyboard.

> **biometric scanner**—A device used to identify a person based on biological data.

Figure 7-5   Badges identify personnel in a facility and grant access to restricted areas.

Figure 7-6   A fingerprint scanner on a keyboard is used to log a user into the network.

Photo credit: Robinson

Remember from Chapter 4, "Organizational Behavior," that privacy screens are used to protect computer screens from prying eyes of nonauthorized people. Also the uninterruptible power supply (UPS) provides just enough power to properly shut down a computer in case a facility loses power.

Environmental Security

Controlling the environment helps to secure restricted areas and increase safety. Several factors can be controlled and altered to help sensitive data remain secured. The following guidelines are used in facilities to assist in environmental security.

The equipment in a data center produces a lot of heat. Ensure that all devices have room for air to circulate through them. The data center should have a dedicated **heating, ventilation, and air conditioning (HVAC) unit**, preferably two for redundancy. The HVAC unit maintains the temperature and humidity to keep the equipment in the data center cool. Recommended specifications are a temperature of 64–80 degrees Fahrenheit with humidity ranging from 30%–55%. The HVAC should be electronically monitored at all times. If the HVAC fails, the heat in the data center could cause significant damage to the devices. A notification is sent to the HIT department in case the HVAC fails in the data center. If there are two HVAC units, daily manual monitoring is recommended in case one unit has failed and the other unit does all the cooling.

> **heating, ventilation, and air conditioning (HVAC) unit**—Equipment designed to regulate temperature and humidity.

Cameras are used for surveillance in addition to security personnel. Usually as closed-circuit TV, surveillance is kept entirely inside the facility. A limitation to surveillance cameras is they can witness only criminal activity; they cannot correct or stop it.

Security lighting is designed to discourage criminal activity by providing sufficient lighting for surveillance. Facilities should have security lighting available at all times. Lighting should be bright enough to easily view objects and activity. Surveillance cameras need to have enough light available to capture images.

Suppressing a fire quickly is critical to data center management. Fire damage in a data center could be catastrophic and make recovering data difficult or impossible if backups are stored on premises or are corrupted. Most states have requirements set by the local fire department. Fire monitors should be placed both under the raised floor and in the ceiling. The alarm should be visual, such as flashing lights, because the noise in a data center from the HVAC unit is very loud. Typically, data centers use an airtight, sealed door that locks automatically if a fire starts. The seal contains the fire-retardant gas or powder used to suppress the fire in the data center. Water should not be used to suppress a fire in the data center. Fire-retardant gas or powder protects the equipment but could seriously injure or kill an employee trapped in the room. A safety switch should be by the door to release the door in case there is a person inside the data center during a fire event. Some data centers have fire retardant material in the ceilings, walls, and floors. This extra precaution delays a fire from breaching into a data center to help preserve the equipment long enough for emergency services to put out a fire outside the data center.

Personnel should not have food or drinks around any computer equipment. Cell phones and magnets should not be placed near any computers or electronic devices. Make sure cables and cords are neatly placed out of pathways or covered to prevent tripping; this is called avoiding a trip hazard.

Generators are used to provide electricity in case the facility loses power from the electric provider. Generators start to provide power within seconds, but even that can be too long for some devices. Usually, the most critical devices use a UPS as well to provide power while waiting for the generator to kick in.

> **EXAM TIP**   For the Healthcare IT exam, you need to be familiar with methods to protect data from destruction.

Using Password Best Practices

> HI001 Objectives:
>
> **5.3   Apply best practices when creating and communicating passwords.**
>
> Communication of passwords, Storage of passwords, Password strength (complexity/length), Password reuse

Passwords are probably the most commonly used security measure. Passwords are so commonplace that it is easy to forget how protective we need to be with them. As HIT technicians we are responsible for communicating to users in the facility the importance to keep passwords secret. Usernames and passwords should not be shared among users; every user should have a unique username and password.

> **EXAM TIP**   For the Healthcare IT exam, you need to know how to properly handle passwords.

Follow these guidelines as both a user and an HIT technician to prevent a breach of HIPAA confidentiality:

- Change all default passwords, especially on servers and network devices.

- Passwords should never be written down and stored in a place that is in open sight or easily found by others.

- Usernames and passwords should never be shared, even if a user needs help remembering it. This includes not sharing with a co-worker or supervisor. If a password is forgotten, the user should contact an HIT technician to have the password reset.

- When a password is created or reset by the HIT personnel, the password must be communicated to the user securely. The best way to communicate a password is in person. If that is not possible, a phone conversation is the next best solution. If you absolutely must, you can send the password through an e-mail, but never send a username and password in the same e-mail in case the email is intercepted. Always make sure you have the right e-mail address and the right user before using this method.

- If possible, set the password to automatically expire with the first log on, requiring the user to reset the password to one that even the HIT personnel doesn't know.

- When resetting the password, users should use a strong password. A strong password is one that does not use easily guessed words and has a combination of uppercase and lowercase letters, symbols, and digits and is at least eight characters long. The password should not contain any dictionary words, any part of the username, or any part of the user's name.

- Group policy in Active Directory (AD) can set certain requirements about the strength of a password, such as including at least one lowercase and uppercase letter, number, and symbol, or character length.

- Group policy in AD can set passwords so that they cannot be reused. This prevents users from using the same password over and over, which contradicts the whole point of changing a password.

- Users should never allow web applications to store a password.

Understanding Encryption Types

HI001 Objectives:

5.2   Summarize the different encryption types and when each is used.

Types: SSL, DES, 3DES, AES, PGP

Communication: E-mail, chat, smartphone, collaboration sites, FTP sites, phone, VoIP, fax

Storage: Flash drives, PCs, laptops, SD cards, external drives, servers, NAS, SANs

Dissemination of PHI

The following sections review the communication that needs to be encrypted as well as a bit more.

Types of Encryption

Encryption can be one of the following:

- **Symmetric encryption**: Uses a single, private key to both encrypt and decrypt data. The private key needed to decrypt the message is sent separately from the encrypted message to the receiving computer, as shown in Figure 7-7.

Figure 7-7   In symmetric encryption a private key is sent with an encrypted message but by a different route.

- **Asymmetric encryption**: Uses different, but related, keys to encrypt and decrypt data. A single key cannot both encrypt and decrypt asymmetric encrypted data. One key is used to encrypt the message, whereas a separate, but similar, key is used to decrypt the message, as shown in Figure 7-8.

Figure 7-8 In asymmetric encryption the key that encrypts a message is not the same key that decrypts the message; although, the two keys may be related or similar.

Secure sockets layer (SSL) is a handshake between a web server and a browser to establish a secure connection. SSL was created by Netscape. SSL uses a public key encryption. When used with HTTP, it becomes HTTPS or HTTP over SSL to secure online transactions, such as with online banking or credit card transactions. SSL can also be used with FTP to create a secure FTP data transfer and authentication. SSL is a symmetric encryption.

> **secure socket layer (SSL)**—A handshake between a web server and a browser to establish a secure connection.

Data encryption standard (DES) is an outdated block cipher from the 1970s. DES uses a 64-bit cipher block considered weak by today's standards. DES uses a 56-bit key that is easily cracked nowadays. What DES offers technology today is the foundation for **triple data encryption standard (3DES)**. 3DES is similar to DES, but it applies the cipher algorithm three times to each cipher block. So 3DES also uses a 64-bit cipher block, but the key size can be as large as a 168-bit key. Both DES and 3DES are symmetric encryptions.

> **NOTE** A cipher is an algorithm that can encrypt and decrypt messages. A block cipher is a cipher that encrypts and decrypts a fixed size, or block, of data.

> **NOTE** An algorithm is a procedure or process of step-by-step rules for completing a calculation or computation.

> **data encryption standard (DES)**—An outdated block cipher that uses a 64-bit cipher block and a 56-bit key.
>
> **triple data encryption standard (3DES)**—An encryption similar to DES but uses a key that can be three times the size at a 168-bit key.

Advanced encryption standard (AES) was first mentioned in Chapter 5 because the wireless encryption protocol WPA2 uses AES. AES is faster and stronger than 3DES if used with a 256-bit key size. AES is the successor to DES/3DES. AES uses symmetric encryption.

Pretty good privacy (PGP) is designed to be used for signing and encrypting e-mail. PGP uses both symmetric and asymmetric encryption. PGP uses a 64-bit block cipher with a 128-bit key. The strength to PGP is that the number of possible keys is so vast that it is relatively safe against hacking.

> **pretty good privacy (PGP)**—An encryption method designed for signing and encrypting e-mail, which uses both symmetric and asymmetric encryption.

> **EXAM TIP** For the Healthcare IT exam, you need to be familiar with different encryption standards and methods.

Communication

In Chapter 4 you reviewed several different types of communication. Some of the following are a review from that chapter with a couple added to learn more.

- E-mail primarily uses PGP to encrypt e-mails and validate signatures.
- Chat is not encrypted and should not be used in the healthcare environment.
- Collaboration sites on an intranet are usually used for employees to share ideas and communicate with each other to complete a project. Collaboration sites are secured because they are only available within the secured network.
- In the healthcare environment, FTP sites should use secure FTP. Secure FTP encrypts both commands and data. Every person accessing a secure FTP site should have a unique username and password.

- Smartphones are commonly used to retrieve work e-mail. Many vendors are also moving toward making their applications accessible through a mobile device as well. These phones should be secured with a power-on password and inactivity timer to ensure if the phone is lost, a hacker cannot access sensitive information. Third-party software can password protect the memory card in the smartphone or even wipe the memory clean remotely.

- VoIP phones are quickly replacing analog phones in healthcare facilities. Because VoIP uses the facility's network and Internet, a facility's network and Internet security protects the phone systems from attacks.

- Some fax services have the capability to encrypt faxes when the fax arrives in an electronic format to be retrieved digitally and not by a printed hardcopy. A fax can be encrypted by using a password-protected PDF format.

Storage

In Chapter 5 you were introduced to several different formats for storing sensitive information. This section focuses on how the data is kept confidential. Storage encryption methods have three goals:

1. Information in storage should remain confidential.

2. Data storage and retrieval should be fast.

3. Encryption should not waste space.

The following list outlines some different types of storage:

- Flash drives can be encrypted using third-party software, which can be run from the flash drive. Some flash drives have a built-in biometric device, such as a fingerprint scanner, to encrypt the data, although this is an expensive option. You can also use software to encrypt data before it is placed on the flash drive.

- Computers that store e-PHI must have password protection and timeout screensavers with locks activated.

- Laptops should have power-on passwords, inactivity timers with password requirements, and encrypted hard drives. Use a privacy screen film on the monitor of the laptop to protect the information displayed from prying eyes in public locations. Most laptops also have a cable lock system that can be used to physically secure a laptop to a location, as shown in Figure 7-9.

Figure 7-9   A cable lock system is secured to the computer and the steel cable is secured to an immovable object in the room, such as a desk or pole.

Photo credit: dpchung

- SD cards should be password protected, which can be done by third-party software.

- External hard drives containing e-PHI should be password protected and encrypted. Some external hard drives come with software already installed capable of encrypting and password protecting the data, but if not, third-party software can be installed to do this.

- Servers should be stored in a secured, restricted area such as the data center. Servers should also be password-protected and require administrative accounts to log in to the server's OS. Remember, users don't need to log in to the server's OS to access data stored on that server through an IS.

- **Network attached storage (NAS)**, as shown in Figure 7-10, is a hard drive storage device used to store data. NAS has its own network address, so other computers on the network can access it to remotely store files. NAS should be physically stored in a secured, restricted location, such as a data center.

> **network attached storage (NAS)**—A storage device connected directly to the network.

Figure 7-10   Typically, NAS devices are hard drives in a data center.

- A **storage area network (SAN)** is an independent storage network separate from the normal LAN. Multiple servers and NAS can store and access data on a SAN. Combining this resource provides better quality and more volume of storage for a server or NAS that might otherwise have limited storage space. A SAN containing sensitive information should be encrypted.

> **storage area network (SAN)**—An independent network separate from the normal LAN designed for data storage.

Dissemination of PHI

The facility's security officer is responsible for the dissemination, or giving out, of PHI when necessary. For example, PHI might need to be shared with the patient, another healthcare provider as a referral, or an insurance agency. All sharing of PHI must be monitored and recorded for six years. PHI may be shared orally, by fax, e-mail, mail, or courier as long as measures are taken to ensure information is secure. Before PHI can be shared with anyone aside from the patient's healthcare providers and the patient, the receiving party must confirm compliance with HIPAA rules and that the information is necessary.

How to Secure Wireless Networks

HI001 Objectives:

5.6   Recognize wireless security protocols and best practices.

WEP, WPA, WPA2, AES, RADIUS, SSID naming, MAC filtering, Site surveys, Access point placement

Although Chapter 5 introduced wireless encryption, this section is a review while still adding more information about best practices to secure a wireless network.

The types of encryption standards that might be used to secure a wireless network are as follows:

- **Wired Equivalent Privacy (WEP)**: Secures data using an encryption key but is a weak encryption because the encryption key is static.

- **Wi-Fi Protected Access (WPA)**: Uses TKIP, which changes the encryption key periodically, but is also a weak encryption because it enables hackers to spoof data, or to falsify data on the network.

- **Wi-Fi Protected Access 2 (WPA2)**: The most current and secure encryption available for wireless networks.

- **Advanced Encryption Standard (AES)**: Used by WPA2, AES is a symmetric encryption that uses keys of 128, 192, or 256 bits.

- **Remote Authentication Dial-In User Service (RADIUS)**: Uses an authentication server to control access to the wireless network.

Additional methods to secure a wireless network other than encryption include the following:

- The service set identifier (SSID) is the name assigned to an access point (AP). A wireless network that contains sensitive information should disable broadcasting the SSID so that it is hidden when devices search for available wireless networks.

- Every computer network adapter, printer, switch, router, or other device that can connect to a network is assigned a unique media access control (MAC) address. When **MAC filtering** is used, a wireless access point keeps a list of MAC addresses allowed to connect to the AP and to the wireless network.

media access control (MAC) filtering—The method to secure a network by limiting which devices are allowed to connect to a network based on a list of MAC addresses kept by the wireless access points.

- Site surveys of the facility document AP locations but can also identify rogue APs. A rogue AP is an undocumented AP and might not be secured properly to be transmitting sensitive data.
- APs should be placed so that the signal range does not exceed the boundaries of the facility.

How to Remotely Access the Facility's Network

HI001 Objectives:

5.5   Identify different remote access methods and security controls.

RDC, VPN, Remote control applications, Terminal emulation, L2TP, SSH, HTTPS, SFTP

Satellite facilities, remote employees, and vendors need to remotely connect to the facility's network. Sensitive data needs to be transmitted to and from remote locations and needs to be secured.

EXAM TIP   For the Healthcare IT exam, you need to know different ways to create remote connections.

The following methods are used to establish the connection.

- **Microsoft Remote Desktop Connection:** As you learned in Chapter 5, **remote desktop connection (RDC)** uses remote desktop protocol (RDP) to connect to another computer to view the remote computer's screen, as shown in Figure 7-11. The RDC connection should require an administrator account, and the remote user needs to grant permission to access his computer.

remote desktop connection (RDC)—A remote connection used to view another computer's desktop in a window. RDC was created by Microsoft.

Window displaying desktop of remote computer

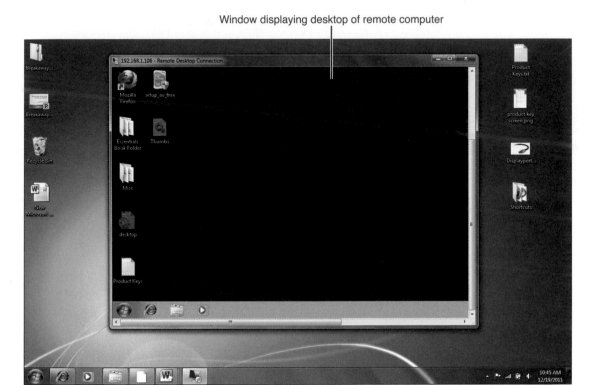

Figure 7-11   Microsoft's Remote Desktop Connection utility enables HIT personnel to remotely access another computer.

- **Virtual private network (VPN)**: A secured, encrypted connection to a facility's network or a specific server from across the Internet. For example, VPN connections are used for remote radiologists to examine medical images or remote medical coders to create claims to send to insurance companies. A VPN can be established through a VPN client, or application, or a VPN tunnel. A VPN connection requires user authentication onto the remote network. The employee is typically issued a computer by the facility that is preconfigured for a VPN connection. Generally, facilities do not want employees to connect using personal computers because the facility cannot control the security of any data moved to the personal computer.

- **Remote connections using third-party software**: Third-party remote control applications are used to connect similarly to an RDC connection between two computers. Using a secure connection is just as important while using a third-party connection as any other remote connection. The remote computer's desktop is viewable in a window on the connecting computer. Examples of third-party remote control applications are DameWare and TeamViewer. Many remote control applications offer features such as file transfer between the remote computers or the capability to record the session.

- **Terminal emulation**: **Terminal emulators** provide a connection to a mainframe computer that holds all the data. The connecting computer or other computing device does not hold any of the data but simply requests to view and manipulate the data on the remote server. The terminal emulator typically looks much like a command prompt window, but some have a graphic user interface (GUI) to make navigating and using the remote data easier.

terminal emulator—A connection to a mainframe computer that holds all the data being accessed. A terminal emulator typically looks like a command prompt window.

The following security controls are used to secure remote connections.

- **Layer 2 tunneling protocol (L2TP)** is a tunneling protocol used to create a VPN connection. L2TP connections are encrypted through the entire connection, from one point to the other, making it difficult to intercept.

layer 2 tunneling protocol (L2TP)—A fully encrypted tunneling protocol used to create a VPN connection.

- **Secure Shell (SSH)** was designed to replace vulnerable and unencrypted connections created by Telnet. The older Telnet and the newer SSH clients are typically used by administrators to remotely control a server. An example of SSH client software is SecureCRT by VanDyke, which an administrator might use to manage a server from a remote computer over the Internet.

secure shell (SSH)—An encrypted tunneling protocol used by client/server applications to connect a remote client to a server. The protocol is designed to ensure confidentiality and integrity of data over an unsecured network.

- HTTPS is a secure version of HTTP that encrypts data sent to and from a web server. HTTPS uses SSL encryption. Used by a web browser.

- Secure FTP is used by an FTP application that is secured using SSL or SSH encryption.

Securing Backups

HI001 Objectives:

5.8 Implement backup procedures based on disaster recovery policies.

Deployment, configuration, and testing of backups

Backup storage: Offsite, courier, and onsite

Methods of secure transfer

Backup inventory

Chapter 5 introduced the different types of backups: daily, differential, and incremental. When implementing backup procedures, you must consider several points of concern to ensure that backups are secured from malicious attacks and available and usable when needed.

EXAM TIP For the Healthcare IT exam, you need to know backup procedures to ensure the availability of data when needed.

Each IS should have an individual backup plan. When creating a backup plan, consider downtime required to make the backup, the backup media available, and the maximum tolerable downtime (MTD). Many backup plans have one full-system backup weekly, biweekly, or monthly followed by differential or incremental backups daily until the next full backup. Deciding which backup to use is determined by the interruption caused by creating the backup. If creating a full-systems backup doesn't interrupt the use of the IS (usually for a small amount of data), doing full-system backups can be performed more often. If the full system backup creates significant interruption, differential or incremental backups can be made in between full-system backups.

Backups can be stored either onsite or offsite. The best practice is to store backup media offsite in a secure and restricted location. Storing backups offsite means a full record of data is kept in two different locations in case a disaster happens at the facility destroying all data onsite. The offsite location needs to be fireproof, waterproof, and climate controlled. The offsite location must be available at all times in case of an emergency during nonbusiness hours. The HIT department should maintain a list of contacts at the offsite location.

One concern with choosing to store backups offsite is getting the media to the offsite location. Either an HIT employee must transport the media, or a paid courier must securely transport the media. Any courier must sign a PHI agreement assuring the courier understands HIPAA regulations. Delivery should be handled using locked bags or carriers. A log should be maintained to show pickup and delivery, when, by whom, and the route taken. Some couriers and record storage companies guarantee secure transfer and storage of backups. These contracts should be signed by both the facility and the vendor and reviewed annually.

Storing backups onsite is much easier to deal with on a daily basis but risks all data being lost if a disaster occurs destroying all data onsite, such as a fire or flood. If the backups must remain onsite, store the data in a secure location that is also protected from disasters, such as a fireproof, waterproof safe. Not all safes are completely reliable in all conditions, so there is still a risk of losing all data. The safe must be locked with a limited number of HIT personnel having access to the backups. If storing backups onsite is only to wait until transportation can be arranged to the offsite location, all safeguards should still be in place and limit the time before the backups are transported to the offsite location.

Backup media should be monitored and replaced regularly to ensure the quality of the media. Rotate and reformat the media as needed to prevent wearing out one media device. The media should always be labeled clearly to save time during an emergency use of the backup.

Disposing of PHI

HI001 Objectives:
5.7   Implement best practices in secure disposal of electronic or physical PHI.
Secure shredding, Degaussing, Sanitizing

In Chapter 3 you learned how to properly dispose of PHI. This section reviews how to dispose of electronic or physical PHI.

HIPAA states that record disposal is the responsibility of covered entities. The covered entity is at fault if any physical or electronic PHI is recovered at any point after the disposal of records. The basic rule is to make sure the data—whether hardcopy or on an electronic device—is unreadable, indecipherable, and cannot be reconstructed.

Physical documentation containing PHI can be shredded, burned, or pulverized. Paper documents and disks, such as CDs and DVDs, containing PHI must be shredded and disposed so that the information cannot be re-created by an unauthorized individual. Use third-party companies when contracts/agreements are in place acknowledging a standard compliance with HIPAA regulations. Usually shredding is done onsite. Cross-cut shredding at two angles is better than straight, vertical lines.

PHI on electronic media is disposed by sanitizing or degaussing the device. Degaussing is the recommended form of destroying any trace of data on electronic media. A couple ways records can be disposed of on electronic media follow:

- Purging or degaussing is when exposure to a strong magnetic field is used to purge data from the device.
- Sanitizing the device is when all data is deleted, overwritten, and reformatted. To overwrite data, irrelevant data (1s and 0s) is written on the memory several times. The standard used by the Department of Defense is if a device contains sensitive data, it must be overwritten at least seven times. Sanitizing is not the preferred method for destroying traces of data on electronic media because the media may have sections that are unresponsive to being overwritten. Data has been proven to still be vulnerable to being reconstructed even after being overwritten as many as six times. Also, sanitizing is a time-consuming process.

> **EXAM TIP**   For the Healthcare IT exam, you need to be familiar with standards in disposing of devices containing e-PHI.

If circumstances warrant the physical destruction of the media before disposal, methods can include disintegrating, pulverizing, melting, incinerating, or shredding the media. HIPPA does not require the physical destruction of media, but it does hold the covered entity liable if any sensitive data is recovered.

HIT in the Real World

This story is from a friend who works in an emergency department.

An elderly patient and her adult son arrived at an emergency department of a hospital. The patient had passed out and broken her nose when she fell in her home. The doctor evaluated her and decided to order an EKG as well as care for her broken nose. Later, the nurse documented that the EKG had been completed using the computer in the patient room. The nurse spoke with the patient and her son for a few more minutes and then left the two in the room alone. A few hours later the patient was admitted into the hospital, and she and her son left the ED.

A couple days later the nurse was approached because the audit trail showing his activity in the HIS revealed that he had viewed the medical records of some psych patients who were not under his care, and there was no reason for him to view their records. He adamantly objected saying he had not illegally viewed any patient records.

The HIT department determined the day and time the illegal activity had occurred and which computer was used to view the patient records. The computer used was in one of the patient rooms in the ED. The date and time stamp showed it happened while the elderly woman with a broken nose with her son was assigned to that patient room, more specifically, it occurred minutes after documenting the completion of the EKG of the woman.

Investigation revealed that the timeout setting on this one computer in the ED had not been activated. All the other computers in patient rooms had the timeout scheduled to lock the computer after a minute of inactivity. The nurse had assumed that the computer had locked while talking with the patient after documenting the completion of the EKG and left the room. The son had noticed the computer was still logged on. He found an interesting read when he somehow navigated to view the medical records of psych patients being seen in the ED.

In the end, the setting was corrected on the computer, and the nurse was reprimanded for not ensuring the computer was locked before leaving the room. Technological safeguards failed the nurse and the psych patients in this story. This is both the fault of the nurse for not checking the computer locked before leaving, but also of the IT department for not checking the setting was correctly applied. There are multiple lines of defense for security of PHI because mistakes are just sometimes going to be made. We must do everything possible to ensure the part we're responsible for works in case a different mistake is made down the road.

Chapter Summary

What Are We Up Against?

- Social engineering is a malicious attack using social skills to manipulate or trick a person who has access to sensitive data, such as PHI, into sharing the information.

- Phishing is when an attacker tricks or manipulates a user to give out sensitive data or into allowing unauthorized programs onto a computer or network.

- The only way to prevent social engineering is to educate employees about how attacks might present themselves and how to avoid falling for the trick.

- Spam is unsolicited contact from an attacker that causes unnecessary network or Internet traffic, which can slow down the network for legitimate uses. Applying email filters and educating users is the best way to avoid falling for spam attacks.

- Malware is any program unknowingly transmitted to a computer or network designed to cause damage. Limiting privileges on the user's account is one way to prevent malware attacks from being successful.

- Spyware is a type of malware designed to secretly collect information on a computer or network. Antispyware is a program designed to prevent spyware from being installed on a computer.

Understanding Permission Levels

- Assigning access to users based on their job role is called role-based access control (RBAC).

- Access is assigned to a specific folder or file. There are four different types of access:
  - **Read**: Can view data but cannot alter data already existing
  - **Write**: Can view and create data but cannot alter data already existing
  - **Modify**: Can view, create, and alter data
  - **Full Access**: Can view, create, alter, and delete data

- An administrator account has full access to the data on a system and can make security changes and other user accounts. Anyone with an administrator account should have separate accounts, one with administrative access to use when needed and another without administrative privileges for daily use.

- AD groups can also affect permissions of computers, printers, and any other device that joins the domain.

Understanding Physical Security

- Servers and other shared hardware is kept in the data center. The devices are kept in locking cabinets in the data center, which has a locking door. Few employees should have access to the data center room. Servers should be accessible only using an administrator account.

- Main distribution frames (MDFs) are located in the server room and manage wiring used for telecommunication. Intermediate distribution frames (IDFs) are located in locked data closets on each floor of a facility to connect the MDF to workstations.

- Printers, scanners, and copiers should be kept far away from unauthorized personnel, patients, and visitors. Security features, such as user authentication, should be activated on the device if available.

- Key fobs display a number or code synched with the network authentication service. The code is used to authenticate a user trying to access a secured network.

- A badge is a card that looks similar to a credit card with a strip or chip that identifies the person assigned to the card.

- Biometric devices can verify a number of unique identifiers of people, such as hand scans, retinal scans, or fingerprint scans.

- The data center should have a dedicated heating, ventilation, and air conditioning (HVAC) unit, preferably two for redundancy, to maintain the temperature and humidity to keep the equipment in the data center cool.

- Security lighting is designed to discourage criminal activity by providing sufficient lighting for surveillance.

- In a data center, fire-retardant gas or powder protects equipment in the event of a fire.

Using Password Best Practices

- Usernames and passwords should never be shared, even with a co-worker or manager.

- The best way to communicate a password is in person.

- Passwords should not contain any dictionary words, any part of the username, or the user's name.

- Passwords should not be reused.

Understanding Encryption Types

- Secure sockets layer (SSL) is a handshake between a web server and a browser to establish a secure connection. SSL can be used with HTTP and FTP to create secure connections.

- Triple data encryption standard (3DES) is similar to DES, but it applies the cipher algorithm three times to each cipher block.

- AES is faster and stronger than 3DES if used with a 256-bit key size.

- Pretty good privacy (PGP) is designed to be used for signing and encrypting email.

- Smartphones should be secured with a power-on password and inactivity timer to ensure if the phone is lost a hacker cannot access sensitive information. Third-party software can password-protect the memory card in the smartphone.

- A fax can be encrypted by using a password-protected PDF format.

- All storage encryption methods should aim for the following goals:

  - Information in storage should remain confidential.

  - Data storage and retrieval should be fast.

  - Encryption should not waste space.

- Network attached storage (NAS), also called a file server, is a server or computer used for storing data.

- A storage area network (SAN) is an independent network separate from the normal LAN designed for data storage.

- All sharing of PHI must be monitored and recorded for six years. Before PHI can be shared, the receiving party must confirm compliance with HIPAA rules and that the information is necessary.

How to Secure Wireless Networks

- Wired Equivalent Privacy (WEP) secures data using an encryption key but is a weak encryption because the encryption key is static.

- Wi-Fi Protected Access (WPA) uses TKIP, which changes the encryption key periodically, but is also a weak encryption because it allows hackers to spoof data, or to falsify data on the network.

- Wi-Fi Protected Access 2 (WPA2) is the most current and secure encryption available for wireless networks.

- WPA2 uses Advanced Encryption Standard (AES).

- Remote Authentication Dial-In User Service (RADIUS) uses an authentication server to control access to the wireless network.

- The Service Set Identifier (SSID) is the name assigned to an access point (AP). A wireless network that contains sensitive information should disable broadcasting the SSID so that it is hidden when devices search for available wireless networks.

- Media access control (MAC) filtering can be set on network devices, such as a switch, to allow only devices with a permitted MAC address to connect to the network.

How to Remotely Access the Facility's Network

- Remote desktop connection (RDC) is a remote connection used to view another computer's desktop in a window.

- A virtual private network (VPN) is a secured, encrypted connection to a facility's network or a specific server.

- Third-party remote control applications are used to connect similarly to an RDC connection between two computers.

- A terminal emulator is a connection to a mainframe computer that holds all the data being accessed. A terminal emulator typically looks like a command prompt window.

- Layer 2 tunneling protocol (L2TP) is a tunneling protocol used to create a VPN connection encrypted through the entire connection, from one point to the other, making it difficult to intercept.

- Secure shell (SSH) is an encryption that ensures confidentiality and integrity of data over an unsecured network.

Securing Backups

- When creating a backup plan, consider downtime required to make the backup, the backup media available, and the maximum tolerable downtime (MTD).

- Best practice is to store backup media offsite in a secure and restricted location.

- The offsite location needs to be fireproof, waterproof, climate controlled, and available at all times.

- Either an HIT employee must transport the backup media to the offsite location, or a paid courier must securely transport the media.

- Storing backups onsite is much easier to deal with on a daily basis but risks all data being lost if a disaster occurs that destroys all data onsite, such as a fire or flood.

- Backup media should be monitored and replaced regularly to ensure the quality of the media.

Disposing of PHI

- HIPAA states that record disposal is the responsibility of covered entities.

- The basic rule of disposal is to make sure the data—whether hardcopy or on an electronic device—is unreadable, indecipherable, and cannot be reconstructed.

- Paper documents and disks, such as CDs and DVDs, containing PHI must be shredded and disposed so that the information cannot be re-created by an unauthorized individual.

- Sanitizing the device is when all data is deleted, overwritten, and reformatted.

- Purging or degaussing is when exposure to a strong magnetic field is used to purge data from the device.

Key Terms

- antispyware
- badge
- biometric scanner
- data encryption standard (DES)
- heating, ventilation, and air conditioning (HVAC) unit
- intermediate distribution frame (IDF)
- key fob
- Layer 2 tunneling protocol (L2TP)
- main distribution frame (MDF)

- malicious software
- malware
- media access control (MAC) filtering
- network attached storage (NAS)
- phishing
- pretty good privacy (PGP)
- remote desktop connection (RDC)
- secure shell (SSH)
- secure socket layer (SSL)
- spam
- social engineering
- spyware
- storage area network (SAN)
- terminal emulator
- triple data encryption standard (3DES)

Acronym Drill

Acronyms sometimes get confusing, especially when a single sentence can have four or five. As an HIT professional, you must know the acronyms and what they stand for. Fill in the blank with the correct acronym for the sentence.

1. An _____ is usually found on each floor of a facility to connect wired workstations on the network to the _____ in the data center.

   Answer: _____

2. _____ chips are mainly used in badges today.

   Answer: _____

3. Usually the most critical devices use a _____ as well to provide power while waiting for the generator to kick in.

   Answer: _____

4. _____ is similar to _____, but it applies the cipher algorithm three times to each cipher block.

   Answer: _____

5. The strength to _____ is that the number of possible keys is so vast that it is relatively safe against hacking.

   Answer: _____

6. _____ has its own network address so that other computers on the network can access it to remotely store files.

   Answer: _____

7. A _____ provides better quality and more volume of storage for a server or _____ that might otherwise have limited storage space.

   Answer: _____

8. _____ is the most current and secure encryption available for wireless networks.

   Answer: _____

9. A wireless network that contains sensitive information should disable broad-casting the _____ so that it is hidden when devices search for available wireless networks.

   Answer: _____

10. _____ connections are used for remote radiologists to examine medical images or remote medical coders to create claims to send to insurance companies.

   Answer: _____

11. The terminal emulator typically looks much like a command prompt window, but some have a _____ to make navigating and using the remote data easier.

   Answer: _____

12. _____ connections are encrypted through the entire connection, from one point to the other, making it difficult to intercept.

   Answer: _____

13. _____ is a secure version of _____ that uses _____ encryption to encrypt data sent to and from a web server.

   Answer: _____

14. _____ states that record disposal is the responsibility of covered entities.

   Answer: _____

15. _____ on electronic media is disposed by sanitizing or degaussing the device.

Answer: _____

Review Questions

1. What is the purpose of spyware?

Answer: _____

2. What type of permission does an administrator account have?

Answer: _____

_____

3. Besides user accounts, what other controls do AD groups control?

Answer: _____

_____

4. What are four methods to unlock secured locks?

Answer: _____

5. What are the recommended specifications for the HVAC in the data center?

Answer: _____

_____

6. How are surveillance cameras limited?

Answer: _____

_____

7. What are three goals for storage encryption methods?

Answer: _____

_____

_____

8. Why might PHI be shared outside of the facility's personnel?

Answer: _____

_____

9. Why are remote employees issued computers owned by the facility?

   Answer: _____

   _____

   _____

   _____

10. What is the goal when disposing of media that contains PHI?

   Answer: _____

   _____

Practical Application

1. Research NAS devices and compare storage capacity, cost, and available encryption software already installed.

   Answer: _____

   _____

   _____

   _____

   _____

2. Use two computers and remotely control from one computer to the other using third-party software or RDC and then exchange files. What freeware software can you use to remote into another computer. What steps did you use to remote into another computer using RDC?

   Answer: _____

   _____

   _____

   _____

   _____

3. Find the wireless access points in the building you're in. What do they look like? Where are they placed? Where is the next closest WAP? Discuss why the placement is good or bad to maintain a secure wireless network. Pictures taken with a smartphone or digital camera will help document your findings.

Answer: _____

_____

_____

_____

_____

APPENDIX A
Answers to Acronym Drills, Review Questions, and Practical Application Exercises

Chapter 1

Acronym Drill

1. HIT
2. HITECH, HIS
3. EMR, EHR
4. MRI, CT
5. VPN

Review Questions

1. A birth center is an acute care facility.

2. Acute care means care for short-term and severe afflictions. Long-term care means ongoing care after a diagnosis.

3. Because they are the most complex of HIT systems. Other facilities will be easier to learn after learning about the hospital.

4. Administrative offices

5. The Radiology Department

6. Inpatient, Outpatient, and through the Emergency Department. The ED is the most common.

7. Outpatient

8. The patient's chief complaint is not life-threatening, such as having the sniffles.

9. To provide accurate and timely information about patients to healthcare providers.

10. The HIT staff must explain technology in ways that the medical staff can understand and also interpret what the medical staff is saying to better support the need for technology.

Practical Application

1. http://healthit.hhs.gov Sponsored by the US Department of Health & Human Services. HITECH was signed into law February 17, 2009.

2. http://healthit.hhs.gov/portal/server.pt?open=512&objID=2996&mode=2. Complete and accurate information, better access to information, and patient empowerment by having access to their own EMR/EHR.

3. Answers may vary. Possible job opportunities follow:

   - Manager, Clinical Information Systems
   - Trainer
   - Sales/Marketing
   - Developer
   - Administrator
   - Programmer
   - Project management
   - Systems analyst
   - Database manager
   - Support analyst
   - Security analyst

Chapter 2

Acronym Drill

1. HIE
2. HIS
3. CPOE
4. HIS, MRNs, MPI
5. ORU, ORM

Review Questions

1. When the local IS support team is small or when an application is supported only by the vendor.
2. The trouble ticket is escalated to a higher-level team to resolve the issue.
3. Both the local IT and the corporate help desk.
4. Health information exchange (HIE)
5. No, billing is an administrative function, and CIS is a limited information system directly related to patient care.
6. To manage patient registration, maintain centralized patient information, provide software for order entry, manage charges and billing, manage scheduling for patient arrivals and procedures, and maintain the master patient index (MPI)
7. An account number is used to track patient information during a patient's visit to the hospital. The MRN is used to track the patient information through all a patient's visits to the hospital.
8. On the HIS.
9. www.hl7.org
10. The interface engine limits the number of interfaces each IS is required to maintain. It also has the capability to forward, filter, and translate data.
11. Because the MPI is located on the HIS and the MPI must be queried to ensure there is no duplication of an MPI entry.
12. The eMAR streamlines the process of administering medicine. It also offers more security by closely tracking individual doses of medicine.
13. CPOE is used for order entry by physicians.

14. An ADC sends a credit message when a patient is charged for medicine he did not consume.

15. Because there are many components that run a lab and each have a special and unique responsibility for fulfilling lab orders.

Practical Application

1.

1. C
2. E
3. G
4. C
5. M
6. F
7. J
8. K
9. I
10. I
11. B
12. H
13. F
14. L
15. I
16. E
17. L
18. D
19. A
20. D
21. D

2.

Photo credits: Lisa F. Young, lightpoet, and diego cervo

Steps:

Step 1.   The pharmacy receives an order via fax, phone, written, and so on.

Step 2.   The pharmacy IS sends an order message to the HIS and the ADC through the interface engine.

Step 3.   The order can be viewed in the physician portal.

Step 4.   When the healthcare provider collects and administers the medicine, the dispense information is sent from the ADC to the pharmacy IS through the interface engine.

Step 5.   The pharmacy IS charges at the time the medicine is dispensed. The pharmacy IS sends charges to the HIS through the interface engine.

Step 6.   The eMAR is updated.

Step 7.   ADC medication credits for ordered yet unused medicine are sent to the pharmacy IS and then to the billing component of the HIS through the interface engine.

3.

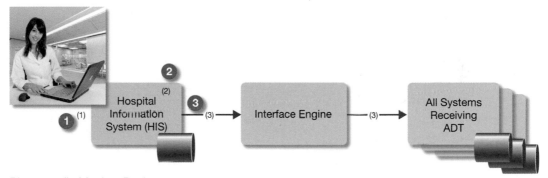

Photo credit: Monkey Business

Chapter 3

Acronym Drill

1. HHS, CMS, ONC, OCR
2. ICD-10, HIPAA
3. ONC, EMR/EHR, HIPAA
4. OCR, HIPAA, e-PHI
5. SLA

Review Questions

1. CMS (Centers for Medicare & Medicaid Services). The current standard is Version 5010.
2. OCR (Office of Civil Rights)
3. Medicare is administrated at the federal level. Medicaid is administrated by states.
4. The Enforcement Rule establishes penalties for violations to HIPAA rules and procedures following a violation, such as investigations and hearings.
5. The goals of meaningful use are to help healthcare providers know more about their patients, make better decisions, and save money.

6. Eligible providers who demonstrate meaningful use receive monetary incentives.

7. A breach can be theft, unauthorized access or disclosure, loss, or improper disposal of e-PHI.

8. A public health record is used for the collection of public health data to be analyzed by researchers.

9. The basic rule of thumb is to make sure the data on an electronic device is unreadable, indecipherable, and cannot be reconstructed.

10. SLAs establish how e-PHI is shared and used, and an SLA establishes expectations of service provided.

Practical Application

1. Answers may vary. The link for the example on the http://www hhs.gov website is http://www.hhs.gov/ocio/eplc/Enterprise%20Performance%20Lifecycle%20Artifacts/eplc_artifacts.htmlSimilar.

2. Answers may vary. However, the link to the hhs.gov examples is http://www.hhs.gov/ocr/privacy/hipaa/enforcement/examples/index.html.

3. Yes, this is a HIPAA violation because Patti Patient's name and medical condition were spoken to be heard by anyone in the waiting room.

Chapter 4

Acronym Drill

1. UPS
2. e-PHI
3. MD, PA
4. PCT
5. NUC, HUC
6. PM, PM

Review Questions

1. A privacy screen
2. Two departments should not share a printer if users in one of those departments do not have proper access to see the PHI being printed by the other department.

3. The user must log off or lock the computer before walking away.

4. Time lockout is not practical for all employees because some have flexible hours and cannot limit their access to only certain hours.

5. IMs should never be used in a healthcare facility because they are not secure.

6. VoIP phone systems offer the extra security provided by using the network security.

7. The MD is ultimately responsible for the medical actions performed on a patient.

8. The system administrator

9. The DBA, database administrator

10. Desktop computers, laptop computers, tablet computers, mobile phones, printers, fax machines, televisions

11. HIPAA allows one exception to never have access issues cause a delay in patient care.

12. The board of directors

13. Having a surgical procedure done at a surgical center is usually less expensive to the patient than at a hospital because the patient does not need to stay overnight.

14. Behaving professionally keeps potentially tense situations calm and helps users feel comfortable coming to you for help with their technical problems.

15. The MRI imaging room is special because no metal objects are allowed to enter the room.

Practical Application

1. Answers will vary.

2. Answers may vary depending on the version of Windows the student uses, but generally speaking, the idea is the same across the different versions. This answer is for Windows 7.

Step 1.   Right-click an open area of the desktop, and select Personalize.

Step 2.   Click Screen Saver. The Screen Saver Settings dialog box appears.

Step 3.   In the Screen saver drop-down box, select any of the options other than *(None)*.

Step 4.   Set the minutes for Wait to 1.

Step 5.   Check the box for On Resume, Display Logon Screen.

Step 6.   Click OK.

3. The Microsoft Support website has a knowledge base entry with these instructions: http://support.microsoft.com/kb/314999.

Step 1.   Use Windows Explorer to locate the Winexit.scr file in the Windows 2000 Resource Kit folder on your hard disk.

Step 2.   Right-click the **Winexit.scr** file, and then click **Install**.

Step 3.   The Display Properties dialog box appears with the Screen Saver tab active. The Logoff Screen Saver entry is automatically selected. Click **Settings**.

Step 4.   Select the **Force application termination** check box to force programs to quit.

Step 5.   In the **Countdown for seconds** box, type the number of seconds for which the logoff dialog box appears before the user is logged off.

Step 6.   In the **Logoff Message** box, type the message that appears during the logoff countdown. Click **OK**.

Step 7.   In the Display Properties dialog box, click **Preview**.

Step 8.   You see the Auto Logoff dialog box. It displays the logoff message and the countdown timer. Click **Cancel**.

Step 9.   Click **OK**.

Chapter 5

Acronym Drill

1. TCP, IP
2. DNS
3. API
4. WPA2
5. SSID
6. DHCP
7. ASPs, SaaS
8. DVDs, CDs

Review Questions

1. An ISP is an organization that offers individuals and companies an entry point to the Internet by way of a WAN.

2. Application layer, presentation layer, session layer, transport layer, network layer, data link layer, physical layer

3. RDP

4. The DNS resolves domain names into the IP address that the network understands to reach the correct computer on the intranet or Internet.

5. Some healthcare facilities do not have the room or finances to house all the servers needed to run health information systems. Cloud computing and virtualization are two techniques designed to reduce the overall costs of these systems.

6. SQL is a programming language used to manage data stored in databases.

7. PHP is an open source, server-side, HTML-embedded scripting language used to create dynamic web pages. PHP script creates a customized web page for each individual viewing.

8. Some of the obstacles might include the following:
   - Signal strength of each AP
   - Shape of the building
   - Types of materials used in the building, such as concrete walls, wooden walls, sheetrock, and lead-lined rooms in the Radiology department
   - Elevators
   - Number of floors

9. A flaw was discovered in TKIP because it reused weak designs from WEP to make it backward compatible. This weakness allows hackers to spoof data, or to falsify data on the network.

10. A router serves as a firewall to act like a middle man to prevent the detection of devices on the LAN by devices outside the LAN.

11. A ping command is used to send a request to another device to find out if the two devices can communicate on the network.

12. A thick client is used when an application is installed on the client computer. A thin client is used when an application is accessed by a computer but not installed on the computer.

13. Security risks, high traffic and load balancing, hardware and software specifications required by vendors, and purging old logs.

14. A differential backup backs up new and changed files and does not mark the files as having been backed up. An incremental back up backs up the files that have been created or changed since the last incremental backup and marks the files as having been backed up.

15. The reference document should include the following:

- Brand
- Model
- Name on network
- Serial number
- OS version
- Static or DHCP IP address (If static, record the IP address used.)
- MAC address for wired and wireless connections
- Applications installed
- Printers installed

16. The antivirus software should have up-to-date virus definitions because new viruses are deployed daily.

17. Certain departments require higher quality or resolution. For example, for picture archiving and communication system (PACS) a larger monitor with higher resolution and quality should be used to view the details of a medical image, such as an MRI.

18. The change management documentation should include the following:

- Device name, model number, and location
- Replacement parts
- Scheduled start and finish time of the change
- Actual start and finish time of the change
- Number of users who will be affected
- The notification of change sent to users affected
- Whether downtime is required
- The results from testing the change
- The rollback plan in case of failure
- Manager or supervisor approval

19. Common peripheral devices found in a hospital supported by HIT technicians include a barcode scanner, document scanner, card or badge scanner, or signature pads.

20. Phones are easily misplaced, lost, or stolen, even more often than laptop computers. Any smartphone with access to e-PHI must be encrypted with password protection and time lockout.

Practical Application

1. Answers will vary. One option is found at http://www.microsoft.com/resources/documentation/windows/xp/all/proddocs/en-us/windows_dos_copy.mspx?mfr=true.

> **1.** Open a command prompt.
>
> **2.** Right-click the title bar of the command prompt window, point to **Edit**, and then click **Mark**.
>
> **3.** Click the beginning of the text you want to copy.
>
> **4.** Press and hold down the **Shift** key, and then click the end of the text you want to copy. (Or you can click and drag the cursor to select the text.)
>
> **5.** Right-click the title bar, point to **Edit**, and then click **Copy**.
>
> **6.** Position the cursor where you want the text to be inserted:
>
> > **a.** In an MS-DOS-based program, or in a command prompt window, right-click the title bar, point to **Edit**, and then click **Paste**.
> >
> > **b.** In a Windows-based program, click the **Edit** menu, and then click **Paste**.

2. Answers may vary. Here is a link for one option: http://www.radmin.com/products/ipscanner/

Chapter 6

Acronym Drill

1. PCP
2. PET, CT
3. EKG or ECG
4. NICU
5. MED/SURG
6. PACU
7. NDCID
8. ICD-10, CPT

9. SNOMED-CT

10. HL7, MSH

Review Questions

1. The EMR is the collection of patient information from all visits at one hospital. The EHR is the collection of patient information from all hospitals the patient has visited.

2. He means the medication should be given immediately.

3. A Level I trauma center

4. A CT machine produces an image with 100 times more clarity than normal X-ray imaging.

5. Because of the strong magnetic field, all personnel, including HIT technicians, must take extra precaution when entering a room with an MRI machine. Absolutely no metal must enter the room because it can cause a dangerous situation as the magnetic field pulls the object to the machine.

6. Obstetricians care for women who are pregnant, and gynecologists care for women at any other time.

7. Pediatrics (PEDS)

8. Occupational therapy (OT) offers rehabilitation to disabled patients to restore meaningful and purposeful activities of daily living.

9. Nuclear medicine deals with the use of radioactive substances for diagnosis, treatment, and research of medical conditions.

10. During registration, the patient may be asked for the following information:

    Full name

    Address

    Employer

    Next of kin

    Billing and insurance information

    Referring and family physician information

11. The CPOE is customized to the doctor's needs because it has the capability to enter prescriptions.

12. Scheduling software specifically designed for healthcare offer conveniences, such as reserving rooms, procedures, and personnel based on the type of procedure or service.

13. Patient tracking software is used to follow and record patient flow through a patient's changing medical status, lab studies, imaging, or other diagnostic and treatment services. Or patient tracking software tracks the physical location of a patient in a hospital using radio frequency identification (RFID) technology.

14. ICD-10 codes describe diagnosis or classification of diseases or illnesses. Current procedural terminology (CPT) describes the procedure or treatments offered by healthcare providers. ICD-10 codes justify billing the CPT codes.

15. A healthcare clearinghouse collects the CPT codes and gives the codes a monetary value. The claim is sent to insurance companies, government agencies, or patients for reimbursement.

16. digital imaging and communication in medicine (DICOM)

17. optical character recognition (OCR)

18. When deciding to suggest when a change should happen, consider all users that will be affected. If the change requires a computer or system to be down or offline, called downtime, choosing off hours might be best to decrease the number of healthcare providers who will be affected. Also consider if support needs to be available in case of a failure during the change. If it is a major change and needs to happen after hours, it may be necessary for support personnel to work during the change to monitor the progress and check for failures.

19. A continuity of care record (CCR) is a collection of CCDs spanning multiple patient visits, and sometimes called patient encounters. Many CCDs can make up a CCR.

20. The vertical bar | separates each field. Two vertical bars together indicate the field is present, but contains no data.

Practical Application

1. The correct order for the change management process is:

    1. A change is requested for an IS.

    2. Change management documentation is created.

    3. Change management documentation is submitted to a CAB.

    4. The CAB approves the change request.

    5. The change is developed in the development environment.

    6. The change is tested for quality assurance in the QA/Test environment.

    7. Users test the change.

    8. The change is implemented in the live environment.

    9. The completed change is documented.

2.

    a. Defibrillator: A machine used to deliver electrical energy to a patient experiencing life-threatening cardiac arrhythmias.

    b. Infusion pump: Infuses fluids (medication or nutrients) into a patient's circulatory system intravenously.

    c. Ventilator: A machine that moves breathable air into and out of the lungs of a patient who is physically unable to breathe sufficiently.

    d. Hemodialysis machine: A machine used to remove waste products from the blood of a patient whose kidneys are in renal failure.

    e. Biochemical analyzer: A machine used in a lab to measure different chemicals or other characteristics in biological specimens.

3. Answers will vary.

Chapter 7

Acronym Drill

1. IDF, MDF
2. RFID
3. UPS
4. 3DES, DES
5. PGP
6. NAS
7. SAN, NAS
8. WPA2
9. SSID
10. VPN
11. GUI
12. L2TP
13. HTTPS, HTTP, SSL
14. HIPAA
15. PHI

Review Questions

1. Spyware is designed to secretly collect information on a computer or network.

2. An administrator account has full access to the data on a system and the administrator can make security changes to other user accounts.

3. In addition to using AD groups to assign permissions to user accounts, AD groups can also affect permissions of computers, printers, and any other device that joins the domain.

4. Keys, key fob, badge, and biometric scanner

5. Recommended specifications are a temperature of 64–80 degrees Fahrenheit with humidity ranging from 30%–55%.

6. A limitation to surveillance cameras is they can only witness criminal activity; they cannot correct or stop it.

7. The three goals of encryption are:

   1. Information in storage should remain confidential.

   2. Data storage and retrieval should be fast.

   3. Encryption should not waste space.

8. PHI might need to be shared with the patient, another healthcare provider as a referral, or an insurance agency.

9. The employee is typically issued a computer by the facility that is preconfigured for a VPN connection. Generally, facilities do not want employees to connect using personal computers because the facility cannot control the security of any data moved to the personal computer.

10. The basic rule is to make sure the data—whether hardcopy or on an electronic device—is unreadable, indecipherable, and cannot be reconstructed.

Practical Application

1. Answers can vary based on findings. A starting point for research is to check popular technology websites that offer product reviews, such as http://www.pcmag.com, http://www.bit-tech.net, and http://www.pcworld.com.

2. Experience can vary. Consider using TeamViewer (free) and DameWare (free trial).

3. Answers will vary.

APPENDIX B
CompTIA Healthcare IT Technician ACRONYMS

ACL	access control list
AGP	accelerated graphics port
AMD	advanced micro devices
ARRA	American Reinvestment Recovery Act
ASC	Ambulatory Surgery Center
ATA	advanced technology attachment
BA	Business Associate
BAA	Business Associate Agreement
BIOS	basic input/output system
BP	Blood Pressure
CCD	Continuity of Care Document
CCR	Continuity of Care Record
CCU	Critical Care Unit
CD	compact disc
CDC	Center for Disease Control
CD-ROM	compact disc-read-only memory
CD-RW	compact disc-rewritable
CDS	Cardiac Diagnostic Services
CFR	Code of Federal Regulation
CMOS	complementary metal-oxide semiconductor
CMS	Center for Medicare Services
CNA	Certified Nursing Assistant
CPOE	Computerized Physician Order Entry

CPT	Current Procedural Terminology
CPU	central processing unit
CRN	Clinical Resource Nurse
CSW	Clinical Social Worker
CT	Computerized Tomography
DA	Dental Assistant
DB-9	9 pin D shell connector
DB-25	serial communications D-shell connector, 25 pins
DDOS	distributed denial of service
DDR	double data-rate
DDR RAM	double data-rate random access memory
DDR SDRAM	double data-rate synchronous dynamic random access memory
DHCP	dynamic host configuration protocol
DIMM	dual inline memory module
DLP	digital light processing
DMZ	demilitarized zone
DNS	domain name service or domain name server
DO	Doctor of Osteopathy
DRP	Disaster Recovery Plan
DSL	digital subscriber line
DVD	digital video disc or digital versatile disc
DVD-R	digital video disc-recordable
DVD-RAM	digital video disc-random access memory
DVD-ROM	digital video disc-read only memory
DVD-RW	digital video disc-rewritable
E/M	Evaluation and Management Code
EEG	Electro Encephalogram
EHR	Electronic Health Record
EKG/ECG	Electro-Cardiogram
EMI	electromagnetic interference
EMR	Electronic Medical Record
ENT	Ears, Nose and Throat
EP	Eligible Provider
ePHI	Electronic Personal Health Information
ER	Emergency Room
ESD	electrostatic discharge
FAT	file allocation table
FAT32	32-bit file allocation table
FBC	Family Birthing Center

FDA	Food and Drug Administration
FQDN	fully qualified domain name
FTP	file transfer protocol
Gb	gigabit
GB	gigabyte
GHz	gigahertz
GUI	graphical user interface
H&P	History and Physical
HCL	hardware compatibility list
HDD	hard disk drive
HDMI	high definition media interface
HHS	Health and Human Services
HIPAA	Health Information Portability Accountability Act
HITECH	Health Information Technology
HL7	Health Level 7
HTML	hypertext markup language
HTTP	hypertext transfer protocol
HTTPS	hypertext transfer protocol over secure sockets layer
HVAC	Heating Ventilation and Air Conditioning
I/O	input/output
ICD	International Code of Diseases
ICR	intelligent character recognition
ICU	Intensive Care Unit
IDE	integrated drive electronics
IDS	Intrusion Detection System
IEEE	Institute of Electrical and Electronics Engineers
IP	internet protocol
IPCONFIG	internet protocol configuration
IPSEC	internet protocol security
ISP	internet service provider
Kb	kilobit
KB	Kilobyte or knowledge base
L&D	Labor and Delivery
LAN	local area network
LCD	liquid crystal display
LOINC	Logical Observation Identifiers Names and Codes
LPN	Licensed Practitioner Nurse
LVN	Licensed Vocational Nurse
MA	Medical Assistant

MAC	media access control / mandatory access control
MB	megabyte
Mb	megabit
MD	Medical Doctor
MFD	multi-function device
MFP	multi-function product
MHz	megahertz
MOU	Memorandum of Understanding
MP3	Moving Picture Experts Group Layer 3 Audio
MP4	Moving Picture Experts Group Layer 4
MPEG	Moving Picture Experts Group
MRI	Magnetic Resonance Imaging
MSCONFIG	Microsoft configuration
NAS	network-attached storage
NAT	network address translation
NDCID	National Drug Code Identifier
NIC	network interface card
NICU	Neonatal Intensive Care Unit
NIST	National Institute of Standards and Technology
NP	Nurse Practitioner
NTFS	new technology file system
NUC	Nursing Unit Clerk
OBGYN	Obstetrics and Gynecology
OBR	Observation Request
OCR	Office of Civil Rights
OCR	Optical Character Recognition
OCR	optical character recognition
ODBC	Open Database Connectivity
OEM	original equipment manufacturer
ONC	Office the of National Coordinator
ONC	Oncology
ONC-ATCB	Office of the National Coordinator[md]Authorized Temporary and Certification Body
OR	Operating Room
OS	operating system
OT	Occupational Therapist
PA	Physician Assistant
PACS	Picture Archiving Communication System
PACU	Post Anesthesia Care Unit

PC	personal computer
PCI	peripheral component interconnect
PCIe	peripheral component interconnect express
PCIX	peripheral component interconnect extended
PCP	Primary Care Physician
PCT	Patient Care Technician
PCU	Progressive Care Unit
PDA	personal digital assistant
PEDS	Pediatrics
PET	Position Emission Tomography
PGP	Pretty Good Privacy
PHI	Protected Health Information
PHR	Personal Health Record
PKI	public key infrastructure
PM	Practice Manager
PM	Project Manager
POP3	post office protocol 3
POST	power-on self test
PPACA	Patient Privacy and Affordable Care Act
PS/2	personal system/2 connector
PT	Physical Therapist
QA	Quality Assurance
QC	Quality Control
RAID	redundant array of independent (or inexpensive) discs
RAM	random access memory
RDP	Remote Desktop Protocol
RF	radio frequency
RFI	radio frequency interference
RGB	red green blue
RISC	reduced instruction set computer
RJ	registered jack
RJ-11	registered jack function 11
RJ-45	registered jack function 45
RN	Registered Nurse
ROM	read only memory
RS-232	recommended standard 232
RS-232C	recommended standard 232
RT	Respiratory Therapist
S.M.A.R.T.	self-monitoring, analysis, and reporting technology

SAN	storage area network
SATA	serial advanced technology attachment
SCSI	small computer system interface
SCSI ID	small computer system interface identifier
SD card	secure digital card
SDRAM	synchronous dynamic random access memory
SIMM	single inline memory module
SLA	Service Level Agreement
SMTP	simple mail transfer protocol
SNMP	simple network management protocol
SoDIMM	small outline dual inline memory module
SOHO	small office/home office
SRAM	static random access memory
SSH	Secure shell
SSID	service set identifier
SSL	secure sockets layer
STP	shielded twisted pair
SVGA	super video graphics array
TB	terabyte
TCP	transmission control protocol
TCP/IP	transmission control protocol/internet protocol
TCU	Transitional Care Unit
UA	Unit Assistant
UPS	uninterruptible power supply
URL	uniform resource locator
URO	Urology
USB	universal serial bus
VGA	video graphics array
VoIP	voice over internet protocol
VPN	virtual private network
WAN	wide area network
WAP	wireless application protocol
WEP	wired equivalent privacy
WIFI	wireless fidelity
WLAN	wireless local area network
WPA	wireless protected access

Key Terms Glossary

account number—The number assigned to a patient to reference the care of that patient for the current visit. The account number is sometimes referred to as an encounter number, accession number, or registration number in different information systems.

active directory (AD)—The Microsoft database managed by the domain controller that system administrators use to control access to the Windows domain. Active directory contains information about users, groups of users, computers on the domain, organizational units, and configuration data.

active server pages (ASP or ASP.NET)—A server-side, HTML-embedded scripting language used to create dynamic web pages. ASP is provided by Microsoft.

acuity—The level of severity of an affliction.

acute care—Care that is given short term and for severe afflictions. For example, a patient experiencing a heart attack goes to an acute care facility.

ad hoc—A network that is wireless, decentralized, temporary, and a peer-to-peer connection.

Adobe Flash—A plug-in or add-on to a browser used to add multimedia graphics to web pages.

adult day care facility—A facility that offers medical and nursing supervision of adults. Patients cannot be at one of these facilities for longer than 12 hours in one day.

advanced encryption standard (AES)—An encryption cipher that uses a block length of 128 bits. The National Institute of Standards and Technology (NIST) adopted AES as an encryption standard.

ambulatory care facility—A facility used for outpatient services. Basically, if patient care takes less than 24 hours, the patient goes to an ambulatory care facility rather than a hospital.

ambulatory surgery center—A facility used for surgical procedures in outpatient services.

anesthesiologist—A physician who is trained in anesthesia and perioperative medicine. Anesthesia means to block sensation to prevent a patient from feeling pain; for example, during a surgery.

antispyware—A program designed to prevent spyware from being installed on a computer.

application program interface (API)—A segment of programming code that can be used by many programs. An API can be a routine, protocol, or tool used to build a software application.

application service provider (ASP)—A vendor that offers an IS provided remotely.

assisted living residence—A facility that offers an apartment-style living situation for patients or residents who need assistance in daily activities. Most assisted living residences have different levels of assistance. A resident might live independently where help is available only if needed, or a resident lives in an apartment, but almost everything is done for the resident.

audit trail—A record of activity in an IS. Audit trails typically record the activity along with a time and date stamp and the username performing the activity.

automated dispensing cabinet (ADC)—An electronic cabinet with drawers containing medications that are placed throughout the hospital for convenient access by healthcare providers to quickly administer medicines.

badge—A card with a magnetic strip or chip that identifies the person assigned to the card.

billing and coding software—Software that receives data from a patient's EHR/EMR, converts the data into billable items, and submits the bill to the insurance company for reimbursement.

biometric scanner—A device used to identify a person based on biological data.

birth center—A facility that offers services for prenatal and labor and delivery low-risk patients. This can be a department of a hospital or a separate facility.

blood pressure cuff—A device used to measure blood pressure. Also called BP cuff, vitals cuff, or sphygmomanometer.

blood work—Examination of a blood sample to test for certain diseases, medications, or other data.

Bluetooth—A wireless communication protocol used to connect personal devices over short distances.

break the glass access—A username and password reserved for emergency use to access patient information.

business associate agreement (BAA)—A contract used between healthcare entities and third parties to establish a mutual understanding of safeguards of e-PHI.

card or badge scanner—A device used for security and convenience that scans a card or badge to transfer data or detect identity.

change advisory board (CAB)—The board within an IT company that decides if a change management request is a benefit to the company or a liability. Also called a governance board.

change management—A process to define a change needed, the steps to take to complete it, the results of the change, and the time frame for completion. Also called change control.

chief complaint—The primary reason a person goes to the ED.

client-server architecture—A network architecture in which client computers rely on services or resources provided by a server computer.

clinical department—A department in a healthcare facility that offers specific medical services for patient care, treatment, or diagnosis. Sometimes called ancillary departments.

clinical IS—An information system directly related to the care of patients. Examples are the information systems for radiology, lab, surgery, pharmacy, and order entry.

cloud computing—Applications and data stored on remote computers on the Internet made available through a browser.

code blue—A code usually used to indicate a patient is in critical condition and requires immediate intervention.

coding—When a patient goes into cardiac arrest where the heart stops beating. Sometimes referred to as code blue.

cold feed—The real-time transfer of data from a source IS to a destination IS that does not receive acknowledgment of receipt of data. The data transfer is not guaranteed in a cold feed. Other data transfers require a receipt of data acknowledgment, called an ACK message, that guarantees the data was received.

communications protocol—The format and rules for exchanging digital messages between information systems.

computed tomography (CT)—Imaging that uses X-rays along with computing algorithms. A patient lies down in a CT machine while the CT machine rotates around the patient producing cross-sectional images (tomography) of the patient's body.

computerized physician order entry (CPOE)—An order entry system designed specifically for doctors' use.

consultation—When a doctor seeks the expertise of another doctor in a specialized field.

continuity of care document (CCD)—A version of a patient's record for transferring relevant data. A CCD is easily read by both a person or an IS.

continuity of care record (CCR)—A collection of CCDs.

controlled substance—A drug or substance regulated by the government. ·

covered entity—Health Insurance Portability and Accountability Act (HIPAA) is designed to protect health information used by health insurance plan providers, healthcare clearinghouses, and healthcare providers. These three entities are classified as covered entities. Basically, a covered entity is anyone or any organization required to submit to HIPAA rules.

current procedural terminology (CPT)—Coding system maintained by the American Medical Association (AMA) to represent procedures or treatments offered by healthcare providers.

dashboard—An application's graphic user interface (GUI) that provides status information at a quick glance and commands to manage the application.

data encryption standard (DES)—An outdated block cipher that uses a 64-bit cipher block and a 56-bit key.

database administrator (DBA)—The HIT personnel responsible for the management of the databases in the information systems used in a facility.

default gateway—The IP address of a router that should receive all requests for communication with computers outside the local network.

dental assistant (DA)—A healthcare provider who helps a dentist perform procedures and prepare patients for dental procedures.

dermatology—The study of the skin and its conditions, including scalp, hair, and nails.

desktop support technician—The HIT personnel responsible for the support of computers and certain peripheral devices in the facility.

dictation—A typed transcript of a recorded healthcare provider's oral report of patient care as spoken into a voice recorder.

digital imaging and communication in medicine (DICOM)—The healthcare industry standard for medical digital imaging. DICOM is designed specifically for image handling, storing, printing, or transmitting. The file extension for this format is .dcm.

discretionary access control (DAC)—A security mechanism where a user has control to grant access to resources owned by the user account.

disk image—The contents of a hard drive including configuration settings and applications stored so the contents can be replicated to another computer.

document scanner—A device used to scan paper documents into an electronic image or document.

domain controller—The server that administers the user account information, authenticates usernames and passwords, and enforces security policy.

domain name service (DNS)—A service that resolves domain names into the IP address that the network uses to reach the correct computer on the network.

dynamic host configuration protocol (DHCP)—The service running on a router or other network device that automatically assigns an IP address to a computer or device when it joins the network.

dynamic IP address—An IP address assigned by DHCP.

electrocardiogram (EKG or ECG)—A test that indicates problems with the electrical activity of the heart.

electroencephalogram (EEG)—A test that measures the frequency of brain waves.

electronic health record (EHR)—Information about a patient's care and health collected and stored electronically. This record is not limited to the visits at only one hospital but is a collection of all visits at all hospitals. The term *EHR* is sometimes used interchangeably with electronic medical record (EMR), although the two terms are not exactly the same.

electronic MAR (eMAR)—The medication administration record (MAR) recorded electronically using hand-held scanners at several locations from the pharmacy to the patient bedside.

electronic medical record (EMR)—Information about a patient's care and health that was previously captured on paper forms and charts, collected from all visits at one hospital and stored in an EMR IS. The term *EMR* is sometimes used interchangeably with Electronic Health Record (EHR), although the two terms are not exactly the same.

electronic protected health information (e-PHI)—HIPAA protects the electronic information that can be used to identify an individual. e-PHI is information created, used, or disclosed about a patient while providing healthcare.

eligible provider—Hospitals or professionals participating in incentive programs must meet meaningful use criteria to be eligible to receive incentive money.

emergency department (ED)—The department in a healthcare facility that treats patients with acute and sudden afflictions. The ED is often referred to as the emergency room (ER) by nonmedical people, but in the healthcare world, it is called the ED.

emergency department IS (EDIS)—The information system that manages patient flow, orders, patient history, record healthcare providers' notes on the patient's visit, and more in the ED. The stage of a patient's visit to the ED, who is caring for the patient, and other information are displayed on the tracking board from the EDIS for convenient reference to a healthcare provider's current caseload.

e-prescribing software—Software used by physicians to electronically write prescriptions for patients.

evaluation and management (E/M) codes—Subcategory of CPT codes that are used to describe the level of care provided to a patient.

examination—When a healthcare provider evaluates a patient and his medical conditions. This might include tests for a complete understanding of the cause of the symptoms. Also called exam.

extensible markup language (XML)—A markup language used to write a new markup language. Using XML, you can create your own HTML tags.

fetal monitor—A device used to monitor a baby before birth, usually recording the baby's heartbeat.

fiber optic—Strings of glass or plastic in a cable where data is sent as pulses of light. Also called fiber.

file transfer protocol (FTP)—A method to communicate over a network electronically. This communication method enables documents to be placed on and copied from a remote server. FTP is great for sharing large files with other people who also have access to the FTP server.

file transfer protocol (FTP)—A protocol standard for exchanging files over the Internet or an intranet.

gastroenterology—The study of the digestive system and its disorders.

general acute care hospital—A facility that offers diagnosis, treatment, or care for patients in a variety of specialties. Patient care is uniquely approached and not all patients are there for the same type of care.

glucose monitor—A device used to measure the amount of glucose in a blood sample.

governance board—See change advisory board (CAB).

graphics interchange format (GIF)—An image file format that supports data compression and animation. GIF supports only 256 colors, so some quality is lost on colored images. The file extension for this format is .gif.

hacker—An individual who maliciously attempts to access electronic information he is not authorized to view.

health information exchange (HIE)—Sharing of patient information among multiple providers. These providers do not need to work in the same hospital to have access to patient information. Currently, this is typically done for hospitals in close geographic locations, but the goal is to make HIE nationwide.

Health Information Technology for Economic and Clinical Health (HITECH) Act—An act of the U.S. congress enacted as part of the American Recovery and Reinvestment Act (ARRA) of 2009. Its purpose is to promote the meaningful use of technology in healthcare so that technology ultimately results in improved healthcare for the patient.

Health Insurance Portability and Accountability Act (HIPAA)—A law created in 1996 to provide a standard set of rules that all covered entities must follow to protect patient health information and to help healthcare providers transition from paper to electronic health records.

Health Level 7 (HL7)—The standard protocol of formatting a message for healthcare interfacing. HL7 is ANSI certified. HL7 operates at the seventh or application layer of the OSI communication model.

healthcare clearinghouse—A business that receives healthcare information and translates that information into a standardized format to be sent to a health plan provider. A healthcare clearinghouse is sometimes called a billing service. Basically, a healthcare clearinghouse is a middle person that processes healthcare information.

healthcare IT (HIT)—The personnel, equipment, and procedures that provide and support the computer systems used in the healthcare environment.

healthcare provider—A qualified person or facility that provides healthcare to patients; for example, a doctor, nurse, or hospital.

heating, ventilation, and air conditioning (HVAC) unit—Equipment designed to regulate temperature and humidity.

home health agency—An organization that offers preventative, rehabilitation, and therapeutic care to patients in their homes.

hospice agency—An organization that offers medical, nursing, social work, and counseling to terminally ill patients in their homes or as an inpatient hospice service at a facility.

hospital information system (HIS)—The primary information system used to manage data flow and maintain databases in a hospital. An HIS usually manages patient administration and order entry. HIS is sometimes called a healthcare information system (HIS).

hot swappable—A device or piece of equipment that does not require a reboot to establish a connection and function.

hypertext markup language (HTML)—A common markup language used for developing web pages.

hypertext preprocessor (PHP)—An open source, server-side, HTML embedded scripting language used to create dynamic web pages.

hypertext transfer protocol (HTTP)—An application protocol that defines how data is sent to and from a web server on the web.

hypertext transfer protocol secure (HTTPS)—A secure version of HTTP that encrypts data sent to and from a web server.

ICD-10—HIPAA mandated a standard electronic format for provider and diagnostic codes. The new standard is intended to grow with the functional needs of the healthcare industry. The http://www.cms.gov website offers more details about ICD-10.

ICD-9—HIPAA mandated a standard format for electronic provider and diagnostic codes. The current standard has limitations that restrict the full use of EMR/EHR software.

IEEE 1394—A standard for a hot-swappable port generally used for transferring multimedia data. Also called Firewire.

information system (IS)—A computerized system used to facilitate the functions of an organization. An IS is a group of components that collect, process, store, and communicate information.

infrastructure— A centralized network. Devices connect to an access point to join the network.

Infrastructure-as-a-Service (IaaS)—A service that hosts hardware remotely needed for cloud computing. Organizations are allowed to use the hardware to host operating systems and software belonging to the organization.

inpatient—A patient admitted to a healthcare facility who stays longer than 24 hours by a doctor's order.

instant messaging (IM)—A method to communicate over a network electronically in real time. Typed messages are immediately viewable by the recipient. IMs are not secured and are sent as plain text.

interface engine—An application that serves as a communications hub and offers services to the messages as they travel through a network. These services include but are not limited to forwarding, filtering, translation, and queue management.

interface—The connection between two information systems for the purpose of exchanging data.

intermediate distribution frame (IDF)—A cable rack that connects and manages wiring used for telecommunication between the MDF and devices such as computers or network printers. IDFs are usually found on each floor of a building in a data closet.

Internet modem—A device used to convert the signal from the ISP to Ethernet used by the router and local network.

Internet protocol (IP)—A protocol used in TCP/IP networks at the network layer of the OSI model. IP is responsible for finding the best path to a destination and breaking down messages into packets small enough to travel through the network and reassembling the packets when received.

Internet service provider (ISP)—An organization that provides access to the Internet.

intranet—The private network that is secured within a facility. All intranets use the TCP/IP suite of protocols also used on the Internet.

IP address—The address used to identify a computer or other device on a TCP/IP network. A TCP/IP version 4 IP address has 32 bits, and a TCP/IP version 6 address has 128 bits.

ipconfig—A command used in the command prompt window to display the TCP/IP network configuration values.

joint photographic experts group (JPEG)—An image file format that supports data compression. JPEG supports up to 16 million colors, but when compressed, the image loses clarity and sharpness. JPEG is generally used on the Internet. The file extension for this format is .jpg.

key fob—A device synched with a network authentication service that provides a code used to log in to a network or other system.

lab IS (LIS)—The information system responsible for orders, charging, and results of laboratory tests.

layer 2 tunneling protocol (L2TP)—A fully encrypted tunneling protocol used to create a VPN connection.

legal health record—Health organizations must retain a health record of patients for use by the patient or legal services.

licensed practical nurse (LPN)—A healthcare provider who completed an LPN program and passed a state exam. An LPN typically assists an RN and provides bedside care. Sometimes called a licensed vocational nurse (LVN).

local area network (LAN)—A small network of computers or other connected devices covering a small area such as a home, business, school, or airport.

lock—When a Windows user is logged on to a computer, but needs to walk away for a moment and does not want to close all programs running to log off, the user can simply lock the computer pressing the Windows key+L. This user's password or a computer administrator's username and password is required to unlock the computer.

long-term care—Ongoing treatment or care. For example, a patient with Alzheimer's goes to a long-term care facility.

magnetic resonance imaging (MRI)—Imaging that uses strong magnetic fields and radio signals to create an image of a patient's body. A patient lies down in an MRI machine and must remain still for extended periods of time in a noisy, cramped space.

main distribution frame (MDF)—A cable rack that connects and manages wiring used for telecommunication between a service provider and intermediate distribution frames (IDFs). The MDF connects private or public lines coming into a facility with the networking devices in the facility.

mainframe—A large-scale computer that supports many users and client computers.

malicious software—Any program unknowingly transmitted to a computer or network designed to cause damage. Also called malware.

malware—See malicious software.

mandatory access control (MAC)—A security mechanism where a user can only gain access to a resource if the security or system administrator grants the access.

master patient index (MPI)—The database of all MRNs and account numbers. This centralized database is responsible to prevent duplication of MRNs and account numbers.

meaningful use—The goals of meaningful use are to help healthcare providers know more about their patients, make better decisions, and save money by using HIT in a meaningful way.

media access control (MAC) filtering—The method to secure a network by limiting which devices are allowed to connect to a network based on a list of MAC addresses kept by the wireless access points.

medical assistant (MA)—A healthcare provider or administrator who is not certified and works under direct supervision of a licensed healthcare provider or office manager.

medical doctor (MD)—A physician who is licensed and trained to practice medicine without supervision.

medical image—Visuals made of body parts, tissues, or organs for clinical study, treatment, or diagnosis.

medical record number (MRN)—The number assigned to a patient to reference the care of that patient for all visits at one particular hospital. An MRN is unique to a patient within a hospital's network.

medical records office—The administrative office that stores and archives patients' medical records.

medication administration record (MAR)—The legal record of medication consumption in a hospital. The MAR tracks all medications in the hospital. Sometimes called drug charts.

memorandum of understanding (MOU)—Contracts are sometimes necessary within an organization between departments or personnel for mutual understanding of the safeguards of e-PHI.

message—The information sent from one system to another.

metadata—Data about data. In imaging, metadata tags files with keywords to easily search for the file.

national drug code identifier (NDCID)—A code assigned to each drug used by the FDA to maintain a list of drugs being produced.

network address translation (NAT)—A router or other gateway device substitutes its own IP address for the IP address of computers behind the firewall that it is protecting.

network administrator—The HIT personnel responsible for maintaining the integrity of the network.

network attached storage (NAS)—A storage device connected directly to the network.

node—A connection point to an IS.

nuclear stress test—A test using both two PET scans and a vascular stress test to test how well the blood flows through the heart of a patient.

nurse practitioner (NP)—A healthcare provider who is a registered nurse who has completed graduate-level education and training. Dependent on state laws, some NPs can work without the supervision of a physician.

nursing home—A facility that provides a residence for disabled and elderly patients who need medical supervision or ongoing nursing care. Patients in a nursing home do not need the level of care required to be admitted into an acute care hospital.

nursing unit clerk (NUC)—An employee of a hospital who assists the healthcare providers in a unit with clerical work. Sometimes called a health unit coordinator (HUC).

office manager—An employee of a physician's office who facilitates the operations of the office.

oncology—Field of medicine dealing with cancer or tumors.

Open Systems Interconnection model (OSI model)—A description of all communication on a network expressed as seven layers.

operating room (OR)—A room in a hospital equipped for performing surgical procedures.

operative record—A complete and detailed accounting of the surgical case happenings from preoperative through postoperative phases. This document is written to be used for legal reference if ever needed.

ophthalmology—The study of the eye and its diseases.

optical character recognition (OCR)—A technology that translates printed lettering into pure text that can be searched and manipulated on a computer.

order entry—A component of an HIS where healthcare providers enter orders for patient care. Orders can be for procedures, imaging, or maybe tests. Order entry is sometimes written as OE but still read as "order entry."

outpatient—A patient who is scheduled for medical treatment, care, or a service. The patient's stay in the healthcare facility lasts less than 24 hours unless being observed. Ambulatory facilities are specifically for outpatient services.

parallel communication—A process of sending data several bits at a time through several streams simultaneously.

patient care technician (PCT)—A healthcare provider who works directly under the supervision of a licensed healthcare provider.

patient census—A recording of the number of patients with the location, registration status, and other data about the patient in a healthcare facility. Patient census usually applies to inpatients or occupied beds.

perioperative IS—The information system that manages patients in surgery. The perioperative IS starts with scheduling for surgery through discharge or transfer out of surgery. The perioperative IS works largely independent from other information systems because there is rarely a need for interaction with the other clinical departments.

pharmacy IS—The information system used by the pharmacy. The pharmacy IS supports but is not limited to order entry, management, dispensing of medications, monitoring, reporting, and charging.

phishing—A form of social engineering in which an attacker tricks or manipulates a user to give out sensitive data or into allowing unauthorized programs onto the computer or network.

phone switch—A server used to route telephone calls in a facility.

physician assistant (PA)—A healthcare provider who is licensed and trained to practice medicine under the direct supervision of a physician.

physician portal—A user interface that accesses the HIS or EHR/EMR. The physician portal is where doctors go to view patient records, add notes, and electronically sign off on charts.

picture archiving and communication system (PACS)—An information system designed to store and retrieve different formats of medical imaging in one location, as well as communicate PACS images to other information systems.

ping—A command used in the command prompt window to send a request to another device to find out if the two devices can communicate on the network.

Platform-as-a-Service (PaaS)—A service that hosts hardware and operating systems remotely needed for cloud computing. Organizations are allowed to use the hardware and operating system to host the software belonging to the organization.

point-to-point connection—A one-to-one interface between two information systems. Point-to-point connections require the IS at each end of the connection to guarantee the delivery and interpretation of the data.

port forwarding—Communication from outside the network is allowed past the firewall only to a specific computer and port.

port—A number assigned to a client or server application that serves as an address to the application, which the OS uses to get network communication to the correct application. Common port assignments are designated by TCP/IP. Also called a port number or port address.

portable document format (PDF)—A widely used file format developed by Adobe Systems used to present digital documents in a printable view on a monitor. PDF files can be viewed using Adobe Acrobat software or many other PDF viewers or editors made by many software companies. The file extension for this format is .pdf.

portable X-ray machine—A mobile X-ray machine that is small enough to be rolled to a patient's room or taken to a patient's house.

practice management software—Software used in small- to medium-sized medical offices for both clinical and business needs.

practice manager (PM)—An employee of a medical practice who facilitates the operations of the practice.

pretty good privacy (PGP)—An encryption method designed for signing and encrypting e-mail, which uses both symmetric and asymmetric encryption.

primary care facility—A facility that contains the private practice of a doctor where a patient receives preventive, diagnostic, treatment, and management services. When a person has an annual checkup, he schedules an appointment with his primary care provider (PCP), such as a family doctor, nurse practitioner, or physician assistant.

primary care physician (PCP)—A doctor who has an ongoing relationship with a patient and provides primary care for that patient.

print server—A server that connects computers and other devices on a network with printers on the same network. Also called printer server.

privacy screen—A clear film or acrylic filter placed in front of a monitor to decrease the viewing angle of the monitor.

private branch exchange (PBX)—A private telephone system. Switches are housed within a facility to provide greater control over the phone system. With a switch, the facility can customize phone routing and assign extensions.

private health record—A health record created and maintained by an individual. Sometimes called a personal health record (PHR).

project manager—The individual who oversees an implementation project, such as installing an EHR/EMR IS in a hospital.

psychiatric hospital—A facility that specializes in the care of patients with mental illness. Services include diagnosis, treatment, care, and rehabilitation. This can be on an inpatient or outpatient basis.

public health record—Researchers need access to health records to analyze data. For this reason a public health record is made available for the collection of public health data in an anonymous manner.

radio frequency identification (RFID)—A technology that uses radio frequency to track or locate a transponder, or tag.

radiology IS (RIS)—The information system responsible for orders, charging, and results of medical imaging.

rapid response—A code used when a patient is about to go into a code blue.

referral—When a doctor refers a patient to go see a specialist.

registered nurse (RN)—A healthcare provider who has completed a nursing school program and passed the national licensing exam.

registration—The administrative office that maintains a patient census of the facility through patient admissions, transfers, and discharges.

rehabilitation hospital or center—A facility that offers care for patients with ongoing recovery from a disability. This can include medical, psychiatric, or physical therapy.

remote authentication dial-in user service (RADIUS)—A protocol and system used to authenticate access to a network. User passwords to the network are sent over the network encrypted using the RADIUS encryption standard.

remote desktop connection (RDC)—A remote connection used to view another computer's desktop in a window. RDC was created by Microsoft.

remote desktop protocol (RDP)—A protocol developed by Microsoft and used with the Remote Desktop Connection utility that allows a user to connect to a remote computer over a network.

risk management—The proactive approach to preventing lawsuits and liability issues due to medical errors.

role-based access control (RBAC)—The assignment of access to information systems based on job title and not individual evaluation for need of access.

router—A network device that separates one network from another. The router logically and physically belongs to both networks.

scheduling software—Software used to schedule services offered that might include features that can reserve rooms, procedures, and personnel based on the type of procedure or service.

screensaver—When a computer is idle for a set time, an image appears on the screen until the mouse is moved or a key is pressed on the keyboard.

secure chat—A method to communicate over a network electronically in real time. Typed messages are immediately viewable by the recipient. Secure chat sessions are encrypted.

secure FTP—A secure form of FTP that encrypts both commands and data. Sometimes called SSH FTP because secure FTP uses SSH to secure the transfer.

secure shell (SSH)—An encrypted tunneling protocol used by client/server applications to connect a remote client to a server. The protocol is designed to ensure confidentiality and integrity of data over an unsecured network.

secure socket layer (SSL)—A handshake between a web server and a browser to establish a secure connection.

security administrator—The HIT personnel responsible for securing data in the facility.

security officer—The hospital employee responsible for determining policies necessary to ensure security of PHI. The security officer is also responsible for ensuring that the hospital staff complies with these policies.

sensitivity label—A classification of how confidential a patient's information is above and beyond HIPAA regulations.

serial communication—A process of sending data one bit at a time through a single stream.

service set identifier (SSID)—The name assigned to a wireless access point.

service-level agreement (SLA)—Contracts used between healthcare entities and third parties to establish how e-PHI is shared and used. An SLA also establishes expectations of service provided.

signature pad—A device used to transfer written signatures into an electronic image.

single sign-on (SSO)—A program that enables a user to enter a username and password once to log in to multiple information systems.

small computer system interface (SCSI)—A standard for a hot-swappable port and storage devices that use these ports. SCSI connections are usually found on servers and are used by hard drives and optical drives.

social engineering—A malicious attack using social skills directed at a person who has access to sensitive data.

Software-as-a-Service (SaaS)—A software delivery method where the hardware hosting the software is housed remotely and organizations are allowed to access the software and that functions as a web-based service.

solutions—Products or programs offered by vendors to provide an answer to a need.

spam—Unsolicited contact that you did not ask for and don't want and might come from an attacker.

spyware—A type of malware designed to secretly collect information on a computer or network.

stat—Derived from the Latin word *statim*, which means *immediately*. It is often used in the medical environment to expedite something.

static IP address—An IP address manually assigned to a computer or device. A static IP address does not change automatically.

storage area network (SAN)—An independent network separate from the normal LAN designed for data storage.

structured query language (SQL)—A programming language used to manage data stored in databases.

subnet mask—A series of 1s and 0s that determine which part of an IP address identifies the local network and which part identifies the host.

superbill—An itemized form used by healthcare providers to indicate services rendered. The superbill is the primary source for creating a claim to be submitted to the payer.

surgical summary report—A brief accounting of the surgical case report for immediate referral during the postoperative phase.

switch—A device with multiple network ports for connecting devices such as computers, printers, or servers.

system administrator—The HIT personnel responsible for the overall health of the information systems in the facility.

systemized nomenclature of medicine—clinical terms (SNOMED-CT)—A medical terminology standard used internationally to create consistency in keywords in medical documentation. SNOMED-CT technology translates several ways to describe the same medical term into a single code.

tagged image file format (TIFF)—A widely supported image file format. TIFF images can be any resolution, color, or grayscale. The file extension for this format is .tif or .tiff.

TCP/IP—A suite of protocols used for communication on the Internet or an intranet.

terminal emulator—A connection to a mainframe computer that holds all the data being accessed. A terminal emulator typically looks like a command prompt window.

terminal services—Applications or even the entire desktop are made available to a user from a remote server. Only user interaction is presented at the client machine and all other processing takes place at the server. Also called remote desktop service.

thread—The interface pipeline that connects two information systems.

time lockout—The capability of software to limit to certain hours of the day and week when users can log in.

T-line—A type of data transmission technology that uses fiber optic cabling. A T1-line transmits up to 1.544 mbps (megabits per second). A T3-line transmits up to 45 mbps.

tracert—The **trace route** command is used to trace the path a connection takes to reach a target host.

tracking board—A display showing the patients in the ED, where they are, and who is caring for them. Because the tracking board contains confidential information, it is for the use of the ED staff only and is primarily kept out of view of the waiting area and patients.

transmission control protocol (TCP)—A protocol used in TCP/IP networks at the transport layer of the OSI model. TCP is responsible for guaranteeing data is received and in the correct order.

triage—The assessment of the level of care a patient needs when she arrives at the hospital used to determine the priority of the patient for being seen by a physician.

triple data encryption standard (3DES)—An encryption similar to DES but uses a key that can be three times the size, at a 168-bit key.

ultrasound—An imaging process that uses sound waves to create a picture of soft tissues inside the body.

uninterrupted power supply (UPS)—A device connected to a computer to provide power for a few minutes in case the power to the facility goes out. These few minutes give the user enough time to save work and log out.

unit assistant (UA)—An employee of the hospital who facilitates the function of a unit in a hospital.

universal serial bus (USB)—A standard for a hot-swappable port. USB standard 2.0 (Hi-Speed USB) is approximately 40 times faster than original USB. USB standard 3.0 (SuperSpeed USB) is approximately 10 times faster than USB 2.0.

vascular stress test—A physical test using an EKG that determines the capability of veins to return blood from the lower limbs to the heart.

Version 5010—HIPAA mandated a standard format for electronic claims transactions. This standard was updated to grow with the functional needs of the healthcare industry. The http://www.cms.gov website offers more details about Version 5010.

virtual private network (VPN)—The secure and private networking of computers through the Internet.

virtualization—One physical machine hosts multiple activities normally implemented on individual machines.

virus definitions—The unique identifiers of a computer virus that antivirus software uses to detect threats and eliminate them. Also called virus signature.

vitals cuff—See blood pressure cuff.

voice over Internet protocol (VoIP)—A method of communication using IP networks such as the Internet. VoIP operates at the application or seventh layer of the OSI reference model.

waiver of liability—A contract used to protect healthcare entities from being inappropriately responsible or sued for harm or debt.

wide area network (WAN)—A network that covers a large area. WANs are used to connect networks together such as when facilities or doctor's offices connect to the Internet.

Wi-Fi protected access (WPA)—A security protocol used on a wireless LAN that uses TKIP for encryption.

Wi-Fi protected access 2 (WPA2)—A security protocol used on a wireless LAN that uses AES for encryption. WPA2 is currently the preferred encryption standard for a wireless LAN.

wired equivalent privacy (WEP)—A security protocol used on a wireless LAN that uses a static encryption key.

wireless access point (WAP or AP)—A device that enables a wireless computer, printer, or other device to connect to a network.

wireless fidelity (Wi-Fi)—The wireless standards used for local networks as defined by the IEEE 802.11 specifications.

Index

F

Q-R

T

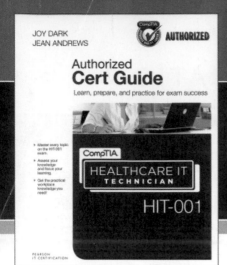

Your purchase of *CompTIA Healthcare IT Technician HIT-001 Authorized Cert Guide* includes access to a free online edition for 45 days through the **Safari Books Online** subscription service. Nearly every Pearson IT Certification book is available online through **Safari Books Online**, along with thousands of books and videos from publishers such as Addison-Wesley Professional, Cisco Press, Exam Cram, IBM Press, O'Reilly Media, Prentice Hall, Que, Sams, and VMware Press.

Safari Books Online is a digital library providing searchable, on-demand access to thousands of technology, digital media, and professional development books and videos from leading publishers. With one monthly or yearly subscription price, you get unlimited access to learning tools and information on topics including mobile app and software development, tips and tricks on using your favorite gadgets, networking, project management, graphic design, and much more.

Activate your FREE Online Edition at
informit.com/safarifree

STEP 1:   Enter the coupon code: WSJBYYG.

STEP 2:   New Safari users, complete the brief registration form.
          Safari subscribers, just log in.

If you have difficulty registering on Safari or accessing the online edition,
please e-mail customer-service@safaribooksonline.com